THE REVOLUTION WILL BE IMPROVISED

Critical Conversations On Our Changing World

Mike Freedman

ANNETTE —
Thank you for your
help and support.
I hope you enjoy the book!

30/11/2017

Mordant Press
2017

First published in 2017 by Mordant Press, a Day 600 imprint

©Copyright 2012, 2017 by Mike Freedman

Mordant Press, c/o Day 600
The Albany, Douglas Way
London SE8 4AG, U.K.

www.day600.com

Cover Design by Ben Gregory

ISBN 978-0-9554727-4-9

For my wife
as everything always is

and for my nieces
Sky, Sunny Ray, Melo and Jupiter
whose world this will be one day

Contents

If one does not have the courage to be hopeless about the world in which they live, then they will never have the courage to be hopeful about creating another world.

Godfrey Reggio

Author's Preface

In 2010, I began researching what would become my first feature documentary, *Critical Mass*, which takes as its subject the impact of human population growth and consumption on our planet and on human psychology. In June 2012, we had a finished film and set about the task of chasing distributors to bring it to an audience.

While making the film, I had recorded several podcasts with people whose work was related, directly or indirectly, with what we were talking about. I fell in love with the podcast format, as it gave me a chance to actually have a conversation with these people, a back-and-forth that by necessity wasn't possible in the structure of a documentary.

After watching the film with various audiences and answering their questions afterwards in person or by email, it realised that, to my delight, I had started a conversation with our audience rather than presenting them with a closed argument or series of data. One of the most common questions, in many iterations, was about where we went from here.

In the film, we had gone to great lengths to present a comprehensive picture of how we got to this point in our cultural evolution, as well as to articulate the numerous social, economic and environmental challenges we see unfolding around us today. It was clear that people wanted to know what was going to happen next, or rather, what we would need to do, as individual humans and collective humanity, to navigate our way through what by all accounts appears to be a landscape rife with crisis, depletion and decline.

It had been a deliberate choice of mine to avoid offering any pat answers or conclusions in the film, as there really are none. There are so many variables and, to quote Donald Rumsfeld in a rare moment of honesty, "unknown unknowns", that is to say things we don't know we don't know, it was not only impossible but dishonest to give the impression that our human story would have neatly tied loose ends.

I had a telephone conversation with Richard Heinberg, the author of "The End of Growth" and founder of the Post Carbon Institute, about many of these future possibilities and unknowns, which I recorded with the intent of editing it into a podcast. When I had the conversation transcribed, I quickly realised that I wanted to preserve that back-and-forth which I see as so crucial to really getting to grips and investigating the many-forked path that lies ahead of us.

The book that you have before you is both a standalone collection of conversations between concerned individuals about the current and possible trajectories of the human enterprise and a companion piece to my documentary, *Critical Mass*. If taken in tandem, my hope is that you will perceive a through-line in story, logic and intention, as we attempt to "put the world to rights". If this is your first experience of my work, I hope that these conversations encourage you to look backwards with interest, towards our recent and distant past, just as I hope that they bring a fresh perspective to your views on the future.

More than anything, I hope that, as the film covered the human story up to the present, this book answers some of your questions about where we might be headed given the choices we are or could be making. I don't hold myself up to be an expert in any meaningful sense, nor do I think that my perspective on world affairs is particularly unique. We all share many or all of these concerns and we all have the curiosity and aptitude to explore them. As the title of this book implies, the future is up for grabs. This can be a blessing as much as it can be a worry. I leave it to you to decide how best to go from here.

Mike Freedman
London, UK

Introduction:
Propaganda And The Battle For The Planet

by David Cromwell and David Edwards, editors of Media Lens

Most of what the public knows about politics, such as foreign policy, the welfare state and the environment, comes from the mass media. But the mass media is a mass *corporate* media. It is mostly made up of large, profit-seeking corporations whose main task is to sell audiences to wealthy advertisers, themselves often corporations, on whom the media depend for a huge slice of their revenues; as much as 60 per cent for the so-called quality press like the Guardian and the Independent.

Media corporations are owned either by wealthy individuals or giant conglomerates, typically with links to fossil fuel industries, the military and financial interests[1], and are answerable to shareholders who are legally obliged to put profits above all other concerns. They depend on governments, the military and big business sources for a supply of cheap, subsidised news. The media are also subject to intense pressures from corporate, financial and other establishment interests that dominate the economy and politics. An oil giant has far greater power to intimidate a newspaper than, say, Greenpeace.

A final factor responsible for the shaping of news output from media corporations is strict adherence to the notion that the West is a bulwark against 'terrorism' and 'Middle East fundamentalism', perhaps even Islam itself. This Western ideology, almost a state religion, is used to generate 'patriotic' hatred of foreign obstacles to Western power and to attack domestic dissidents as 'apologists' for 'terror' and 'extremism'. It acts as a control mechanism that forever portrays 'us', more particularly 'our' leaders, as the global 'good guys'.[2]

This corporate media system, misleadingly called 'the mainstream media', therefore projects a view of the world that favours elite interests, business and financial aristocracies, and Western state actors; in other words, the narrow sectors of society with huge power over the rest of us.

The above-described five factors or 'news filters' – ownership, advertising, sources, flak and anti-terrorism (or anti-Communism during the Cold War) - is a summary of the 'propaganda model' presented by Edward Herman and Noam Chomsky in their book, 'Manufacturing Consent'.[3] The model is arguably one of the most successful ever proposed in the social sciences, and also one of the most ignored; at least, by media elites and academia. In essence, the corporate media is a system of propaganda for the powerful.

'The Kind Of Newspeak That Would Make Orwell Proud'

'Propaganda' sounds like a lumpen, defunct term from a bygone era. It evokes the Nazis, Stalinism and tinpot Third World dictatorships. We don't normally associate the word with modern Western leaders and political parties. This is a convenient and necessary illusion that serves powerful Western elites very well indeed.

The Russian-born filmmaker Andre Vltchek relates his experience of appearing in the media in different countries. He says that when he speaks in China, he does so uncensored:

> 'I was on CCTV – their National TV – and for half an hour I was talking about very sensitive issues. And I felt much freer in Beijing than when the BBC interviews me, because the BBC doesn't even let me speak, without demanding a full account of what exactly I am intending to say.'[4]

Vltchek continued:

> 'people in the West are so used to thinking that

we are so democratic in terms of the way our media is run and covers the stories. Even if we know it's not the case, we still, subconsciously, expect that it's still somehow better than in other places and it is actually shocking when we realize that a place like China or Turkey or Iran would run more unedited or uncensored pieces than our own mainstream media outlets. Let me put it this way: Chinese television and newspapers are much more critical of their economic and political system than our television stations or newspapers are of ours. Imagine ABC, CBS, or NBC coming on air and beginning to question the basics of capitalism or the Western parliamentary system.'[5]

The same goes for the BBC, as Vltchek noted above, even though it may not initially appear that the propaganda model should apply here. For example, the BBC may not ostensibly be driven by purely commercial values; it is publicly funded through the licence fee, after all. However, the BBC has to challenge for audiences in a highly competitive economic market. Moreover, it does have a commercial, money-making subsidiary called BBC Worldwide Limited which in the year to March 31, 2012 made a profit of £125m on a turnover of £1.116bn.[6]

True, the BBC is not a grasping business corporation in quite the same sense as a profit-driven conglomerate like News International, Shell or General Motors. However, it is run by a director-general, and overseen by the members of a BBC Trust, all of whom typically come from a strong establishment background with close ties to industry, banking, financial and other elite interests.[7]

As the former Guardian journalist Jonathan Cook notes:

'And the BBC is really owned by the British government, which decides on its level of income through the licence fee. Even a perusal of the BBC Trust members shows that they are heavily drawn from the establishment, with half of the current board having received honours from the Queen. The other half can presumably look forward to an honour when they retire from the trust.'[8]

It is therefore extremely unlikely that anyone who represents a strong challenge to the established order would come within sniffing distance of a senior managerial role at the BBC.

Given the close ties between the BBC and the state, and the monarchy-tipped hierarchical class system, it is hardly a surprise that the BBC is the most patriotic and state-supportive of all the major media outlets with its heavy coverage of events like Remembrance Day, Trooping the Colour, royal visits at home and abroad, anniversaries of the Queen's 'ascension' to the throne, Dunkirk, the Battle of Britain, D-Day, the Falklands War, and other trappings of a militaristic 'constitutional monarchy'.

As just one of countless examples of BBC News propaganda, Emily Maitlis opened the flagship BBC2 Newsnight programme on August 11, 2008 with these words after Russian forces had invaded Georgia:

> 'Hello, good evening. The Russians are calling it a "peace enforcement operation". It's the kind of Newspeak that would make George Orwell proud.'[9]

Sceptical comments of this kind are never heard when the BBC relays US or UK propaganda about the 'peace enforcement operation' in Afghanistan or Iraq. No BBC journalist would dare to declare such government claims 'the kind of Newspeak that would make George Orwell proud.' This double standard cannot possibly be considered consistent with the declared commitment of BBC News to remain 'impartial'.

Sinister Facts And Unpopular Ideas

Remarkably, BBC professionals nevertheless manage to believe that the 'news service' they provide really is impartial. An example is Maitlis's later assertion that:

> 'The one thing I've learned is to question herd-thinking, received wisdom.'[10]

In fact, this is one lesson that Maitlis has most definitely *not* learned in the course of a successful BBC career. A journalist who has truly learned to question received wisdom, and actually tries to hold power to account, will find themselves labelled 'unreliable', 'crusading', 'emotionally involved' and 'unprofessional'.

Noam Chomsky summed it up once when interviewed for the BBC by Andrew Marr.[11] If you watch the video, you can see that Marr struggles to grasp the propaganda model of the media which is being patiently explained to him by Chomsky.

In some exasperation, Marr challenges Chomsky:

> 'How can you know that I'm self-censoring?
> How can you know that journalists are...'

Chomsky interjects:

> 'I don't say you're *self-censoring* - I'm sure you believe everything you're saying; but what I'm saying is, if you *believed something different*, you wouldn't be sitting where you're sitting.'

In other words, if Marr really was the 'crusading', adversarial journalist he believes himself to be, he would not have had an influential position making documentaries for the BBC. (Marr was political editor of the Independent at the time; later he was the paper's editor, and he subsequently became political editor of the BBC).

The propaganda model describes the political economy of the corporate media. In a sense, it explains the big picture of media structure and performance in a profit-driven economy. It is not the last word on how the media operate at every level of detail; nor did the authors intend it to be so.

Chomsky himself often broadens discussion out from the propaganda model and points to the importance of the socialising effects of the education system from a very early age, the heavy pressures to conform to mainstream society, show obedience to authority, and so on. Professionals in all fields learn to toe the line when rising up the career ladder.[12] Open criticism of established power is not welcome and often punished.

Along the way, 'successful' journalists come to internalise the limits of permissible reporting and commentary.

Chomsky puts it this way:

> 'In an unpublished introduction to *Animal Farm*, Orwell wrote that "The sinister fact about literary censorship in England is that it is largely voluntary. Unpopular ideas can be silenced,

and inconvenient facts kept dark, without any need for any official ban." The desired outcome is attained in part by the "general tacit agreement that 'it wouldn't do' to mention that particular fact," in part as a consequence of media concentration in the hands of "wealthy men who have every motive to be dishonest on certain important topics." As a result, "Anyone who challenges the prevailing orthodoxy finds himself silenced with surprising effectiveness." '13

Whatever Happened To The Greens?

Consider the fate of the Green movement which, in the 1980s, was a major source of hope for genuinely radical and sustainable change in society. In 2012, the acclaimed biologist and conservationist Edward O. Wilson put the scale of the environment crisis bluntly:

'We're destroying the rest of life in one century. We'll be down to half the species of plants and animals by the end of the century if we keep at this rate.'

Wilson, then 82 years old, addressed the young directly:

'Why aren't you young people out protesting the mess that's being made of the planet? Why are you not repeating what was done in the '60s? Why aren't you in the streets? And what in the world has happened to the green movement that used to be on our minds and accompanied by outrage and high hopes? What went wrong?'14

Wilson did not link the withering of the Green movement with the corporate nature of the media system delivering environmental news to the public. But in fact this corporate domination of the mass media is a disaster for truth and even survival. Clearly, the corporate media is quite literally not in the business of alerting humanity to the real risk of climate catastrophe and what needs to be done to avert it. On the contrary, it has a profound short-term interest in suppressing the scale of the problem and the need for action.

Yes, token moves may be made towards renewable energy by fossil-fuel giants, but only so long as they can retain, indeed strengthen, their economic power and opportunities for yet more profit. The radical overhaul of energy generation and consumption necessary for a sustainable future would require the transfer of economic power from elite institutions, like the banks, oil companies and their political backers in government, to genuinely democratic, accountable institutions acting outside of corporate and elite control.[15]

So what can we do? Obviously, we need to build and strengthen grassroots efforts to raise public awareness of the issues confronting humanity, and to challenge the powerful interests that are crushing so much of the planet's people and ecosystems. However, we at Media Lens are proposing a crucial difference from previous approaches.

For years, activists in left and green circles have argued that we should work with or within corporate media to reach a wider public. For example, in 2004, Tony Juniper, then executive director of Friends of the Earth in the UK, revealed an all-too complacent view of one of the traditional standard-bearers of liberal reporting in Britain:

> 'The Guardian is certainly considered the voice
> of progressive and sound environmental
> thinking both in the UK and in Europe.'[16]

Juniper was referring to an ad-filled newspaper that daily pushes mass consumer advertising of the most destructive kind, such as '2 for 1' transatlantic flight offers. When we asked Juniper why Friends of the Earth fails to address the inherent bias in corporate media reporting in any of its campaigns, he told us that 'Friends of the Earth's response is not to abandon the mainstream media' but to 'debate both with it and the corporate interests that lay behind it, for example through our work on corporate accountability.'[17] In reality, corporate 'accountability', as part of something called 'corporate social responsibility', is a cynical public relations campaign that has been foisted upon people, even as big business has sent global consumption through the roof.

We asked the same question of Spencer Fitzgibbon, then press officer for the Green Party in England and Wales. He responded:

'If we made general sweeping criticisms of the media, we'd just piss off journalists who would then be less likely to write about us. This would not be a functional way for a political party to behave.'[18]

It seems clear to us that after decades of accelerating planetary devastation and lip service to the Green movement, the frail argument of working with or within corporate media has been weakened to the point of collapse. By a process of carefully limited corporate media 'inclusion', the honesty, vitality and truth of environmentalism have been corralled, contained, trivialised and stifled. Why should progressives continue to provide a protective sheen of a 'wide spectrum of views' to a destructive and hugely biased corporate media system that filters and suppresses any genuine sustained challenge to the status quo? Corporate media 'inclusion' of dissent concedes influence and control to the very forces seeking to disempower dissent.

While the power of the internet remains relatively open, there is a brief window to free ourselves from the stifling limitations of the corporate media and to build something honest, radical and publicly accountable. Climate crisis is already upon us, with much worse likely on its way. The stakes almost literally could not be higher.

David Cromwell and David Edwards are the editors of Media Lens (www.medialens.org), a UK-based media analysis website. Media Lens received the Gandhi Foundation Peace Award in 2007.

The Release Phase
with Richard Heinberg

"How do we build the institutions and the attitudes now that will lead to more collaboration, more co-operation, more sharing as scarcity really bites?"

Richard Heinberg is a world-renowned author on the topics of peak oil, post-growth and resource depletion, most notably for his books "The Party's Over", one of the first books about peak oil, "Peak Everything" and "The End of Growth".
I met Richard when we were both on a discussion panel at the Mountainfilm in Telluride Film Festival. We hit it off and have stayed in touch since then. We spoke over the phone after he had recovered from a bad cold.
He speaks in what they call "high American", the region-less newscaster accent. He leaps from subject to subject as if chasing the answer, following an internal instinctive logic rather than merely a line of inquiry. It is clear from the way in which he expresses himself, and in the warmth of his tone, that his interest in these topics is emotional as well as intellectual.

Mike Freedman: I was wondering if you could tell me what you see in the current events going on around us, particularly what's happening in Europe with the financial crisis, what's happening in America with the ongoing political and social crises. Just today, we saw news from India, they're having an extended power cut because their power grid is outdated and overwhelmed and also because they don't have the inputs. I was wondering what you thought were the kind of salient topics from your book and from your research that can clarify what's going on around us.

Richard Heinberg: Right, well over the past few decades economic growth has been the main goal of economies and political leaders. Of course growth is something that has really been a recent phenomenon. It's not like economic growth was the main target of political leaders back in the 13th century. It's since the industrial revolution, since we got this tremendous hit of cheap abundant energy from fossil fuels that we've been able to have economic growth on an annual basis.

So we got used to it and made it the be-all and end-all of political and economic existence. But now that fossil energy is getting harder to come by, economic growth is also getting harder to come by so for the past few decades what political leaders have done in order to stimulate growth is to increase debt. And not initially government debt but initially consumer debt. Household debt. Making it easier for people to take out loans that they ultimately couldn't repay for houses, bigger cars and all the rest.

So here in the US, for the last forty years, debt has grown faster than GDP in every single year[1]. Debt has outpaced GDP growth by about three hundred percent overall. So we're in a huge debt crisis that's monumental in scale. It overwhelms any previous historic example of a debt bubble. But it's showing up first and foremost in Europe because of the way the Euro was set up.

Usually how countries get out from under a debt bubble on a national basis is by devaluing their currency. But the seventeen members of the Eurozone are unable to do that on an individual basis. So the countries with the worst debt problems are being thrown to the wolves basically in order to pay off the banks that hold that debt. This is a problem that can't be solved by normal economic means. We're going to ultimately see massive defaults across the board. The banks are insolvent, big banks are insolvent fundamentally anyway, so propping them up merely prolongs the pain and takes away the resources that the rest of society will need to adjust to a post-growth future.

So that's what's going on in Europe and what will be playing out in the US economy over the course of the next few months. Of course in the US we have this big reset coming at the end of the year where, it sounds so crazy to explain to folks outside the US: in order to refinance US government debt last year, the President and the Congress made a deal whereby at the end of this year unless they can agree to some major spending cuts, some mandatory, really austere spending cuts, tax increases will kick in to artificially balance the budget. Right now the US government is spending about a hundred billion dollars a month of deficit spending. Effectively that is keeping the economy from imploding. If we take that away then next year, the US economy will just go into freefall. So it's likely that some last minute deal will emerge but this is like a national game of chicken that's playing out that would be incredibly comical if it didn't have such dire implications for the US and the rest of the world. So, you know, that's kind of the overview from an economic standpoint.

From an environmental standpoint, US crops are withering on the vine as the worst drought in decades takes hold throughout the American Midwest[2]. Over half of the US is in a drought right now and the severity of the drought increases with every passing week. You can attribute it directly to climate change or indirectly but very clearly we have entered a new era in which we can't count on agriculture to produce food in the quantities and with the regularity that we've been accustomed to. So that of course raises the whole question of global carrying capacity[3] which is what your film takes direct aim at. We've set ourselves up for assuming increasing population, increasing per capita consumption and yet we live on a finite planet. The result of that is population overshoot and a bottleneck which we're entering right now.

MF: One of the examples I've used when I've given presentations or done Q&As in the past is that if there was an elevator that has a plate inside it that simply says 'Maximum capacity: Fifteen Persons or Three Thousand Kilos' or whatever it says, the sixteenth person is neither welcomed into the elevator nor actually attempts to get on. The sixteenth person knows that it's dangerous to be there and the other fifteen people know it's dangerous to let the other person in.

The challenge that we have in the world as it appears to me is we have a situation where we don't have a hard and fast carrying capacity because it's so tied up in elements of lifestyle and consumption and where people live and how they're used to living and how their mindset is pliable to changing into accepting other lifestyles. So the idea of carrying capacity, which it seems has been anathema to the mainstream scientific and political establishment for some time, it's difficult to get a handle on in a way that you can put across to the public sympathetically because either you come off as saying there are too many people, some of them need to go and someone needs to make these hard decisions about who goes which is kind of the eugenic argument which is not one which I am personally invested in or sympathetic to. Or you kind of get sucked into this negotiating tactic where people begin to describe each other in terms of metrics. People can consume this much CO_2 or this much water and so you get bogged down in the statistics and we forget that these are human beings having a qualitative experience of the world, not merely a quantitative one.

So it's interesting that while we seem to be having very straightforward quantitative problems in terms of food, in terms of oil, in terms of provision of the basics to people around the world, ultimately the challenge is a qualitative one. How do we jettison those aspects of our lifestyle and of our mindset that are ultimately destructive to ourselves, to society and to the planet and how do we preserve those elements of our lifestyle that really speak to the genuine quality of life for human beings?

You used the phrase 'post-growth' earlier, and it's a challenge because it's not only about describing problems as they are occurring now but it's also about really replacing a fundamental social narrative which has been dominant for so long that people don't even know that it's questionable, let alone what can replace it, right?

RH: Yeah.

MF: In your work, which I enjoy very much because it is very much rooted in a sense of compassion for human beings, it's not a kind of blithe assumption that some people just need to die off to make space. You are definitely about understanding quality of life issues. How do you see, going forward, a healthy way of presenting this new narrative? What is a post-growth narrative?

RH: Well, as you say, we need to concentrate on and preserve the aspects of life that from a human standpoint really give us the most satisfaction. That doesn't mean consumption, enormous houses and fast cars. It means the quality of relationships with one another, with our communities and with the environment around us. We can have a lot more of that kind of quality of life without consuming more stuff. So that's what we need to be measuring rather than GDP. We should be measuring Gross National Happiness or have a 'genuine progress indicator', something along those lines. There's a lot of discussion amongst economists about alternative indicators and that's very important.

One of those qualities I think that we really need to focus on is just an overall sense of co-operation and collaboration. Right now we see a tremendous emphasis in politics on wedge issues, basically driving people apart and increasing competition. Valorisation of competition, 'You gotta be more competitive' and so on. But as we confront scarcity, we are going through a bottleneck and one way or the other the chances are the human species is going to be winnowed out, but does that have to be a winner-take-all, ultra-competitive kind of experience? Because if it is, we'd probably experience some kind of undershoot. In other words, a "die off" of humanity will be much more extreme than it would actually have to be if we were to approach scarcity with a co-operative, sharing attitude.

We're capable of both. The evidence is very strong that, especially in times of crisis, people tend to band together and co-operate. So how do we set ourselves up for that? How do we build the institutions and the attitudes now that will lead to more collaboration, more co-operation, more sharing as scarcity really bites? And less of the kind of really deadly competition that we're actually seeing right now.

MF: What's interesting about what you just said, which I happen to agree with you, is this need to make the case for co-operation as an aspirational, social trait. We've been told that human beings are superficially co-operative and fundamentally competitive, which is to say that we're able to form villages and societies and team up when we need to take down a boar but underneath this, as Edgar Rice Burroughs called it, the "thin veneer of civilisation"[4], beats the heart of the ancient primate who is always looking for advantage and who is always looking for selfish gratification.

Whereas it seems to be the exact opposite to my mind, that human beings are superficially competitive but fundamentally co-operative. This is something that we haven't really been told.

It hasn't been elucidated for the public or in the mainstream sciences. This game theory geopolitics that we've ended up with, this zero-sum game that you're talking about where it's not necessarily that it'll always get better if there's more, it doesn't necessarily follow that things have to be worse if there's less. This kind of, not only capacity but proclivity for co-operation among people at a fundamental level is also kind of a tool that's been used against us by power systems, by hierarchies, by vested interests because we tend to go along. We're a species that is context-based. We've a tendency to accept at face value what we're told about what's happening and we just kind of get on with our lives and raise our children and make sure we have enough to eat and that we're dry when it rains. In general that keeps us ticking over because of this fundamental co-operative nature. Ironically, we find ourselves co-operating with people who have exactly the opposite of our best interest at heart. This is a very striking example of what I believe you're talking about. We've been told a story about people and a story about our society which not only isn't true but actually runs counter to the way we actually are and actually could be.

RH: In a situation like what we have right now where basically the interests of the majority of people are being sacrificed to prevent the banks from suffering the loss resulting from their bad debts, whether we're talking about Greece or Wall Street or Spain, the same basic dynamic is working out. The natural inclination of people I think would be to band together to co-operate, to stop that from happening, to act in the interest of society as a whole. Revolution, I guess you could say, is a co-operative activity.

So how do governments prevent that kind of co-operation from happening by creating other kinds of co-operative opportunities like getting everybody together to go to war with some other country. I think that's unfortunately a likely strategy that the elites could use in the years ahead in order to avert the de-legitimisation of their own regimes and of the economic system.

So once again, as you're saying, our basically co-operative nature can be used against us and I think the tonic for that is to develop systems of trust at the grassroots level. Whether it's local economic systems, local food systems, getting people talking to one another across our fence lines in our backyards. Neighbours talking to neighbours regardless of political affiliation. Get away from the wedge issues, talk about what's in our genuine collective best interest.

MF: Well, America is a particularly striking example of this exact bizarre paradox of the way power structures behave. In a way, they kind of cannibalise themselves because of that exact tactic you said about preserving legitimacy. People only accept authority as long as the authority is legitimate in some way, either because it's based on some semblance of democratic process or because people simply feel safer when that authority is in place. Whatever the case is, legitimacy is obviously a fundamental part of preserving any power structure, especially a hierarchical one like we have. But then you see these methods by which it gets chiselled away. You have corporate lobbyists who are lobbying to prevent regulating environmental degradation. What that does is it makes the government seem weak because it is unable to prevent the degradation on the one hand but at the same time trust in the government is at an all-time low so people don't trust the government to regulate. So there's this kind of lose-lose structure to this behaviour pattern which is very counter-intuitive. You would assume that if business is, as they claim, long term because they want to be a functioning, profitable corporation for fifty to a hundred years then they would know that a massive agribusiness conglomerate will have no future if there is catastrophic climate change, catastrophic water scarcity or catastrophic crop loss due to soil deterioration.

So, we're in this bizarre zero-sum game where even the people who are perceived as the elite or are perceived to have that legitimate power seem to be making choices that are not only opposed to our best interests as the people or the constituents but even their own long-term best interests because of some short-term goal that never really gets discussed and is very difficult to pinpoint.

RH: You know, one way of describing the situation we're in is in terms of resilience theory[5]. Resilience theorists talk about the adaptive cycles that are characteristic of systemic development in nature, in evolution or in human societies. Within the adaptive cycle, one of the key phases, they call it the 'release phase'. They describe it as a rapid, chaotic period during which capitals, which could be natural capital, human, social or financial capital, tend to be lost and novelty can succeed. I think that's a useful way of describing the period that we're entering, the post-growth period. Some people would call it collapse, I think that's a little bit too simplistic a term. It implies that everything falls down, that's the end of the story. Of course it's going to be a much more complicated story than that. Unless we face actual human extinction, which may be a possibility but certainly not a certainty unless that's the outcome, then there's something that comes after. What we should be talking about is a process, not just a once-and-for-all event.

I have a theory. I'm looking for evidence either to confirm or disconfirm it, a hypothesis if you will that in human societies as they approach the 'release phase', as they approach this chaotic period in which capital is lost, fear and competition tend to be exacerbated. The elites are very fearful of losing what they have. They've attained maximum concentration of wealth at this point and they're very fearful of losing that. So a sense of competition driven by what we today call wedge issues becomes characteristic of this immediate pre-release phase.

But then once release actually occurs, then society regroups fairly quickly on a co-operative basis. You can even see it in the financial world. When a country is striving to avoid default then people experience in some ways the worst of all possible worlds because there's extreme austerity and competition within social classes and all the rest. But once the country actually defaults, then the economic system reorganises itself pretty quickly and life goes on.

So I think that's where we are right now. It's a really painful place to be. But it's not gonna last forever.

MF: I spent a good year and a half to two years of my life researching and making the film and several people I interviewed described, especially the peak oil side of things, this kind of five stages of grief concept. And you do find yourself going through that but what's also interesting is that many people, I believe, and I found myself falling prey to this to a certain extent, get to the point where it's almost comforting believing that collapse is this immediate threat that is conclusive. And you find yourself thinking, well OK, so Armageddon is going to happen on Tuesday but what if I wake up on Wednesday and I still need to get by and do my thing? That collapse can be almost this vicarious pornographic thrill. That we're on a ride and it's all gonna crash out. Just accept it and have fun and then when it ends it ends but then obviously the next day you're going to need to eat, your kids are still going to need shoes.

So did you find that when you first started working on these kind of issues around peak oil and decline, collapse and deterioration, did you find yourself falling prey to that? How did you go about beginning to look toward the days after rather than focussing on the build-up to the crash?

RH: Interesting question. My first book back in 1989 was a book called 'Memories and Visions of Paradise'[6] which was a book about world mythology and prophecies. Mythologies of a lost golden age, prophecies of days of tribulation and the end of the world. In some ways it was a study of how the human mind tends to create these dichotomies and scenarios of extreme perfection or disillusion. We're still doing that. We have this inbuilt tendency to totalise information and reality usually is somewhere in between.

I see this working out in people's psyches all the time. Either it's denial, the sense "oh well, our current system, it will go on forever, of course we'll always have economic growth" and " oh yeah, we'll have problems here and there, we'll always have wars somewhere but it will never affect me and my family". A person can flip very quickly from that kind of attitude to the attitude that says "oh, the world is just teetering on the brink and it's all going to fall apart and within six months we'll have complete chaos in the streets and you won't be able to take money out of the bank and that will be the end of it" .

That kind of totalising attitude keeps us from actually doing the real work or preparing circumstances that will enable us to get by more successfully in times of increased scarcity which is what we are actually facing. In some places at some times it's going to feel like collapse, there's no question, but that doesn't mean that nothing will come after that. If you look back at civilisations that collapsed in previous eras, most civilisations have gone through that process at least once and on occasion several times. It's a process. People come out the other side of it usually poorer and often fewer of them but they regroup, they re-organise and life goes on. That's what we should be thinking about: how we want this to go, how we want this reorganisation to proceed and what could be the best outcome at the end of it.

MF: You segued neatly into another key issue which I find very fascinating. It applies both at the international level when we talk about 'borderless' issues like resource decline, climate change, water cycle issues etcetera and also at a national and even local level, we talk about "we need to do this", "we need to do that". It seems that, more so in the past two hundred years since the advent of industrialisation and also faster than we have in the past, we've really committed ourselves to a centralising principle whereby we have concentrated power in fewer and fewer hands. We've concentrated decision-making in fewer and fewer hands. We've reinforced the strict hierarchical principles that Western civilisation has been organised along for quite some time now.

When environmentalists or politicians or academics discuss the challenges we face going forward, when we discuss things like "we need to do this", "we need to do that", it's always fascinating to me that we've come to this precipice in part because of the alienating and unaccountable features of the centralised, hierarchical, top-down system that we use; all of the suggestions seem to be based on preserving, at some level and in some manner, that exact same hierarchical, highly centralised, top-down structure.

When it comes to the UN talking about a climate agreement or Colin Campbell's oil depletion protocol idea[7] or the rest of them, the idea that organisations need to make these moves for the public good, when you don't have the legitimacy, when the public doesn't believe that the power structure has our best interests at heart, we're in a position where we're facing evidently worldwide huge loss of confidence in exactly the structures that many people are arguing need to be strengthened in order to get us out of the problem we're in.

So the question is: how do we resolve this issue where it's obvious that there are many, many people and that a minority of them are intimately acquainted with the problems we are looking at and therefore in order to respond speedily to these problems, we're looking at a minority of people making decisions that affect the majority in a sweeping manner in effectively a fast and ultimately less than accountable manner? This is really the worry. That we haven't really had a functioning or healthy democracy for some time, if we ever did. It seems all of the suggestions, like the way the Athenians used to hire a tyrant in times of crisis, all of the suggestions seem to focus on less due process and more very fast decision-making by very few people who 'know what's best'. This is deeply worrying if one would suggest that the actual structures of hierarchy and centralisation have a central role in exactly the predicament we're in.

RH: Well stated. The good news is that history is moving in favour of decentralisation at this moment. The reason I say that

10

is centralisation of power requires energy. Ivan Illich, philosopher, wrote a book back in the 1970s called 'Energy and Equity'[8] in which he proposed that the higher the energy flow-through in a society, the more inequitable that society is likely to be. In other words, a hunter-gatherer band have very, very little energy that they use. Absolute minimum for cooking their food and that's about it. Build a campfire at night to sit around and that's about the extent of it. It tends to be very egalitarian.

In order to have a city, you have to have a lot of energy expenditure for transportation of resources from the periphery to the centre, the transformation of those resources into commodities and distribution of them. With the fossil fuel era, the amount of energy flow-through has gone off the charts compared to anything in any previous human society and therefore we've been able to fund urbanisation, centralised power structures and economic inequality, all at a scale well beyond anything seen in any previous historical epoch.

As energy quality declines, as fossil fuels become more expensive, less available, lower quality, higher environmental costs, higher investment costs, all the rest, the result of that is it's going to be harder and harder to maintain the levels of economic inequality and the kind of centralised power relationships you were talking about.

That's of course why the elites are so frightened of this moment in history. They see or they feel, intuitively at least, the direction which all of this is headed toward: decentralisation, levelling, relocalisation, and it doesn't feel very good to them. That's the inevitable direction of history. So we should be planning for that and rather than assuming that all of these problems have to be solved at the absolute apex of power by really smart people with Harvard degrees sitting around tables making decisions for the rest of us, I think we have to start looking at ourselves and our neighbours and figure out how we're going to build the structures that are going to get us through this bottleneck.

MF: But then I suppose the question is whether one believes that the recourse of power under threat is greater collaboration or whether the recourse of power under threat is authoritarianism or totalitarianism?

RH: You see plenty of evidence of the latter right now. The criminalisation of dissent and the militarisation of the police are trends that we're seeing in most countries right now. They lead only in one direction.

MF: This is exactly, again, what I find particularly worrying. Let's assume for the moment that what is referred to as 'Western, free-market, liberal democracy' is mainly a marketing exercise. Let's just make that wild assumption and put that to one side. Frank Zappa once said that "When the expense of maintaining the illusion of freedom becomes too high they will simply move all the props, raise the curtains and you'll see the brick wall at the back of the theatre". It seems that the West, which has sold itself as this bastion of democratic and free-thinking values, is being the most eager to dispense with those trappings as soon as it is facing straitened circumstances. This obviously is very worrying because it means that we are governed by marketers, rather than marketeers, who are willing to stop pretending when things get rough. We're having the same problem here [in Britain]. The Metropolitan Police, for the first time ever, went public with the fact that they are ordering a record number of tasers.[9] So the British bobbies who have been unarmed throughout the age of firearms with the exception of a single firearms unit of anti-terrorism police, the British bobbies are now going to be carrying tasers. We had our Home Secretary here after the riots in August say "We don't want to see water cannons on the street but ..."[10]

It's the relationship of the abusive drunken husband, "Look what you made me do!", and it seems that this is the trend that we're seeing. As conditions become more strained, as people's creature comforts are threatened by legitimate environmental and resource constraints, governments are stepping on dissent, slowly eroding the legal structure that protects people from government interference and attack. Not so much that there's an overt shift to some kind of fascist system immediately, but by the time, further down the road, some event takes place where these draconian laws come into play in full, the legal framework that could have repealed or constrained these new measures has been removed.

This is the real worry. How do we as individuals within society, with our voice and our communities, use our rights to free speech, to free inquiry, to accessing information, to challenging structures, to speaking the truth to power if these freedoms are inevitably eroded or entirely constrained by the social conditions that are created right now? In that situation it is doubly difficult to actually change something, surely because this crackdown serves to entrench the power of the elite you are describing rather than to say "Look guys, we're going to need some fresh ideas. Let's have some sweepstakes."

RH: It's a really tough question because of course some folks will say "Well, what we need to do then is directly confront the power elites". In my mind that's engaging on their terms. The power elites have the money, the guns, the PR professionals, you name it. And even though it's possible to point to 'people power' overwhelming the elites in specific situations, Tahrir Square and so on, but take that example: in Egypt the people tossed out Mubarak, now the military is largely in the driver's seat and we'll see how all of that works - it's a process.

That's really the point. It's a process and unless the people build structures of collaboration and mutual support then just toppling the citadel of power at the pinnacle of the pyramid really doesn't accomplish that much because what happens is the folks at the next level of the pyramid pop up and keep the pyramid going as best they can. The only way to change the shape of the pyramid of power is by changing the way the whole economic process works from the bottom up. That means we have to contemplate a different way of life because if we want to maintain by any means necessary our current industrial way of life of cars and shopping malls and all the rest, it's going to be hierarchical and it's going to be highly unequal just by the very nature of the system itself. If we really want to get through this bottleneck and preserve the best of humanity, the best of human nature, we're going to have to, in the process of building that new future, exercise those qualities of co-operation and compassion and all the rest that we want to see. They have to be part of the process of thinking and designing our lives at the most basic level.

MF: When the Occupy thing was taking off here in London at the end of last year, I wrote an open letter to the protesters. One of the things I said was that there really is no more 'good guys' and 'bad guys'. That's a dead paradigm when we're in a situation like this. We're simply either people who know what's happening or people who have been misinformed. The protestors being in a square surrounded by riot police feel that they are under attack by some kind of monolithic establishment but the irony of the way our system is at least supposed to work is that if the protesters represented the establishment the police would be facing the other way and would fight tooth and nail to protect them.

13

So the social structures and ideas that I would hope the rule of law and associated institutions are based on are about creating tools rather than weapons. The police will defend what they are told to defend by the establishment that they represent. The fact that they are defending people who are behaving in an unsympathetic manner against people who want to change the system for the better is a co-incidence of the structure rather than the failing of the police as humans.

So when we see this kind of militarisation and reduction of the ability to dissent, we see these structures that are meant to be social tools are becoming political and economic weapons. The danger obviously is that, before we can change them, we may get ourselves to a point where if a new party or a new way of thinking took root they would no longer bend themselves to the will of the people. They would not be tools. They would be weapons in the hands of the people that have changed the rules to suit themselves.

RH: So many paradoxes: if folks act in their own economic self-interest at a moment like this, what they really should be doing is becoming more self-sufficient. Growing more of their own food, sharing with neighbours, getting out of debt and so on. But if everybody did those things the result would be economic collapse. The system depends on everyone consuming more and more and taking out more and more loans all the time. That has to grow in order for GDP to grow and so on. So for people to act in their own self-interest is to undermine the system. For them to act against the only way to keep the system going is for them to act against their own self-interest.

MF: Like gay Republicans?

RH: Yeah, right. So sorting this out won't be something we do overnight. It's going to be a process by which more and more people gradually wake up to see what their real self-interest is and the system isn't going to like it. I think people growing veggies in their backyard and keeping chickens may seem at some point, in some places, as subversive or even criminal, because it's clear if you're going to be an obedient member of the system, what you need to do is consume, go into debt and shut up. Fewer people are going to want to do that.

MF: Positive Money[11] here in the UK, I don't know if you're familiar with their work, but I would consider them to probably be the most important advocacy organisation in the UK today because they're working to reform the money creation system here in Britain - obviously, one of the bitter ironies of having a debt-based money system as we do is that as people pay off their debts the money supply shrinks which creates exactly the recessionary conditions that make it more likely that people won't spend as they focus on paying off their debts.

RH: Exactly, yeah.

MF: So like you said, someone who pays off their credit card instead of buying a new Hummer is betraying the system as it is even if they are doing, objectively speaking, the right thing. I suppose it's the paradox of democracy. If we all become like Mazlow's pyramid where we're the highest pinnacle and we're developing ourselves because all the other needs have been taken care of, we'll come to a position where more and more of us find that the system that allowed us to become the people that think like this is actually destroying people who think like this.

RH: So the secret I think is to do the right thing anyway.

MF: Was it St. Augustine who said "Give me chastity and give me constancy but not yet"?[12]

Thinking Outside The Death Camp
with Derrick Jensen

> *"This is not a human problem. It's a civilisation problem."*

Derrick Jensen is one of the most controversial environmentalist authors working today. His books capture a deep passion for nature and a raw sense of loss for what mankind has left behind as we've formed industrial, urbanised societies. To sum up Derrick's work and beliefs succinctly, his own words are perfectly suitable:

> "Every morning when I awake I ask myself whether I should write or blow up a dam. I tell myself I should keep writing, though I'm not sure that's right."

I interviewed Derrick for what was originally intended to be a podcast, during the early portion of production on Critical Mass, but the audio quality of the recording was so poor that it sat, unused, until I remembered how apropos it would be for this book. In print, his ideas can seem forceful or caustic, but over the phone his voice is gentle and patient, qualities belied by his strong views on humanity's behaviour and future prospects. He signs every email, no matter how trivial, with the words "Thank you".

16

Mike Freedman: I know that your area of interest is the impact of civilisation itself. I'm reading 'Against The Grain' by Richard Manning[1] right now and he has a lot to say about how civilisation itself is almost a pathology in terms of how it's affected our behaviour. Do you think you could explain to me how you see the role of civilisation in the way that we behave as people?

Derrick Jensen: Well, why don't we start with a definition of civilisation. In my work, I define civilisation as a way of life characterised by the growth of cities, by people living in numbers large enough to require the importation of resources. Two things happen as soon as you require the importation of resources. One is that your way of life can never be sustainable because if you require the importation of resources it means you've denuded the landscape of that particular resource. As your city grows, you'll denude an ever-larger area. All we have to do is look at the history of civilisation to see this. One of the first written myths of this culture is that of Gilgamesh deforesting the plains on all sides of Iraq. Prior to the beginnings of this culture, Iraq had cedar forest so thick that sunlight never touched the ground. The Arabian Peninsula was oak savannah. Greece was heavily forested, North Africa was heavily forested, Italy was heavily forested. What this culture does is destroy forest and destroy land bases. It does that to continue to grow "the machine", as Lewis Mumford[2] put it.

So one of the things that happens is your way of life can never be sustainable. I live on Tolowa Indian land. The Tolowa lived here for twelve thousand and five hundred years; if you believe the myth of the Tolowa, then they lived here since the beginning of time. Either way they lived here for an awfully long time and they didn't destroy the place. The place was a paradise when the first Europeans arrived here. The Europeans have been here en masse for about a hundred and seventy years and the place was trashed and that's what you see everywhere. This is not a human problem. It's a civilisation problem.

The other thing requiring the importation of resources means is that your way of living must be based on violence. Because if you require, 'require' being the key word, require the importation of resources and the people in the next watershed over won't trade you for that resource that you need, you will take it. Trade will never be sufficiently reliable if you require the importation of resources. So this means we can all become junior bodhisattvas and the US military would still have to be

17

huge because how is it going to get access to the oil that they need to run the economy?

So that's on one level. Then there's another level too. There are many unquestioned assumptions in this culture. One of them is that civilisation is what it means to be human. There have been some strides at least in the linguistics of racism over the past forty to fifty years. No longer is it acceptable in polite society for anyone but the most open racist to call someone a 'nigger'. Yet with women, it's acceptable to call someone a bitch. So women, it's still acceptable to defame them. Another group it's still acceptable to really demean, in academic circles certainly, is indigenous people. I was having an unfortunate bit of discourse the other day and I was talking about indigenous peoples living sustainably and he said 'Nobody wants to go back and live in caves'. There are those advertisements on television, 'So simple, even a caveman can do it'. What that is, that is an explicit, racist attack on the only ways of living that have ever been sustainable, which is indigenous small-scale horticulture and hunter-gatherer. Those are the only ways that have ever been sustainable. Yet there's this bigotry in this culture that presumes that civilisation is what it means to be human.

There was a scholarly article not very long ago, they were saying that there was a civilisation in the Amazon and the way they noticed is because there were moats, forts and other signs of militarism, which is a pretty significant acknowledgement on their part that civilisation equals militarism, but we'll leave that aside. They said "Until then, we only thought that hunter-gatherers lived in the Amazon with their short, nasty, brutish lives". This culture has a huge hatred of the natural, which includes humans who live in the natural world.

We can take it in a different direction if you wanted to, which is talking simply about population. Someone who influenced me a lot, and you can't interview him because he's dead, is John A. Livingston.[3] He wrote how we often think of cities as places of sensory overload where you go there and you're just assaulted. Your senses are assaulted by all the lights and all the sharp corners and all the cars and all the sounds and everything. He actually says that, and this really makes a lot of sense to me, that instead they're places of sensory deprivation. The reason is because every sensory perception that you have when you're in a city, almost every sensory perception, is either created or mediated by human beings. What happens to people in sensory deprivation? They begin to hallucinate. So John A. Livingston says, and once again I agree, that most of our ideologies and most of the things we think and talk about are hallucinations. They're insane, literally. They're delusional.

A great example of this, we can come up with examples all day long but a great example of this is what do all of the so-called solutions for global warming have in common? What are the mainstream solutions? What they all have in common is they all take industrial capitalism as a given - the natural order must conform to industrial capitalism. That is literally insane and being out of touch with physical reality because without a real world you don't have any social system. Any sane social system must take the natural world, the source of all life, as primary, and the social system as secondary to that.

Another great example of this is: I was getting interviewed one time by this horrible, right-wing, anti-environmental radio interview person. I had no idea going into the interview what he was like. I agreed to do the interview and then it ends he was what I just described. I was talking about how ninety percent of large fish in the oceans are gone, how salmon are getting hammered and sharks are getting hammered, migratory songbirds are getting hammered. I kept saying all these things that any of us who are paying any attention at all know and he kept saying "No, that's all fine Derrick, but let's get back in the real world". I thought I was describing the real world but I realised part way in that he was actually describing the real world for himself. For him the real world is industrial capitalism. That's how they use it, they say "what are you going to do when you have to go out in the real world?" Now what they mean is "what you gonna do when you have to get a real job?" Industrial capitalism is not the real world, it's a social system. The real world is the songbirds I actually hear right now chattering and the wind that I hear in the trees. That's the real world. That's where life comes from.

Another thing that civilisation does, like any good abusive system, it puts itself between us and the source of life. That's what any abuser does. If you have someone abusing his wife, one of the things that is absolutely standard is that they will cut their wife off from all support systems. They will make the victim reliant upon them. The reason is because no one in their right mind is going to stay with an abuser unless they don't perceive themselves having a choice. It's one of the things this culture has done systematically is insert itself between us and the real world. Once again, if you want to go that direction we can talk more about that. I'm not really sure what direction you

19

want to go so there are a series of directions that are possible. Wherever you want me to go is fine.

MF: I never intended to embark on an ecological journey of discovery. I actually was intrigued by an experiment that I found out about and began reading up on by John B. Calhoun in the fifties, sixties right through the seventies when he was working at The National Institute of Mental Health in the US. You've probably come across it at least in reference through some of the things you've read. He put rodents into various enclosures, gave them plenty of food and water and nesting material, let them reproduce and simply observed the population dynamics. His interest was in the human or population ecology of it. What happens to a social structure when population density reaches a certain point? If predators are absent, if food is plentiful, if survival pressures are taken away, what other stress factors are there in a society whether it's rodent or human? That was his main thrust.

I started reading up on the experiments and seeing so many parallels to the situation we're in. The alienation that we feel, the density that we live in. Exactly like you said, this mediated connection to the world around us. That's why your initial leap that civilisation means cities is very interesting because the city is the best example of what Calhoun was looking at. A city is like an enclosure. People go there, they're kept safe from predators. Your ability to obtain food, water and nesting material is directly related to your financial capital and nothing else. So you could effectively say those things are abundant in that sense. So what happens to people in that 'enclosure' of the city? The conclusions you come to are very similar in that sense, that cut off from any relationship to the life support systems that brought us there in the first place, we develop a series of pathologies, whether you want to look at them as hallucinations or coping mechanisms. The fundamental byproduct is that we are in an unnatural situation. Effectively that is what I took away from what you were saying. The way you see it is the real world is the world that we have built a box within, to protect ourselves. So when we talk about that, I guess you could call it the pathology of civilisation, do you see in the world around us and I mean the natural world, the stresses that we've placed on the environment, whether you want to talk about climate change, resources, fossil fuels even just human behaviour, the ability of human beings to relate to others, do you see a peaking of these pressures where we have to evolve in terms of our thinking and in terms of our behaviour in order to get over the hump? Or do you think that we are looking at some kind of deterioration if we're going to learn anything?

DJ: I don't think most people are going to learn. I think most people are irredeemable. Lundy Bancroft wrote a book called "Why Does He Do That?: Inside The Minds of Angry and Controlling Men" and he's done work with abusers, in terms of helping their partners. In his book he makes some great points. One of the points is that there's a tremendous recidivism amongst abusers, that they almost never change. One of the reasons that the rate of recidivism or the rate of continuation of abuse is so high amongst perpetrators is that it's based on entitlement. They are gaining tangible benefits from their behaviour.

The same is true for members of the elite worldwide by which I mean most people in the United States, people who are rich on a global scale. We're the beneficiaries of this ridiculous system. You have a computer, I have a computer. I have a telephone, you have a telephone. I have a hot shower, you have a hot shower. Which is not to say "it's our fault", I want to be really clear about that. I'm not one of those people who believes you can have personal change equal social change. I'm not saying that at all. The cliche about addiction is that addicts don't usually change until they hit bottom. One of the problems is that people who are addicted to entitlement actually don't hit bottom. They cause everyone else to hit bottom.

I do talks in front of four hundred people, six hundred people, nine hundred people all the time and I ask "How many of you believe this culture is going to undergo a voluntary transformation to a sustainable way of living?" Nobody ever says yes. Like one person in five years has said yes. The answer is we don't know. One of the reasons we don't know is because we don't talk about it. The reason we don't talk about it is we're all so busy pretending we have hope.

So back to your original question, yeah, I see the world collapsing around me right now. Five years ago it was so loud from frogsong outside my house that you couldn't have a human conversation. Now I'm lucky if I hear three or four frogs at a time. Amphibians are collapsing, populations are collapsing worldwide. Salmon. There used to be salmon runs so thick you couldn't see the bottom of the stream and I'm lucky if I see two or three salmon. Even banana slugs, all I know is my own experience. I don't know if anything is happening to banana slugs on a larger scale. I moved here ten years ago and at night and at certain times of the year you'd squish them because you just couldn't avoid them. Now, if I walk about half a mile, maybe I'd see three banana slugs. All of them are big. The last three or four years has been reproductive failure. I don't know why. I don't know if that's only right here or if it's on a larger scale. I was talking to some guy from Washington and he said he hasn't seen banana slugs in five years. I was talking to somebody else who lives about ninety miles south of here and he said he still sees banana slugs all the time and he sees babies too. Everything is collapsing around us and everything is going faster and faster. We continue to see the same rhetoric that we've seen in this culture for the last two thousand years of Christianity. "Well, God gave us this world to use so we're gonna use it!" I see no cessation.

The only slight slowdown that I saw, even of carbon emissions, was when the economy went down. So the only thing that is going to stop this is the entire collapse of civilisation, whether it happens through peak oil or whether it happens through ecological collapse or whether it happens because some of us are smart enough and brave enough to actually bring it down ourselves.

MF: There is a very real sense of addiction to a lifestyle. Like you said, an addict doesn't stop until he hits bottom. The first step of overcoming addiction is admitting you have a problem, to use another cliche. We as a community, whether it's local communities, whether it's the global community, we've only really in the past couple of years begun to even pay lip service to the idea that there might be a problem.

So, when I look at this, there's this addiction factor that I find the most worrying because until the drug of choice is withdrawn there's no incentive to overcome or to develop. I also keep getting reminded of a quote, I think it was George Santayana who said "A fanatic is one who redoubles his efforts whilst forgetting his cause". I feel like maybe once, when we started planting food and living together and there was this kind of organic development of civilisation as you describe it, it was more people turning up and going "Oh, there's fresh water, there's food, these people seem nice, I'll stay."

DJ: Actually that's not so accurate. From the beginning it's really been based on militarisation. Going back to the addiction thing, yeah, I agree.

MF: I read "Critical Path" by Buckminster Fuller and in that he lays out the premise that basically all land ownership is fundamentally an extortion racket that just turned into something that was around for long enough that people forgot that it was extortion and just figured that it was the way things were. You build a cabin, you fish from the local river, you plant a few potatoes in the backyard and then this guy shows up on horseback and says "Give me potatoes every month or I'll burn your cabin down". Kapow! All of a sudden this guy ends up being the regent of the area. How do we develop as a community, as a civilisation? If civilisation is to have hope, it needs to begin to deliver civilised values.

DJ: Like the anthropologist Stanley Diamond wrote, civilisation is based on conquest or broad repression at home. That was the point I was trying to make earlier about civilisation. If civilisation continues, there will be no life on the planet because civilisation is systematically, functionally and inherently based on drawdown, on population and on continued growth. It's been that way from the beginning because if you have a way of life that's based on drawdown of your carrying capacity, based on the destruction of your land base, that means you must be militaristic because you're going to have to continue to take other places and you will be expansionist because you've destroyed your own land base.

I was doing a talk down in Los Angeles a couple of weeks ago and one person asked "But if the United States overshot its carrying capacity and they need to import these resources, can't they just go ahead and take them? They need them". I said the fact that the United States has overshot carrying capacity is not the problem of the people of Peru. It's not everybody else's problem except of course if the people of the United States have a lot of guns. So my point is that any way of life based on growth must be militaristic and also unsustainable and it will crash. We will be undergoing a crash. Economically the crash has already begun.

MF: There are three main ramifying factors: population growth, economic growth and consumption. They all seem to reinforce each other. If more people are around every year, you need more goods and services even if they're of the most basic kind simply because the sheer numbers demand more supply.

In that sense we have had what Herman Daly[4] calls uneconomic growth. You end up with these vast disparities

23

between people having immense amounts of consumption and other people who may, in that very tricky economic sense, be better off than they were fifty years ago but they still proportionally have not seen the gains. There's never enough to go around so either we all keep walking and the music never stops or the music stops and some of us don't have a seat.

DJ: Yes, I agree. The primary victims of this are (A) land-based people around the world whose lands are stolen to make more chairs for those who are still playing musical chairs and (B) the natural world which is destroyed to make these additional chairs. And the people of the future, as the whole thing collapses. Every day that goes by, the carrying capacity of Earth for human beings is decreased.

MF: I really like that idea that you're cutting down forests in one place to make chairs in another. I was looking at the calculations of the Global Footprint Network, the people who developed the ecological footprint. They calculate bio-capacity, which is the ability of nature to supply and absorb, then they also calculate consumption. Countries in sub-Saharan Africa are places with tremendous bio-capacity and not only has consumption there stagnated whilst ours has just gone through the roof but what you're seeing is an actual decline in the bio-capacity. We're damaging the future prospects of that environment to supply anything to the people who live there, let alone us.

So we're screwing ourselves. You can pump the oil out of Venezuela, you can dig the gold out of Congo, dig the diamonds out of South Africa, strip mine, dig coal out but eventually there's going to be no more places to outsource to. There's going to be no more places to import from. I know your answer, it's just that I feel like there must be, because when you said that people are irredeemable -

DJ: Most people.

MF: Sorry, most people. When I speak to people about these things, when I'm on the train or walking around and I start a conversation with someone, there is this awareness that everyone has - we all feel like there's something going on, it's just that it's never been articulated in a broadly accepted way. So I think that we've been categorically failed by the information systems that are supposed to engage us about the world we live in. I think that most people who you believe are irredeemable, maybe they just haven't been given the information with which to comprehend the gravity of the situation.

DJ: Well that's the function of the corporate media. There's a great line by Henry Adams from maybe a hundred years ago: "The press is a hired agent of a money system set up for no other reason than to tell lies where the interests are concerned." What you were saying before about the addiction - that verb, 'addict', comes from the same root as 'to enslave'. It was originally a Roman term meaning 'to bind'. A judge would deliver an edict that would 'addict' you to whatever term or whatever sentence you were going to be 'addicted' to.[5]

I used to teach in a prison and my students would say that at first the drug would serve them and then later on they were serving the drug. Lewis Mumford really made the same point and Frederick Winslow Taylor[6] did to - excuse the sexism, this is him not me: "In the past, the man was first; in the future, the system shall be first". That's one of the things that I see happening all the time.

I used to have this hobby of asking people if they like their jobs and about ninety percent would say no. What does it mean when the vast majority of people are spending the vast majority of their waking hours doing things they don't want to do? It's all crazy. All of this crap that's happening is not even really to serve human beings but rather to serve the system. The system is out of control. It's just insane.

MF: I read a quote by M. King Hubbert[7], obviously of peak oil fame. After he discovered the peak curve scenario he started working out ways of doing things differently. One of the things he suggested was that in order to curtail the damage that excess energy consumption brings with it, we should do away with the economics of perceived value and instead have an economics of energy credit, in the sense that whatever the energy allowance of each person was, that was their "right" as a member of the global community to consume X amount of energy. If we understood what energy was needed for everything we would then live within that energy trading system. He said the biggest stumbling block to that was the work ethic, which is this kind of instilled programme.

DJ: It's not just that. Traditionally, and you can find lots of

25

quotes in my books and in anthropological studies too, for many indigenous people prior to their conquest by this culture, their life was far more full of leisure. Even modern San Bushmen living in the desert still only work an average of three or four hours a day but for their sustenance. There's a great line by Kuikoi, a member of a people who have since been driven extinct; he was asking the Europeans who were invading their land "Why do you work so hard? We have these wonderful trees that give us fruit. We have these wonderful streams that we drink from and so, why should we work?" You can't really argue with that.

So it isn't simply a position of privilege. It is, within this culture, a position of privilege to not have to be a stevedore or a coal miner but that was our birthright as living beings. I hate nature programmes for any number of reasons, one of which is they don't show that crocodiles spend all their time asleep or hanging out or just sunning themselves. The same with lions. Everybody just spends their time playing and hanging out. I'm not saying that violence doesn't happen, of course it happens, but it's nowhere like in nature programmes. I was watching this awful nature programme recently, they were showing these crocodiles going after anything that moved and they had one throwaway line: "The crocodile may eat somewhere between once a month and some of them can go up to six months without eating." All we ever see when we see nature programming is them going after somebody but the truth is twenty-nine days out of thirty they're not killing anybody. Anyway, back to the original point, I agree.

MF: It keeps coming back to balance. I felt you out about how you see a way out of this and I think it's pretty clear that you feel like it's not only that most people will need a sudden cessation or a dramatic decline in order to snap out of the situation we're in, it's the only way to preserve an extended future for humanity. Is that correct? Do I understand you right?

DJ: Humanity and non-humanity, for anybody really. I don't think that humans are particularly more important than other beings. That's one of the hallucinations that cities make us have. It's the belief that humans are fundamentally separate. I was up in Victoria doing a talk last week, brought up by the Indigenous Governance Graduate Program, and I was talking to some of the Indians there. One of them was talking about a song that his people sing which is:

26

"We are the salmon, the salmon are us;
Where the salmon go, we go."

He meant that song in a really fundamental sense. If the
salmon die, the people die. So as far as us having a future, us
being me or redwood trees or forests or oceans or whomever,
you can call it what you want, civilisation, the growth economy,
industrial capitalism - they need to go.

There's a great book called "The Nazi Doctors" by Robert J.
Lifton. In this book he examines how it was that people who
had taken a Hippocratic Oath could still work in Nazi death
camps. What he found was that most of the doctors who
worked in the death camps actually cared very deeply for the
health of the inmates. They would do whatever they could to
keep the inmates alive. They would give them an aspirin if they
were in pain. The would hide them from the collection officers
who were going to kill them. They would give them an extra
scrap of potato. They would do everything they could except for
the most important thing of all: they wouldn't question the
existence of the death camp itself.

Environmentalists, we do whatever we can to protect this or
that species or this or that piece of ground. We do everything
except the most important thing of all which is to question the
existence of industrial capitalism itself. So long as you have this
death camp culture, turning the whole world into first a work
camp and then a death camp, it's going to continue doing what
a death camp does.

Two and a half million children die of starvation every year
because of the economic activities of empire. Most countries
that have famine, they're actually net food exporters. We heard
of the great Irish potato famine. They were actually exporting
grain at that time. So people, when they're dying of starvation,
are almost always dying of colonialism. This culture is a death
cult. We're making massive human sacrifices on the altars of
economic exigency. Madeleine Albright said about the death of
half a million Iraqi children in 1990s: "That's the price we're
willing to pay".[8]

MF: But you're not paying it.

DJ: Yeah, exactly. There is always somebody else who can
sacrifice, which is awfully convenient.

MF: We have a system that excludes any calculation of

quality, whether it's quality of health, nutrition or human experience or even just the natural world, ecosystem experience if you will. If we exclude any kind of qualitative analysis in the only metric we use, which is our economic system, it's like you said, working in a death camp where you think you're being a good person because you sneak an extra piece of potato to the person whose testicles you just removed. What you're really doing is you're still living in a death camp and working for someone who's performing unspeakable crimes.

It's been an incredible journey you've been on in terms of the research you've done, the books that you've written, just in general your thinking is very free-flowing. You don't seem to be limited by a lot of the self-imposed guidelines we use in our thinking. Was there a single thread that you tugged at that led you on this journey? What was it that made you first look around at a city or what we were doing and go "Wait a minute what's wrong with this picture?" and "How can it be another way?" What was it that snapped you out of it?

DJ: Thanks for asking. I guess there are three different directions. One is, when I was about seven, second grade, these fields near where I lived were converted into a subdivision. I remember thinking - of course it wasn't in this language - this can't go on forever because if you continue to convert wild spaces into human neighbourhoods eventually you're going to run out of space. That's easy logic even for a second grader.

Another part is that my father was extremely abusive. My brother has epilepsy from blows to the head. He broke my sister's arm. Raped my mother, my sister and me. I remember thinking 'if his behaviour doesn't make him happy, why is he doing it?' I ask the same question now - if all this nonsense, all this frenetic coal-mining, child labour, everything else isn't making people happy then why are they doing it? It doesn't make any sense to me.

The third strand is my first degree was in physics and I didn't really like it at all. That's when I asked people if they liked their job and like I said ninety percent said no. So, I started to really question the wage economy. If it's not making us happy why are we doing it? I would ask all my fellow students 'Do you like going to school? Do you like the idea of working for an oil company?' A few of them would say yes but almost all of them would say "no, but when I get out of here I'm going to buy myself a nice car." A lot of them were already planning on retirement. That seemed crazy to me.

28

An environmentalist friend of mine said a lot of environmentalists begin by wanting to protect a specific piece of ground and they end up questioning the foundation of Western civilisation because once the questions start they don't stop. It was the same for me. I was questioning the growth economy, I was questioning abuse and I was questioning the wage economy, an economy where you have to get a waged job. I started to question, and just like the others, you end up questioning the foundations of Western civilisation. That's what you end up with.

It's just like when you start asking 'why do men beat up women?' You're going to end up questioning the foundations of patriarchy. So for me it's really been asking those questions. I appreciate you saying I'm not so much limited by constraints on thinking and I take that as a real compliment. It doesn't take a cognitive giant to figure out that any way of living that's based on the use of nonrenewable resources won't last. It doesn't take courage to say the world is being killed when ninety percent of the large fish in the oceans are gone. That's pretty basic.

Those in power, they keep promising all these things and the question is "Would you buy a used car from this person?" They sold you five thousand cars already, each one of which drove fifteen feet before the wheels fell off, and you're going to buy another one?

MF: I recorded a podcast with my niece, who is ten years old, and she didn't know anything about my film, anything about what I was working on. Einstein said "You don't understand anything until you can explain it to your grandmother". I figured if I can explain what I'm doing in a way that is understandable to a ten year-old then either that's a very smart ten year-old or it's clear enough that anyone can get it. We recorded for an hour, we had a chat and at the end of it she was a hundred percent clear on everything. There was no confusion, there was no rejection, there was no kind of imprinted incredulity of "it couldn't be like that". She was finishing my sentences. I'd say "So what happens if we keep doing this?" and she said "Well we can't because there's not enough space. If you keep doing that there's not enough food".

I get this sense that there is a fundamental understanding, a relationship that we hallucinate our way out of. From my own personal experience growing up, being "educated", there is this consistent reinforcement and confusion about your own internal compass versus the compass of propriety, of 'the norm', of the direction we are going. You get to the point where you doubt yourself. You look at something and go "Wait a minute, that's just fucked up!" and then you start thinking "wait, but there's this, there's that..."

I think that we're taught not to believe our internal compass. Whether you want to call it an alarm bell, a sense of the world, whatever. It gets confused by all these external factors that we're told need to be taken into account, when really it's just a matter of looking at it like you said: if it's not working, why are we doing it? Whatever the purpose of doing that thing is, it's not happening. So why are we doing it?

DJ: R.D. Laing has a great line about how, to maintain the military industrial complex, we have to destroy our capacity to think and to imagine. It is imperative that you start with the children because without the most thorough brainwashing, their dirty minds would see through our dirty tricks. So we need to turn them into imbeciles like ourselves.

I wrote a book called "Walking On Water" which is about the education system. The first sentences are:

"As is true for most people I know, I've always loved learning. As is also true for most people I know, I always hated school. Why is that?"

One of the things I come up with is that the reason school takes so long is because children don't give up their wills easily. It takes twelve years to sufficiently break their wills to prepare them for a life of painful employment. The fundamental purpose of school is to get you to obey authority.

One more thing is that I've asked a lot of seven, eight and ten year-olds "So how do you stop global warming that's caused in great measure by the burning of oil and gas?" They will say "You stop burning oil and gas." I'll ask a reasonably intelligent thirty-five year-old who works for a green high-tech consulting firm "How do you stop global warming?" and they're probably going to give you an answer that does not benefit the natural world but instead benefits green high-tech consulting firms.

MF: Everyone keeps coming back to the fact that you need to educate ecologically, compassionately from childhood or else you still end up with generation after generation of eighteen year-olds who want the iPhone and the car and the job and the house and none of it actually solves the underlying problem, which, like you said, is that we're performing cultural cannibalism. We're consuming our life support which in effect is consuming us, like Saturn devouring his son.

An Empty Space Where My Offspring Would Have Been
with Les Knight

> *"I really like people. Some of my best friends are people."*

Les Knight is the founder of the Voluntary Human Extinction Movement which takes as its central principle the idea that humans should cease reproducing entirely and slowly go extinct, leaving the biosphere to the rest of nature. I came across his website and ideas during the research for *Critical Mass* and, after he was also mentioned to me by Alan Weisman, the author of *The World Without Us*, I decided to get in touch with him.

My concern was that he would be interested purely in shock value or in the comedic/satirical aspect of voluntary human extinction but instead I found a quiet, considerate man who gave deliberate and thoughtful answers to my questions. Nothing about him was cavalier or outrageous.

In fact, as I write this introduction to our conversation, I feel that somehow what is outrageous is that he managed to present the idea of voluntary human extinction as entirely reasonable. No mean achievement, and perhaps an indication of how serious our current predicament really is.

32

Mike Freedman: How did you come to start the Voluntary Human Extinction Movement?[1]

Les Knight: Well like a lot of people I saw the environmental destruction and ecosystems being converted to human uses and I realised that the more of us there are the less wildlife there is and eventually I realised that if we completely stop breeding we would go extinct and the rest of the biosphere could recover. I think a lot of people have followed this same basic train of thought guided by compassion for other life forms and arrived at this conclusion. I just gave it a name but other people have come up with this idea as well.

MF: Why extinction? We also have the idea of stability, even, although it is unpalatable to discuss, reduction. Extinction is a very emotive term, is it not?

LK: Well it sure is, although we are causing the extinction of so many other species that we really do not seem to be all that concerned about. The Atlantic Great Whale is gone and yet when it comes down to just one more species, us, people start taking notice that it is a significant finality.
There are supporters of the movement who agree that for now the intentional creation of one more of us by anyone anywhere cannot be justified. There are volunteers like myself who realise that as long as there is one breeding pair of us we could be right back where we are now in a very short time.

MF: I think it was Garrett Hardin[2] who said that 'the freedom to breed is intolerable'. Now that is a very loaded way of putting it. I interviewed a guy who said the difficult challenge is how to find a way of preserving both the planet and the human enterprise while making sure that the human enterprise is worth preserving. For instance something that is a totalitarian system like in China where women have their menstruation registered etcetera, that is not a particularly brilliant system that is worth fighting for. What you are effectively saying is rather than agonising over what kind of human system is worth sustaining, really the only way for the planet to be sustainable is for us to be gone.

LK: Yes, that is right. We are incompatible with the biosphere. We have evolved into a virtual exotic invader even in Africa where we originated. Everywhere else on the planet we are by definition exotic invaders. A totalitarian society is not necessary. We are a voluntary movement, obviously.

We are lacking reproductive freedom around the planet. The freedom to breed is very well-established except in China and even there, there are so many exceptions that their birth rate is about the same as the U.K. What we really need is the right to not breed respectfully. Hundreds of millions of couples who are on the planet do not want to create more than they already have and yet they are denied the basic human right to not conceive. Probably 80 million unwanted pregnancies occur each year. Rather than starting to think how we can restrict people's breeding, let us see how we can guarantee people's basic right to not breed.

MF: There is almost a parallel with the smoking ban here in the U.K. I have had arguments with friends of mine who are either smokers or who style themselves as libertarian and the argument I put forward is the smoking ban is not about limiting the freedom of smokers, it is about respecting the freedom of people who do not want to smoke. A smoker can still buy cigarettes and have a puff but if I want to go out to a bar with my wife or with some friends, I do not have to breathe smoke in. So really what you are talking about is a kind of freedom born of restraint rather than simple lack of rules?

LK: We are suggesting that people think before they breed and I think if people thought before they smoked, they might not. It is a similar thing. Both are pretty unnecessary in today's world.

MF: Desmond Morris[3] said stabilising the human population should not be such a hot potato because seven billion of us is a big enough genetic pool that we are not going to die out. That we have won, effectively.

The word 'voluntary' - social pressure to have children is to your mind just as unacceptable as the pressure not to. So how do you square the dire situation we find ourselves in with that voluntary aspect?

LK: Well yes, we are really in rather dire straits. We are into overshoot of the carrying capacity of Earth's biosphere for our kind by quite a bit. At least 25%, some say as much as 40%. We cannot continue this for very long. Our population continues to increase by 200,000 a day. This results in a diminishing of everyone's standard of living.

So back to that smoking thing again - it shows that while you have a right to breed, it encroaches on other people's right to clean air, water etcetera.

Even with the word 'voluntary' on there it is very difficult for people to understand that all we are saying is that we should stop breeding. It is like a company that wants to reduce their labour force but does not want to fire anyone. They just let the retirees go and do not hire more. It would be the same thing here, rather painless. We just live our lives out and disappear. I came up with this by following a train of logic guided by compassion for all living things. I receive emails from people saying 'I thought I was the only one who thought this way', so people do feel alone when they think of this but once it is realised it is hard to see that we could possibly live in harmony with the planet.

MF: Using your corporate metaphor, is it more of a voluntary obsolescence rather than a voluntary extinction?

LK: Well, we are obsolete but it is voluntarily accepting the fact that we are obsolete. Actually we have never been viable entities as far as the biosphere is concerned. Even before we became homo sapiens we were using fire to alter ecosystems.

MF: So you see humans as an invasive species from the get-go?

LK: Well yes. We caused massive extinctions all over the planet, everywhere we went. Now we're continuing to do it as there are more and more of us. We really can't help it. It's hard to tread lightly on Planet Earth when you have 14 billion feet.

MF: There are accusations of misanthropy against the environmental movement on the whole and particularly against people who are vocal about population concerns, that these people, like yourself, are anti-human. That you do not like people. I am curious to ask whether that is true or whether you see it a different way?

LK: I definitely see it a different way. There are misanthropes in the movement for sure but most of the people who are anti-human are not concerned about some voluntary method of increasing reproductive freedom. In fact the involuntary human extinction movement seems to be gaining a lot more traction than the voluntary human extinction movement.

I really like people. Some of my best friends are people. I think we have a lot in common, but just because you like people does not mean you should create more of them. Same with children. I really like children. That is one of the reasons I am never going to make one. We have got so many we are not taking care of, how can we in good conscience make more to take care of when we have got tens of thousands dying of preventable causes every day?

MF: It feels like there is this bizarre Orwellian distortion of meaning where people in favour of economic growth, corporate power, financial well-being, industrial development and all of the things that are contrary to a viable ecosystem are painted as being in favour of humanity because they favour all of these trappings of human enterprise.

LK: A human-centred perspective of the planet. The other perspective is earth-centred, where humans are one of tens of millions of species which are all valuable in their own way. We are valuable too and obviously we are pretty special. But when we see ourselves as just one of many, our whole perspective will change.

MF: Do you see a through-line here from anti-scientific thinking right back to the Catholic Church's resistance to the idea that the Earth was round? Then they were like 'OK, it is round but at the centre of our solar system' and then 'OK, it is not at the centre of the solar system but man is the most important species.'

You are talking about seeing ourselves as one more species among many rather than something that is fundamentally exceptional.

LK: I think in some ways it is a moral maturity. As we are infants, we are the only thing that exists and in a short time our parents exist and then our family exists. As we mature, more and more exists. Some people stop at the nation state and find their identity there, others find their identity internationally and eventually see the whole world as one human family which is the way I like to think of ourselves. There are seven billion in our family and some of us are not getting enough to eat. We really need to change that.

If you continue one step further, you see the entire biosphere as part of our family and you are concerned with that. So that is the progression I see towards thinking of ourselves as one of the millions rather than the top of the heap.

MF: Can you describe some of the resistance that you have had to your ideas? You have said that you have been going for thirty years - you must have had quite a journey along the way.

LK: Almost all of the opposition is just misunderstanding. Once they realise that all we are saying is that people should think before they breed and have the ability to not breed, it is hard for many people to disagree with that. It is just a basic freedom that we all want.

However, the idea that we should not create more of ourselves does seem very threatening to those who want to do that or have already done that. I think that on some level they realise that they should not be doing that and that is why they are so sensitive to being made more conscious of the fact that they really should not create more of us. So they are bound to be resistant to the idea that maybe they should take care of the babies, children or even the adults that are already here. We do not need to create more of them.

MF: Walk me through your scenario. Your movement gains traction and people choose not to have children. Couples adopt instead and eventually we have an ageing population. Walk me through how you would like to see the human story play out.

LK: If everyone has the ability to not procreate and then realises that they should not procreate, there will be fewer and fewer of us every year. As there are fewer of us, there will be more of everything for everyone. Conflicts have always been over resources since before we became Homo sapiens. We are continuing it now at a huge rate. We are fighting over resources. That is what the unrest is in the world. So we could achieve world peace if there were fewer of us and we could share everything. We could also increase wildlife habitat instead of decreasing it. The human-free zones could increase little by little. Not just Chernobyl but places where we could go but do not go.

Eventually we would all disappear. That is the idea. We could continue on with our technology. We do not have to go back to being cave people or whatever we were in ancient times. We can continue progressing technologically and enjoy the fruits of all of the wonderful things that we have.

MF: You touch on something that is key - a more circumspect approach to the environment, a slightly more delicate balance between people and the planet, is painted as being anti-scientific, anti-technological, anti-progress as if somehow by saying civilisation is damaging one is saying that civilisation should not happen.

Do you feel that humans are simply an invasive species that like a virus eventually has to be eradicated if the host is to survive? Or do you see it more as a kind of loss of knowledge of ourselves, that somehow we were once in equilibrium and we have gotten further and further away from this idea of ourselves as part of a whole?

LK: We have always adversely impacted the ecosystems that we have found ourselves in. There was never a time that we can look back and say this is a time where we lived in harmony with the planet and with each other. I do not think we can look back and say agriculture was when we made our mistake so let us go back to a pre-agriculture time. There just are not resources for 7 billion people to become hunter-gatherers unless we hunt and gather each other, which I do not think is going to be a very pleasant situation.

MF: How do you sell an idea to people that involves them accepting an eventual eradication of people?

LK: Well that is a difficult sell for sure but it is a philosophical one. We will all pass away in due time and far sooner than this voluntary extinction could ever occur. So it is more of an emotional attachment to something in the future that they will never be around to see anyway. It is culturally induced and can be overcome.

MF: At each key phase in the human story it seems that we have given something up and moved on to something else. We went from being hunter-gatherers to being agriculturists so there were more of us and with more of us we learnt more about each other than in the tribal situation when we were simply members of the same tribe with the same beliefs and the same language.

Each step has involved us giving something up and gaining

something. What do you think we have given up, what do you think we have gained and why do you think we should give up more in order to regain something that we lost?

LK: I do not see this as giving up. I see it as a gain for everyone. What we have given up in our excessive breeding is individuality. We have lost value. The more there are of things, the less they are worth across the board. As there became more and more of us we did not value each other as much. I do not think that the mass murders that we call wars could have ever occurred if we were still just 150 people, which is about as many as our minds are wired to accept and understand.

However, even then we would go out and kill other tribes as ours increased more than the resources allowed. So the idea of killing 'the other' has been with us all along. Now it seems to be much easier.

It is difficult to identify with people in other parts of the world who are being killed. They are dying so we have to, in order to live with ourselves, distance ourselves from the fact that they are members of our family. We are killing our own children. That is part of the motivation of wanting to improve our population density so we will not be killing each other over the resources.

MF: Is the Voluntary Human Extinction Movement at a point where it sustains itself or do you need to do day job work on the side to keep yourself ticking over while you do the project?

LK: There is no organisation. It definitely does not sustain itself. There is no income. It is whatever individuals want to do to share the message. If someone wants to set up a table and pass out information and answer questions they can do that. I am just one of the volunteers even though I have become known as a spokesperson and I maintain the website. Anybody could do what I do. There is no leader of the movement. We are all leaders, leading the world to a better place.

MF: Your logical journey, assessing where the stress points of human existence have been so far and then concluding that there are a lot of us and when we compete for resources we kill each other, has a fairly uncontroversial conclusion. But your emotional journey also interests me. As a person you must still have that in-built biological clock. As a man, as a child growing up, what has the emotional ride been for you?

LK: I grew up in a large family, there were five of us but it was a small town and so although the family was large, the town was small and I felt connected to everyone. We all pretty much knew each other. Kids going down the street would be known to everyone. It was a strange combination of a small town and large family that forged my understanding of human interaction.

As far as emotional, I have been a step-parent and enjoyed the privilege of being a parent and I think it is a wonderful endeavour for those who feel like taking it on, but it is not for everyone. Society thinks that everybody should pair up and have offspring somehow, even if you are gay. Even if it means outsourcing it to India for IVF and getting a surrogate mum. People are really desperate to have this biological offspring. It is not something that we are born with. The urge to create a new one of us is cultural. The urge to nurture one of us once they are here probably has a biological component. I sure felt it was biological when I bonded with my step-daughter.

MF: If one wants to see oneself as part of a human family, you either replace or find those human connections with non-blood relatives. If you have the urge to nurture and look after another human being, you do not need it to be yours. You can adopt a child from an orphanage or from a country that has a collapsed society where children are not being looked after. Do you think that maybe this is part of human evolution - to reach this crisis point and lump together and look after each other along human lines rather than bloodlines?

LK: This may have been all along what we have done. People have taken care of other people's offspring. The idea of a child being ours, having our DNA, is fairly modern. In tribal societies quite often everybody raised the kid. They had a special bond perhaps to the mother because that is where the nurturing and feeding originally began. They probably would not know who the father was and there was no concern about them being biologically the same genetic material. The bloodline became so important where we had our class systems. If you are going to have a divided society by class it is really helpful to do it in some way that is obvious. Lineage is a pretty convenient way of doing it. Skin colour helps, but they are all artificial constructs to maintain a stratified society. If we see all of ourselves as one then a stratified society is lessened.

We can obviously form bonds with those who are not

genetically related to us. There is an organisation here in Oregon called 'Love Makes A Family' and that pretty much sums it up. What else do you need? So they promote gay adoptions and people just getting together and forming a family based on love.

MF: Do you think that religion is a natural obstacle to the acceptance of human limitation because it casts man as an exceptional creature?

LK: Most religions do place humans as exceptional creatures and their gods are usually in the form of humans but the churches are really the obstacle, not the religion itself. The religions are belief systems that include care for each other. Almost every one of them, in fact every one of them I can think of, has the golden rule of doing unto others as you would have them do unto you.
So the religions themselves can be force for good. It has been the churches that have perverted those religions into self-serving institutions and have waged wars and done things that are not at all part of the religion. Once you have got somebody blindly believing it is easier to get them to do things that they would not normally do.

MF: Again, coming back to your idea that man is the invasive element, it is almost as if when man begins to build a human construct around the concept of the divine or the spiritual that the process begins to break down and becomes destructive.

LK: Yes, that is it. We make it artificial instead of natural and the more artificial or man-made it becomes, the further away it is from the natural. Which is why we as modern humans are trying so hard to get back to the natural through whatever ways we can - owning pets to help us stay in touch with our animal side, taking vacations in what is left of wildlife habitat. A lot of times it is watching a nature show on TV which may be better for nature because we stay home.

MF: Nina Paley had an interview with Chris Korda[4] where he said that it is almost as if we are in the process of downloading animals by filming them, that we are abdicating our real world responsibility to preserve life by preserving them artificially on film. We go "OK, we can watch a film about a polar bear now so if they die out we haven't lost anything."

Do you feel that we have been so successful at creating representations of the real world that we have begun to or already lost our connection to what parts of the world are real? We describe a hurricane as causing x amount of dollars of damage rather than human cost. Is that a process that you have seen happening over the course of your life?

LK: Yes. We confuse symbol with reality constantly. The best example is money. It is just a measure of wealth. It is not wealth itself. Other things too such as flags. In the US it is a sacred object so people are very sensitive about treating this piece of cloth properly while at the same time the real country gets trashed. So there is a confusion of symbol and reality that is seriously a problem in our culture. In our worldwide culture especially as we have more animals downloaded on TV, we think we can re-create them, like Jurassic Park: "you know, well, we could just bring them back."

Well, the problem is not bringing them back from the dead, it is finding a place for them today. In Oregon we are trying to reintroduce wolves.[5] The cattle ranchers and the sheep farmers do not like the idea of introducing wolves because they are going to eat their livelihood. So there is a conflict between human uses of the land and natural wildlife using the land.

MF: It feels like we are succeeding our way into oblivion. That natural process of preserving life has turned into preserving only human life at the cost of everything else to the point that there will not be room for anything else.

LK: We can look back throughout history and pre-history and see that every major civilisation has collapsed[6] and we can see why. We now are on a global course to have a collapse of civilisation because we are all so entwined.

We exceed the resources, our population gets too large, there is no place left to take over in order to accommodate our increased population size and there is a collapse. This time it is going to be a bit larger because we are all so intricately connected. The economic collapse is a good example of that. It was not just one country, it was all over the world. This shows how it can be if we continue as we are and it does seem like we will continue as we are. I see very few indications that we are going to turn things around. We are continuing in the direction of an involuntary human extinction, a collapse of Earth's biosphere. At least a collapse of civilisation will give the biosphere some recovering time but in a few thousand years we could easily be back where we are today. Maybe then the collapse of the biosphere will take care of it. So the alternative to waiting for involuntary human extinction is for us to voluntarily and peacefully phase ourselves out, restoring as much as we can of the biosphere as we go and enjoying our lives as best we can.

MF: Do you think there is a happy medium somewhere in there? That somehow, rather than voluntary extinction it is more of a voluntary balancing act? If you removed all the pro-natal policies and all of the anti-contraceptive policies based on whatever politics or ideology and simply had a world where people did not have to have kids they did not want and if they did want to have kids they did, do you think that we would be able to maybe get down to number that could live within the biosphere with other species or do you see it really as we are headed for a catastrophic collapse anyway?

LK: We do not seem to have gotten the message in the past. The Native Americans in America realised that the species that they were eating had disappeared and I think that had a lot to do with their ethic of respect for other life forms but they continued to impact the environment. It is just how we are with fires and agriculture.

As far as us getting down to a sustainable number, only about seventy-five thousand years ago we were down to about fifteen thousand people or fewer.[7] We know from DNA analysis that was about how many Homo sapiens there were. Something caused us to go through a bottleneck. Fifteen thousand people for the entire planet is a fairly sustainable number. Seventy-five thousand years is not that long. I think as long as there is one breeding couple, Earth's biosphere is in too grave a danger.

MF: If humans are not here then the consciousness that we credit ourselves with will not be here to experience the world. It is the old 'tree in the forest' question: why would we choose to sacrifice ourselves entirely for a world that effectively for us would no longer exist if we were gone?

LK: Right. It would not make sense unless we had an Earth-centred perspective. With a human-centred perspective it does not make a whole lot of sense and that is why we need to make that one last step in our emotional maturity.

We are all going to die. That is something that people are

consciously resistant to even though people say 'yes, I know, I am going to die but some of me will live on in my child or some work that I have done will continue on.'

Well, you know, it does not really have to continue on. That is kind of a nice thought. As long as there are humans I would like to leave something for them but I would really like to leave something for the rest of creation as well, like an empty space where my offspring would have been. I think that is the best thing I can give for Planet Earth.

MF: But isn't that a big ask, to get from a human-centric to a bio-centric view of life? It would be a really healthy step for people, I do not think anyone would argue with that, but won't we be better as people if we can do better while we are here instead of just saying we cannot be trusted so let's get rid of ourselves?

LK: We are on our way out. Even if not one more of us were born we could pretty much trash the planet before we are gone. So, we do need to become better people. It is so far from here that I won't be around to say 'yeah, what the heck, looks like we have got it together so let's make a few more of us and keep this thing going'. Maybe it will get to that point. Just because we never have does not mean we never will.

MF: Does the human story have a happy ending for you?

LK: Well it does, yes. As there are fewer of us we will take care of each other better. Life will be so much better for everyone. We will live out our lives as we always have and disappear as we always have. I think that is a very happy ending. That is the ending we are all going to have anyway.

MF: The primary cognitive dissonance of the human condition is that we are all born with a profound love for life and the knowledge that we are all going to die. Somehow I think this at the back of our minds does something to drive us crazy. On one hand we want to love, live and have great experiences. Maybe I'm an idealist but I see people as fundamentally intriguing fascinating lovely creatures that just want a life. But the knowledge of our mortality just makes us do crazy shit while we are in the process of rocketing to the grave.

Do you see that as a component of the human condition? Are we really talking about overcoming the limits of the human condition rather than the limits of nature?

LK: Or overcoming the limits of our own nature. Our emotional brains are running the show and we use our frontal lobes to justify what our emotional brain demands of us. Part of that is a fear of death. One of the things we can do to overcome that is give ourselves the illusion that we are going to live on by creating another person with as much as possible of our specific DNA. That satisfies the emotional part of our brain and that is what rules.

MF: I don't buy the idea that to respect life we need to stop living. I see the way humans affect the planet and each other but I do not know if I would go so far as to say therefore humans do not belong in nature if nature is to survive. Surely the great project of life has a place for us or else we would not be here now. How do you square that?

LK: I do think we have a place. There have been what are known as super-predators, so good at being a predator that they kill their food supply and of course then they go extinct as well. We seem to be the ultimate super-predator. We are using up our life support system and we will not survive beyond that. We are in the sixth great extinction on Planet Earth since life began three and a half billion years ago and this one, unlike all of the rest, is caused by one species. That is us. It seems only fair to me that after causing so many other species to go extinct that we follow suit.

Who Wants To Live Forever?
with Aubrey de Grey

"The whole question of increasing the population burden on the planet by lowering the death rate, be it by medicine or anything - we have a duty to humanity of the future to give them the options."

I emailed Aubrey through the website for the SENS Foundation[1], where he is the Chief Science Officer. I had seen him on "It's Only A Theory", a fairly typical BBC panel show where guests put forth a theory which is debated and then either accepted or rejected by the panel. Aubrey's contention on the program was that the world's first 1000 year-old human had already been born. At the time, neck deep in a film about human population, he seemed like exactly the man to speak to.

We met in the upstairs function room of a pub in Cambridge. He is heavily bearded, rake-thin and intelligent in a completely unpretentious way. He conducted his entire interview while holding a pint of good British ale, just below the camera's field of vision.

As we were editing the film, it became clear that the thrust of our narrative would deal with the past and the present. Aubrey's work deals with, as he puts it, "the development of rejuvenation biotechnologies, which is to say the application of regenerative medicine to the health problems associated with ageing", obviously a matter of interest for the future. This made our long and interesting conversation in that pub in Cambridge simultaneously fascinating and entirely unusable for the film. Such is the brutality of the editing process.

As with Derrick Jensen, our conversation lurked in one of my hard drives until the idea for this book made it suddenly not only usable but essential.

Mike Freedman: One of the first questions I wanted to ask: What impact has modern medicine had on life expectancy and quality of life?

Aubrey de Grey: There have really been two phases of the impact of modern medicine and modern lifestyles on longevity. The first phase began in the middle of the 19th century and continued, in the Western world, until about World War Two. That phase consisted of the improvement in hygiene and the availability of very simple medicines, the sort we're all familiar with: vaccines, antibiotics, things like that. Between them, those technologies allowed us to reduce the impact of very early death, in infancy or in childbirth for example, down from an enormous number. Something like forty percent of all live births in the UK used to die before the age of one back in the 18th century. We reduced that down to a very small amount, maybe one or two percent of births, so that of course made a big difference to the proportion of people who lived to the age of sixty, to the age of eighty etc. which is how life expectancy is calculated.

If, way back in the 18th or 19th century, you got to the age of thirty, then your probability of getting to the age of sixty or seventy or eighty didn't change very much over that period. It really did start to change more recently; during the second half of the twentieth century, we started to see a lot of effects that were not necessarily medical but more lifestyle and prosperity associated - better nutrition, especially better prenatal nutrition. Things like that have an effect right through the whole of life and allow people to live a lot longer.

So we've seen a slower but nevertheless very significant increase in longevity during the past fifty, sixty, seventy years.[2] The real question is whether we are coming to the end of that phase now and what will happen if we do.

If we look at the situation with infectious diseases, the impact of hygiene, vaccines and antibiotics and so on, we have pretty much solved the problem. We can't increase life expectancy more than a tiny amount more by further improvements in those things because the incidence of death from those things is already so low. We may have got to the stage where we'll see a small extra benefit but there's only a small margin left. So in order to see a big addition or increase in longevity we would have to have some third new technology, new phenomenon that would actually deliver that.

MF: Considering the length of human life as it is now and the pressures of population that we have on the planet right now, why is this an important area of research?

AdG: I think that, in order to think clearly about the impact of any technology, but of course especially medical technologies on global population, we have to stand back and be honest about our actual priorities. The fact is at the moment we are, in general, quite keen on having kids. The main reason why there is a population problem is because we're having kids faster than people are dying. This year, for example, the rate of death is less than half the rate of birth. The number of people born last year is more than twice the number that died. So of course you can see that we have got a problem.

But actually that ratio is falling already because it has been seen that without any exception, in every single society in which women have become better educated and more emancipated and generally given more opportunity, the fertility rate, which is to say the average number of children that a woman has in her life, falls very sharply.[3] Now, that's pretty interesting.

If we look back at the situation in the late 19th century when we suddenly discovered the impact of hygiene and vaccines on the ability for infants to survive into childhood and adulthood, the impact was very great and we had a big population spike. It didn't matter too much at that time in terms of the environment because we just didn't have enough people on the planet to be able to make the impact on the environment that we're making today. It was still a pretty big shock but, lo and behold, it was very brief. People started having fewer kids awfully quickly.

If you stood up in 1800 and said "I think that when we cure all these infectious diseases, we are going to have to start wearing these repulsive rubber contraptions whenever we have sex", everyone is going to laugh at you and they are going to say "There is no way we're going to do that", but of course everyone started doing it pretty damn quickly. It was only because children are expensive. It wasn't because of any sort of draconian one-child policy or anything like that.

So, society is very hard to predict. Society's reaction to new technology and to new situations is very hard to predict but one thing we do know is that nobody likes getting sick. Even if they're elderly. Nobody wants to get Alzheimer's Disease, nobody wants to get cancer or cardiovascular disease. When you ask people "OK, how badly do you not want to get Alzheimer's Disease?" they'll say "Pretty damn badly!". Of

48

course, if people say "How badly do you want to have kids?" they'll also say "Pretty damn badly" but we just don't know where the balance lies. Of course, the balance is in the context of all the other enormous technological changes that are happening in society all the time.

So, the whole question of increasing the population burden on the planet by lowering the death rate, be it by medicine or anything - we have a duty to humanity of the future to give them the options, to maximise their options.

One option that we have today is to prevaricate and hesitate and be terribly scared of the development of new technologies that might lower the death rate because we would then be increasing the pressure on the environment. The fact is that it's only pressure on the environment if a lower death rate is not accompanied by a lowered birth rate and the lowered birth rate is a choice that humanity of the future is entitled to make. It's between doing that or us not using these technologies we might have developed that would lower the death rate in the first place.

So it seems to me that the thing we're absolutely morally obliged not to do is to hesitate. It's to not make decisions on behalf of humanity of the future and say we don't think you're going to want these therapies therefore we're not going to develop them. If we do that then we're for practical purposes condemning humanity of the future to an unnecessary degree of suffering, an unnecessarily early, painful death. We just have no right to do that. It is up to them to decide whether these therapies are for them. We have a duty to develop them and give the humanity of the future that choice.

MF: There is an interesting balance there. Obviously you want the most people to have the best quality of life possible. That's the humane answer. The word 'irresponsible' is a bit strong but I think without recognising the population pressure, it is a disingenuous line of -

AdG: I think that the population pressure that will arise from really dramatic success in combating ageing is probably the number one but nevertheless just one of the sociological and psychological consequences of such technologies. I completely accept that people in all walks of society but especially people who are spearheading the development of that work, people like me, have a moral obligation to think about these things and talk about these things and make sure that these things are not

49

in any way forgotten.

The difficulty at the moment is the opposite. The difficulty at the moment is that people are inclined to say that this technology will in some sense obviously be a bad thing in such and such a way whether it be population, living forever, people getting bored. They don't think about them in the proper context. So, I see my position as a scientist as certainly not in any way sidestepping or ignoring these issues but rather as framing them appropriately. Giving professional sociologists, economists, theologians the right information about what is likely to happen in the future and roughly how soon so that they can actually debate and analyse these issues without doing it in a vacuum, where it is functionally irrelevant because it doesn't actually make the right assumptions about what technology is going to occur. This not only applies to professionals in these areas. It also applies to policy makers and to the general public.

MF: Technologically speaking, because I assume that is what you meant, what's happening in the near and the long term future? What development, in terms of progress? What's going on now?

AdG: The trajectory of longevity in the industrialised world over the next several decades goes, in my view, in two phases. What I'm expecting to see is actually a levelling-off of the rate of increase of longevity that we've seen over the past fifty or so years. I mentioned earlier that that rate of increase has been slower in that period while we were benefitting from things like prenatal nutrition than when, in the prior period, we were benefitting from things like the dissemination of antibiotics and better hygiene. I expect that we are in the process of reaching diminishing returns with respect to what we can deliver from technology, medicines and lifestyle improvements that already exist.

Therefore there will be a levelling-off. In twenty-five to thirty years I think we have a fifty percent chance or so of developing a whole new raft of medical technologies to be applied to the problems of age-related ill health that will make everything take off again. This time the take-off will be much more dramatic than it was in either of the previous phases. The reason it is going to be so much more dramatic is because it is going to be focussed on regenerative medicine.

Regenerative medicine is a very fashionable area already in

medical research and even in actual medical application because it involves repair. It involves taking people who have suffered spinal cord injury and fixing them up so that they can use their legs again or giving people a whole new heart using tissue engineering. It's a very exciting and very glamorous area of biology and that is great. But at the moment it really only can be applied to acute injuries of the sort I just listed. In the future, my belief is that the panel of different types of regenerative medicine will progressively expand. We will get to a point where everything that goes wrong in the body during ageing, whether at the organ level, cellular level, even at the molecular level inside or between cells, can actually be amenable to such work. In other words, we will be able to restore, at all these levels of organisation, the structure of the body to something like how it was at a younger age.

We will be genuinely rejuvenating people. Taking people who are already in middle age or older and actually getting them back more or less into the state that they were in as a young adult. That means is two things. First of all, these people will not get the scary diseases of old age like Alzheimer's and cardiovascular disease and type 2 diabetes. The second thing is that we won't get any of the other things that distinguish the physical and mental capacity of an elderly individual from a young adult. We won't get all of the things that we don't really call diseases but are still bad for us, like loss of muscle mass or decline of function of the immune system.

For all practical purposes, we will be young adults again. That means that our chances of just dying in our sleep at ninety or even at a hundred and ninety will be no different than our chances today of dying in our sleep at the age of thirty. In other words an extremely small chance. That is why there will be a side benefit of an increase in longevity but I do want to emphasise the words "side benefit". The purpose here is to keep people healthy. I do not work on longevity. I do not work on keeping people alive. I work on keeping people healthy; keeping people alive will be a side benefit.

MF: That's one question I wanted to ask actually. Right now there are seven billion people on the planet, two billion of whom have no clean drinking water or sanitation or even enough food. It seems to me that the real battleground is quality of life not length of life. So it is interesting that you make that distinction.

AdG: I think it is extremely important to scotch at the outset any idea that we are talking about extending low quality life. We're talking here about improving the quality of life and it just so happens that the way we are going to improve the quality of life will be a way that also has this side benefit of improving the quantity of life. That is a side benefit because, let's face it, when you're healthy and vigorous and virile, you don't want to die tomorrow. If people who are in that state are keen on dying soon, we think they have a problem. We have a word for it - we call it "suicidal" and we are rather pleased in general that organisations like the Samaritans exist that are rather good at changing the minds of people like that.

So, the question is: does that general belief that suicidal tendencies are a bad thing apply only to young people? Of course not! It applies to healthy people. It applies to physically healthy people. There is a good deal more ambivalence in society with regard to suicidal tendencies or the wish to die when one is in a terminal and untreatable state, physically. When one is in a good state physically there is no argument. It is absolutely imperative to be honest about this, to be honest with ourselves about this question. The fact is, health is good. People tend to want to stay alive while they are healthy and people tend to want to stay healthy while they are alive. The two things go together.

MF: What you're saying is that euthanasia is not the moral question people think it is but it is merely a practical question. If your future quality of life is low enough you won't want it; if you can increase the potential quality of life, you remove the moral debate because if you are not ill then it is just a plain suicide, it's not a decision to end a terminal condition.

AdG: Nobody has considered the idea that euthanasia would be something that physically healthy people should actually be in any way encouraged or even not discouraged to contemplate. I think that the view society has of suicidal tendencies in people who are physically healthy is pretty much universal. I don't recall ever meeting anybody who feels that people in anything other than the most extreme degree of physical ill health should contemplate or engage in euthanasia or suicide.

MF: It would seem to me that the medical and scientific aspects of your research would be best put into a broader, social/population-dynamic context. I would assume you've done research on the social framework and the social outcomes.

AdG: There is so little we can actually know about how society is going to work even twenty years from now, let alone fifty years from now when we see some significant impact on the age structure of the global population as a result of therapies that work on ageing. The internet, desalination technology, better vaccines that stop people from getting malaria - these technologies make an enormous difference to the way that we prioritise things, the way that we think about the importance of particular ways of living or the problems that result from particular ways of living.

I think it is extremely likely that fifty years from now we will be able to have a much larger number of people on this planet without an environmental impact than we can today. Clearly at the moment the number of people we have on the planet exceeds the amount that, with current technology, can actually maintain the environment in a stable situation. That's why we are seeing so many changes, but I think technology is going to catch up. The question however is not whether technology catching up is going to work or how soon that is going to happen.

The question that we have is: given our profound ignorance of the answers to those questions, what should we do to maximise the options that humanity of the future have? Ultimately, certainly in the context of medical technologies against ageing, the answer is perfectly clear. We have to develop these technologies as quickly as we can because otherwise we are condemning people in the future to death.

MF: The projection that Western, wealthy populations will begin significantly ageing, do you think that that might have something to do with the interest in this kind of research?

AdG: I am quite sure that at the moment there is an enormous amount of money to be put into diseases that affect people in the West rather than diseases predominantly solved in the West and only really affect people in the developing world. There is no real argument about that. At some level that is just a feature of how humanity is. We tend to be a bit selfish and a bit parochial. It is a bad thing but it is the real world. The more we can do about it, the sooner we can fix that, the better, but that's the starting part. However, ageing is a bit of an exception to that. Everyone has ageing, yet people are mysteriously unable to focus on that fact and actually do anything about it.

I've thought and written a lot about why that is. Essentially, we are so scared of ageing that the only way we cope is by pretending that we are not scared at all, generally by finding a way of putting it out of our minds. As and when we come close to developing therapies that are really going to work against ageing, the probability is very high that a lot of people, policy makers and the public for that matter, in the developed world, in the industrialised world, will tend to focus on what these therapies can do for them and less on what these therapies can do for people in the developing world.

However, remember that we are talking about a few decades out from now. First of all, the developed world is going to be a lot bigger than it is now. At the moment people don't tend to include China and India as part of the developed world but they sure as hell are catching up. They are catching up in a whole bunch of ways; for example, the fertility rate in China and India is plummeting faster than it is in the industrialised world. That's pretty nice news.

These countries are going to have quite abundant wealth to be able to provide these technologies to their entire population as and when those technologies arrive. One thing that we have to remember when we look at the economics of all of this is that therapies are going to pay for themselves really well. At the moment, high-tech expensive medicine is a lose-lose situation. You only slightly extend the lives of people who have these very prevalent age-related diseases, you spend a lot of money doing so and then you still spend a lot of money keeping the people alive in a frail state before they die, same as you otherwise would have done if you had not used the medicines to postpone that period. In this case we will be postponing that period indefinitely. People will never get into the frail, expensive state that they suffer in the last year or two of their life these days. We will be in the glorious position where the therapies we are giving these people are paying for themselves. It is keeping these people out of hospital, out of care homes and keeping them so healthy that they are continuing to contribute wealth to society which will pay for the therapies that keep them in that good condition in the first place. So the economics are very clear.

Now, if we go to the extreme end of the spectrum and look at the real developing world, say sub-Saharan Africa, in which I think it is fair to predict that there will still be a considerably lower standard of living even thirty or fifty years from now than there is in the developed world, then the question comes "What are the balances?" and "What are the priorities?"

At the moment, the priorities are rather different because a high proportion of people die from causes that have nothing to do with ageing. A much smaller proportion of people get to an age where they need therapies against ageing. Remember that these therapies that I have been talking about, that I predict will be developed in the next few decades, are therapies that can only be applied to people who are already in middle age or older because they will be bonafide rejuvenation biotechnology and therefore people who are younger simply won't need these therapies. In fact, the actual expense involved in giving these therapies to everyone who needs them, even in the developing world, will not be as daunting as one might initially think.

MF: Your work is very linked to population issues, intentionally or not. How linked do you see them?

AdG: The thing that one really needs to take into account when focussed on the impact of medicines against ageing on population is that it is going to be gradual. Even if we eliminate death completely at any age, people would only get one year older per year. It's going to take a long time before we have people who are significantly older than what we have at the moment. It is going to take a very long time before it ceases to be the case that the birthrate is the dominant driver of population growth rather than the death rate. I mentioned that the death rate at the moment worldwide is actually less than half of the birth rate. Roughly speaking, a hundred and fifty thousand people die each day, something like three hundred and fifty thousand people are born each day. If we wanted to really fix the problem of population growth worldwide, then we could eliminate death completely, all causes of death, not just the one I am working on, and we'd have no population growth at all if we halved the birth rate. Even if we halved the birth rate only in the developing world, we would still have pretty much no population growth even if death were eliminated. That's the right way to think about it.

Something very important to incorporate into this analysis is that the birth rate should not just be measured in terms of the total number of children that the average woman has during their whole life. What also has to be absolutely, fundamentally taken into account is the average age at which they have those children and especially the average age at which they have their first child.

55

Women across the industrialised world have been progressively having their children later and later. In terms of the impact of therapies against ageing, there is one enormous thing that we have to take into account that comes down to one word: menopause. The reason why we are not seeing an even greater increase in the average age at which women have their first child is because it is then or never. You have got to do it in your late thirties, early forties or else you are screwed.

So, one of the things we are not going to have anymore is menopause. One of the things that we are going to be fixing by putting people back into a young adult state is they are going to be fertile, safely, as long as they like. That means the reason they are currently having children later, things they want to do with their life before they do this terribly time-consuming thing, are going to continue to apply longer. Women are going to end up having their children a decade later and a decade later.

If one does the mathematics on this one can discover that the impact on the birth rate is humongous. We may actually, rather paradoxically, see that the elimination of ageing has a positive impact on the slowing of population growth.

MF: So you mean a woman who waits until she is thirty-five to have a kid will wait until she is sixty-five to have a kid.

AdG: Or seventy-five.

MF: So she will have almost a full lifetime of youth followed by parenthood.

AdG: I think the best way to describe this in more detail is that because women will have so much choice, complete open options as to when they have their kids, they will have them on a time frame that is not defined by their age. A lot of women will still continue to have kids in their twenties but a lot of women who are currently having their kids in their thirties will have them in their seventies instead.

This is not something we can look at psychologically because different people are different. We only need to look at it demographically. It is very hard in my view to argue from current data that we would not see a very rapid increase in the average age at which women have their first child, because the rate at which people have over the past few decades increased that age up to the barrier of menopause has been so enormous.

MF: So you are talking about stopping the biological clock.

AdG: We are certainly talking about stopping the biological clock completely, both in terms of ageing of the body in general and in terms of ageing of the reproductive system. So we are certainly talking about elimination of the biological clock when we talk about menopause.

MF: So the idea is, like you said - paradoxically, by getting rid of the natural barrier to endless fertility you actually get people to wait even longer, creating more breathing space in population increases.

AdG: The most important thing about this actually is that it is front-loaded. By delaying, they will reduce the birth rate in an earlier year in favour of a later year.

MF: Can you give an example?

AdG: It is pretty hard to do that. This is something we have not done in enough thorough quantitative detail to be able to publish, so it is not something I can point you to a paper on yet. We will be working on this a lot over the next couple of years. We want to develop the technologies that are going to be needed but we need to develop the understanding of the social, psychological and philosophical implications at the same time.

MF: The research you are talking about, will it have an impact mainly in the West, at least in the immediate future?

AdG: I do actually want to emphasise that I do not think there will be very much delay in the dissemination of these technologies, when they get developed, to the world in general. What is going to happen is that there will be a period of at least a decade, very likely to be more like two or three decades, between the point when people accept and realise that these technologies are coming and the point when they actually do arrive. That period of anticipation is going to be the period of real turbulence when a lot of the changes in priorities and policies are going to occur. People are going to be preparing for that point and indeed hastening that point. There will be what I like to call a bona fide "war on ageing". There will be an enormous amount of resources thrown at the development of these technologies and the development of the infrastructure to deliver these technologies as widely as possible when they are developed. So, I think that all of the difficulties that we can foresee today, in terms of the economics of making sure that people actually get these therapies, will be front-loaded. They will happen in that anticipatory period and by the time the technologies finally are safe and effective to use, everything will be in place.

We will be in a position twenty or thirty years from now, when anti-ageing technologies are perhaps developed, that we will not be the same that we are now in terms of other technologies. Therefore we would be absolutely wrong to blithely think about the impact of the end of ageing in a context that is defined by technology as we know today.

MF: A lot of the people talk about what they call technological optimism, the idea that because we have had huge advances in the past hundred years, the logic goes that the rate will only increase as it has over the past thirty and in the next hundred years we will come up with stuff we cannot even imagine now and we are going to be OK because of it.

AdG: I am not a fan of technological optimism. I think that it is very dangerous to presume that everything will be alright on the night. If we look at climate change for example, I think that is the fundamental difficulty right now. It is not so much that people feel that climate change does not matter, it is actually that people feel "Well, OK, we can't do anything yet but technology will come along and save us in the end so we can't get terribly excited about no longer using incandescent light bulbs. We'll just get on with our lives and hope for the best and everything will be fine."

I don't agree with that at all. I think that is extremely dangerous. Technology usually does come along in the end but only usually. The argument that I am giving with respect to the moral imperative to develop technology against ageing does not rely on certainty that technology is going to come along to make it OK. It only relies on non-certainty that those technologies are not going to come along. All I am saying is that since there is a significant probability that the world will be very different thirty to fifty years from now, we need to take that into account in determining what we do today to give humanity of the future options that they would not have if we did not develop technologies today.

58

MF: You said you can't think of the ageing issue in terms of today's technology looking forward, but isn't your expectation rooted in what we have now readily available: cheap fossil fuels, energy infrastructure that functions, enough water to go around that can be put to industrial and scientific uses in addition to domestic usage? With water depletion, food shortages, other political aspects that come with that, if you are going to look forward and say that people should look forward, what about what is happening now? We are talking about a projected shortfall of oil by the US government in the next five years, the human population going up by thirty percent in the next forty years, not having enough food for the people we have now, not having enough water and not actually making significant advances in industry and agriculture to account for the difference. So isn't your outlook informed by the relative abundance of the necessary components now?

AdG: My outlook on the way that the future works is only formed on the basis of current technologies and shortages to the extent that I perceive difficulties in improving on those technologies. For example, if we look at the idea of energy shortage due to exhaustion of fossil fuels, we are of course well aware that there are at least three types of ways in which those problems would completely go away. One being the development of technologies that would be able to extract fossil fuels that are currently uneconomical to extract. Two being the development of much more large scale use of other sources of energy such as wind, wave power and geothermal energy that are currently neglected because we have easier ways to get energy. Number three being the development of technologies that are still in the future, the primary one being nuclear fusion which will essentially eliminate the problem of energy shortage.
There are an awful lot of different ways in which things could come right. I am not saying that one of those things is definitely going to come right. What I am saying is that it is irresponsible to presume that none of them will come right even over a period of several decades, which is what we are talking about when we are talking about any impact of medicines that affect ageing.

MF: The main flaw in the alternative energy ideal is that at some point of input there is still a reliance on fossil fuels; once fossil fuels become scarce or at least prohibitively expensive, that line of technological development will be closed at source.

Rather than a failing of science it will be a failure of physical input. I am not a pessimist but I see the logic in that. Basically you still need oil to produce wind turbines. You still need oil to build nuclear power stations. You still need oil to build photovoltaic cells. You still need oil to run drilling equipment, to build the offshore rigs that are technologically advanced to dig oil out that is now uneconomical -

AdG: That sounds like nonsense to me. There are some ways of extracting energy that today costs less to extract in terms of how much energy you use than the energy you extract and there are others that cost more. The others that cost more are being developed precisely to reach a point where they cost less. It's all a matter of the way in which these things dovetail together over time. Sure, there is going to be a fluctuation in the equation, so to speak. There is the possibility that one might reach some sort of crisis point where the things that used to be cheaper to extract suddenly become more expensive. That is just one scenario. It seems to me to be extremely arbitrary to suggest that is necessarily going to happen, especially since people understand that it obviously could happen and therefore they are predicting against it and trying to develop other technologies as fast as possible.

MF: I understand. I am just curious because the way you couch it is a very passionate and plausible way of seeing it.

AdG: I don't mean to be passionate here. I want to make sure that you understand that if the way I am saying things is passionate it is just because of frustration at people's myopia, at people's tendency to think about particular aspects of the future in isolation when it is obviously ridiculous to do so. It is essential to understand all of the various potentially dramatic changes in our technological options over the coming decades together and furthermore to understand all of that in the context of our uncertainty as to the rate at which those technologies will be developed.

Then, with that whole package, to actually stand back and say "What are our actual priorities?" Ultimately when you ask people what their priorities are, health comes fairly high on the list. People do not want to get sick.

MF: I had a conversation with a friend of mine about GM crops and he was saying "Everyone says it safe. It is unscientific to resist progress just because it is different". What I said was "What is anti-scientific is to rush a technology out before - "

AdG: I'd like to say something about that. It seems to me that the discussion that we are having about the potential impact of technologies that could dramatically change the game in a whole bunch of areas is very distinct from the discussion on technologies that sound terribly dramatic but actually are much less dramatic in terms of what they deliver over and above what else already exists.

GM crops is a fine example of the latter in my view. Crops that have been genetically modified not to get particular diseases are good but they don't qualitatively change the game in the way that the development of nuclear fusion or ways to extract fossil fuels from shale in an economical manner would.

In the case of these relatively less game-changing technological advances, the argument in terms of the cost-benefit analysis is completely different. It is completely correct to be much more circumspect and cautious in introducing such technologies and in disseminating them. I certainly think it is a good thing that there is a wide spectrum of opinion across the world. Different classes having different attitudes to different technologies because what it does is it allows things to be test run in a manner that does not in any way enforce or impose technologies on people when they do not want it.

Still, I think that the cost-benefit ratio needs to be taken into account. It is absolutely correct to say that we do not know very much about the impact that a particular new species or a new genetically modified version of a species would have on the ecology in a particular area. There have been plenty of celebrated train wrecks with regard to the introduction of unmodified species over the last century or two. So we know that we can make mistakes in these areas and I think that caution in these sorts of things is absolutely correct.

The technology that we have been mainly discussing would very dramatically change the way that society works, the way that humanity goes forward. The work I do on the defeat of ageing, work on nuclear fusion or desalination, these are things that will qualitatively alter our options and therefore the safety, the cost-benefit ratio is very different. We are also at an earlier stage. It is the development of the technology as opposed to the dissemination that I am focusing on here. I feel that once the technology is within range of being developed and therefore dissemination is something that is worth talking about and thinking about, one has a better chance of making the right decision because one is doing so at a point where one knows what technological advances in other areas have occurred in the interim and have changed the context of all of this.

None of that can impact the argument in favour of developing the technologies in the first place when they could end up giving us options that would massively improve people's quality of life.

MF: There are certain qualities associated with ageing that are not put in the same column as downsides, not a propensity for disease, weaknesses or loss of memory. Things people associate with the elderly: more wisdom, more circumspection, more of a reflective attitude -

AdG: Perhaps I should explain that I am not working on ways to make elderly people dumber.

MF: That is not what I meant. Do you think that those aspects of being elderly are something that comes from the experience of living that long or do you think it is also down to the fact that when your body begins to let you down, when you are a little closer to the end than you are to the beginning, you begin to have those attitudes? By removing the imminence of death as a motivation for greater acceptance and understanding of life, is there the chance that all we will end up with in the main will be everyone acting like twenty year olds?

AdG: I think that is complete bollocks. There is absolutely no chance whatsoever that the upside of being elderly today, the wisdom, the long view, the ability to actually contribute to a society by thinking differently than a younger person might do, would in any way be eliminated or even challenged by the development of therapies that keep elderly people healthy. It seems to me to be very clear indeed that the only reason why we see these upsides as we might think of them is because we are very nice to the elderly right now. We pay them money to do nothing from the age of sixty five because we are very sorry for them and we are very sorry for them because they are about to die. That is not going to be true anymore in a post-ageing world. What that means is that we will be motivated to restructure society to ensure that everybody is in a position to maximise the utility to society that comes from the knowledge that they have.

It will still be the case that people who are progressively more elderly will be more knowledgeable, experienced and able to contribute intellectually to different aspects of life. They will be able to do so that much more effectively by virtue of the fact that they will still be thinking quickly, still be able to remember stuff and still be physically and cognitively youthful.

MF: In a sense what you are saying is about a more circumspect approach to reproduction, egalitarian attitude to consumption, more respect for the resources we use instead of burning them and thinking they will always be there. I think that the idea that someone lives for a very long time gets rid of the idea that someone else will clean up the mess.

AdG: Too much is made of the idea that part of the problem with our attitude to the environment today is our short life spans, that these things happening are bad but they are happening very slowly and therefore it won't be our problem. I do not think there is much truth in that argument. I think personally that if there were truth in that argument then we would see that young adults would care more about the environment than the middle-aged or the elderly would, but I do not see any evidence of that.

I also think that when we look at what does drive the priorities of a young adult, we do not see it being driven by the fact that they have only got fifty or sixty more years to live. We see it being driven by peer pressure and self image. They want to make sure that they do stuff that they feel has some merit as measured by what other people are doing. It is a more short-term, instantaneous thing rather than life planning.

We need to look for an alternative way of describing how the impact of anti-ageing medicines on lifespan will have knock-on impacts in terms of our attitude to the environment. It will be much more complex than that; we will have a lot more respect for the environment but the reason we will have it is not because of fear, that we are going to have to live in this screwed-up world but rather the opposite. I think the word "empowerment" is the right word to use. We are so negligent about the major problems that the world faces, such as climate change, because we feel powerless to do anything about them. We feel ultimately that no way we are going to be able to fix this problem so let's just not think about it too much.

That is exactly how we think about ageing. It is always how we have thought about ageing. Ageing is something that has been with us since the dawn of civilisation, so the attitude that I

63

am talking about here has become pretty entrenched. The only way we are going to be able to fix that is by fixing the technology. By actually developing technology that shows us that our fatalism about ageing was wrong. My strong prediction is that when we do that, when we have developed therapies that really work against ageing, really banish the oldest and most powerful problem that humanity has ever experienced, that we will feel far more capable as a society of actually tackling other really hard problems.

I am not just talking about climate change. I am talking about all of the things we are discussing: pandemics, water, desalination. I bet that we could have definitely developed nuclear fusion by now if we had actually taken the trouble but there were a whole bunch of drivers for why we have not. We did not need it, we have got enough fossil fuels, but we did not really know if it was possible and we did not care very much. It was OK for governments to spend fifteen years trying to decide where to put the bloody research laboratory.

I would like to say a word about the atomic bomb because it is always brought up as an example of something we wish we had not invented. We wish we could uninvent it. Nuclear power is all very well but the physics that underlie nuclear power have led to these weapons that are terribly dangerous and terribly problematic.

I think it is extremely wrong, extremely incorrect to use this as an example that underlies pessimism or fear about development and dissemination of other technologies. The thing about the atomic bomb is that it is a technology with which a very small number of people can do a very large amount of damage in a very short amount of time. If you do not have all of those three things, if it is not something a small number of people can do, if it takes a long time for them to do or the damage that they do is not very large then it is just not in the same ballpark at all.

If we look at all of the other technologies that we are discussing here, technologies that might have an impact on the environment whether in the short term or in the longer term, we can see that they do not fit into that pattern. So we can be pretty damn certain that, whatever the scenario we end up in a few decades hence after we have developed anti-ageing technology or nuclear fusion, we will not be in a position where we are unable to to back out. We will not be in a position where the technology can be misused in a manner that nothing can be done about it. We will be able to decide as society, not necessarily as a global society, maybe different societies will make different decisions, what to do with the technology, whether to use it, how to use it in a manner that just does not have the same scale of risks that we see with nuclear technology.

MF: Do you think you could encapsulate the timeline of this particular line of technology?

AdG: As with any ambitious, long-term technology the timeline is highly speculative. It is more speculative the further out in the timeline we look, obviously. I think it is pretty possible to give at least a top-level timeline for what I think is going to happen and roughly when.

The first step in this timeline will be the point at which results are obtained in the laboratory, not in humans but in mice, that convince expert opinion in general that we have a proof of concept, that it is only a matter of time before regenerative medicine is applied comprehensively to the problems of human ageing and we can bona fide rejuvenate people.

I think that that point is very likely to be reached within the next ten years. All of the technologies that we are working on and that we are getting other people to work on at the moment are geared towards that. We do not do any work on humans. We work towards getting proof of concept in mice. The reason I think that is so important is of course mice are mammals, their body plan is not all that different from the body plan of a human being and I know scientific opinion in general is that if we can get something to work really well in mice then the chances are we can get it to work really well in humans.

No one will want to actually put a number on how soon we are going to work in humans but they will agree with the statement that it is only a matter of time. That in my mind is the milestone that matters the most. It is going to be complete pandemonium. Everyone's attitudes and retention of the presumption that this is just never going to happen will vanish overnight. Incredibly quickly, over a period of weeks, we are going to see a change that outweighed anything we have ever seen before in technology.

What is going to happen is that policy makers, opinion formers, are going to say "Fuck me, this actually sounds like quite a good idea. I don't want to get Alzheimer's either". It is going to become impossible to get elected unless you have a manifesto commitment to put very serious money into a "war on ageing". People are going to accept a very substantial reduction in their standard of living for a while just in order to end the slaughter as soon as possible. It is going to be like that. It is going to be war, except we are all going to be on the same side.

That is going to be a very different world than any of us have experienced except the people who were alive in World War Two, I guess. Really, it is going to be pandemonium. People are going to be working as hard as they can to make this happen. My job at that point will be done. There will be people out there far better than I am at all of the things I am reasonably good at and I will be able to retreat into glorious obscurity.

Perhaps fifteen years after that, there will be the actual delivery of these technologies to humans. At that point, of course, people are going to get treated, things are going to happen fast. The critical point I want to come back to is that in that interim period there will have been the putting in place of not only the technology to make sure that the medicines actually get developed as soon as possible but also the technology to make sure those medicines can be disseminated across the world as broadly as possible and as quickly as possible.

So by that time we will be in a position to blow a whistle and, BANG, people will not have ageing anymore. I am simplifying but I am not simplifying all that much. After that we will see all of the gradual changes that will result from the inevitable changes in age structure. We will see a shift, but people will be only getting older one year per year. We will not have thousand year old people for nine hundred years or more, let us remember that.

Let us also remember: a sufficient number of decades in the future, we have no idea what other technologies are going to be around, what the availability of those technologies is going to mean for the choices that we make on how to use these anti-ageing technologies, how to cope with population growth etcetera.

Cyberia: The Security-Industrial Complex
with Professor Ross Anderson

"I am concerned that we may be heading from being a state that can watch anybody to being a state that can watch everybody."

I came across Ross Anderson's work when he was quoted in a newspaper interview about the impact of digital surveillance on society. Living as I do in the UK, which has 25% of the world's CCTV watching 0.1% of the world's population, issues of privacy and surveillance are of great interest to me personally as well as within the scope of this book.

It seems perfectly reasonable rather than paranoid (and this in itself is worrying) to state that the future will see more surveillance, more intrusion by state as well as corporate entities into personal privacy, perhaps even to the extent of the compilation of 'super-databases' which catalogue everything from our hair colour and address to our preferred brand of toothpaste and public transport usage. The manner in which that data is gathered and protected from unwarranted perusal fall well within Ross's expertise.

He is Professor of Security Engineering at Cambridge University and literally wrote the book on security engineering. The book is called Security Engineering. He chairs the Foundation for Information Policy Research, Britain's leading internet policy think tank. Despite being incredibly busy, he agreed to speak with me twice over the course of a week in August 2012.

If you want to get the most realistic impression of him, try reading his answers with a slightly impatient Scottish accent.

NB: This interview took place before the Snowden leak and the subsequent publicity surrounding the ways in which personal information is gathered by corporations and governments. His concern about the mass collection and storage of this data proved extremely prescient.

Mike Freedman: There are several aspects of your work that I was hoping we could explore. The first is a kind of overview of the field of information and cyber security as it has sprung up recently and how you have seen it develop around you.

Ross Anderson: Information security is a field that started off from academic beginnings in the 1970s with pioneering work on operating systems security at MIT and in cryptography at Stanford, MIT and Xerox, the development of public key cryptography in particular. There have been academic conferences in the field now for thirty years - the IEEE Symposium on Security and Privacy started off in that year.

Since I became involved in the field as an academic, and in the eighties I was a practitioner, the field has expanded enormously. From perhaps twenty relevant conferences in 1992 there are now probably over two hundred. You should look at the IEEE Security and Privacy newsletter to get some feel for the scale and scope. It is a bit like a fungus expanding in a forest - as the mushrooms grow outwards, the nutrients get exhausted, the ring gets bigger and bigger. So the scope of information security research has become ever wider. One of the things we found to be very interesting and profitable from the research point of view is to look at how information security problems arise and are solved in one industry after another as they have moved to working electronically or online.

For example, the healthcare industries used to keep medical records on bundles of paper and now this is done electronically, which has raised all sorts of interesting problems of privacy and safety.

Another example is utility metering. In the old days if you had a pre-payment meter in your house you typically fed it with coins and a man would come round once a month and empty the meter. Nowadays these meters are run cryptographically - you buy a magic number from an ATM or a petrol station, you type it into your electricity meter and bingo, you have another couple of weeks of energy available.

As these applications come along, they raise all sorts of fascinating engineering questions. We have come to realise that they raise policy questions as well because very often systems fail when the people who are responsible for maintaining the system aren't the same as the people who suffer when it fails. This has given rise to significant problems with, for example, the resilience of the internet. Who is responsible for supplying the excess capacity that is needed to provide that resilience? It has given rise to issues with the protection of consumers in banking transactions. In many countries, banks dump liability for fraud onto merchants, cardholders or both. The incentives facing the issuing banks and the acquiring banks are not the same, so an acquiring bank might, for example, find it economic to give merchants cheap terminals that are vulnerable to fraud because the resulting fraud will be spread largely over many of their competitors rather than affecting them directly.

So security has grown from a discipline that thirty years ago was founded on cryptologic mathematics and the design of operating systems into one which touches a very wide range of disciplines: hardware engineering, software engineering, economics and even psychology. That is one of the things that has kept working in information security interesting for me personally.

MF: You raised exactly what I was hoping we could get into. As more and more of the daily operations of life become digitised, and now we are seeing a move towards cloud computing for much of storage as well, the issue of information security as it pertains to privacy becomes, as you said, a matter of psychology and economics as much as it does a matter of engineering.

RA: It is also a matter of power because security is not a skill. It is not something that you sprinkle onto systems like pixie dust. Security is always something that exists only in the context of a threat model. From the point of view of the person who owns the system, the threat is often not Chinese hackers but that their customers might arbitrage the product or might go elsewhere. So you see information security being used to support business models, to lock people in and to do other things that regulators might not approve of.

Another fact in the information goods and services industry is the tendency to monopoly. Right from the beginnings of the industry, with firms like IBM, we have seen the tendency for platform vendors to become large and dominant. We then had Microsoft, we have Google, we have Facebook. There have been similar games played in mobile platforms, telecoms switchgear and elsewhere.

You see it also in consumer firms. Ebay and Amazon are each dominant in their field. There are all sorts of policy questions about what happens in a world where more and more of our goods and services are supplied or mediated through firms that

69

are so large and powerful that they are not responsive to individual consumers or even most governments.

MF: Essentially we are talking about a bottleneck. The same issue that caused a lot of antitrust and anti-monopoly legislation to be brought in, in this country and in the US.

RA: There are some echoes of the issues that exercised US politicians between the 1870s and about 1900, as the first antitrust framework in the USA was elaborated in response to the robber barons.[1] It is not quite as extreme of course because that framework already exists. You already have the Federal Trade Commission you have the Director General of Competition in the European Union.

But many of the issues are more difficult to deal with because of the global nature of the businesses concerned, the speed with which the business models evolved and the fact that most governments are not at all confident or even competent when it comes to dealing with information technology.

MF: So the issue of power is particularly pressing as applied to the economics and the psychology of a lot of these technologies, right? Because they have their own economies of scale, their own economic priorities and people can be moulded to buy into these systems if they are marketed to in the right way. They can be made happy with a government bringing in quite intrusive measures. If they are fooled or influenced by the way a company markets its products then they can be induced to give more and more of their data, as with Facebook and cloud computing.

This centralising principle which, as you pointed out, is present in a lot of the internet companies, this way of consolidating more and more data into fewer and fewer hands, what kind of ramifications do you see that having for the future of our privacy in particular?

RA: Facebook is an interesting case because if you use Facebook you are not their customer, you are their product. The customer is the advertiser. Facebook's incentive is to provide you with the illusion of privacy, with the illusion of being in a private space surrounded by your friends so you will supply as much information as possible which they can sell to the advertisers. Given this economic imperative, the psychology that is then applied to provide the illusion of privacy follows automatically and in fact this is not just a Facebook thing, this is something that was common to the forty-odd companies that duked it out in the social networking arena until Facebook won. It is not a particular CEO, it is just the dynamic of an industry. That is how the entire social networking industry grew up.

The problem facing regulators is, if you are going to have a social networking industry of the same sort of shape as Facebook, then it is going to suck out an awful lot of people's private information and sell it to advertisers.[2] What can you realistically do about that?

The big public policy debate at the moment is about the Data Protection Regulation in the European Union which is supposed to replace the Data Protection Directive from the 90s, with an updated privacy law which will give member states less wiggle room to do bad implementations of it. The UK in particular did a poor implementation of data protection law because it wanted UK companies to be more competitive and more able to wheel and deal with personal data the way American companies do. This irritated the European Commission, so there's a struggle in Brussels at the moment about the wording of the new regulations which will update the law.

MF: Very present in information technology, and I also find it frustrating when it is not addressed openly in manufacturing as well, is the way in which the construction of the device dictates the way that it is used. For example, before he passed away, Steve Jobs made it perfectly clear that to him the computers of the future would not have hard drives. Everything would be stored in the cloud. If people are only sold devices that require the use of a completely central storage system for all of their data which can be accessed by god knows who for the purposes of god knows what, then it is almost as if the customer is forced into this position.

RA: Well, the forces that compel customers are quite diverse and quite interesting. Three years ago when we got some new students, they told us that they were interested in researching the privacy of social networks and I said 'Why is that?'. One of them said "maybe you guys don't understand this, but in university nowadays the use of Facebook is really compulsory because that is where the party invitations come from". If you're not into Facebook you miss party invitations, you don't meet girls, you don't have kids and so your genes die out. The

71

Facebook refuseniks are just going to be deleted by evolutionary processes.

When social forces like that are harnessed to create monopolies or to uphold monopolies it is an interesting case where you can't blame it on the marketing people but the structure of an industry. It is entirely unclear what sort of regulatory response is even possible, let alone appropriate.

MF: The way you put it about evolution fascinates me. A lot of these technologies have market and commercial forces behind them but also seem to be emergent. We developed the internet at a point where, as society, we required a new way of communicating, same with mobile phones. All of this stuff seems to me to come out of an ever-growing need to maintain the burden of communication across the web of society. That point about the students is very compelling.

If evolution is a part of it, in the sense that an ever-increasing complexity of communications technologies giving ever-increasingly monopolistic corporate interests the possibility for ever-increasing centralisation and monopolisation of data, then people are in an evolutionary trap, right? We need these systems to maintain the integrity of society as a functioning entity but at the same time we are preyed upon by the very interests that make that integrity possible.

RA: Yeah. The forces that we are talking about have not yet been operating over evolutionary timescales and one should be aware of what happened to Karl Marx's predictions back in the 1840s. He predicted that increasing centralisation of capital would lead eventually to the collapse of the capitalist system as we knew it. Now that failed to happen for a number of reasons and one of them was technological progress. Sure, the railway companies that were flourishing in the 1840s ended up being consolidated into a few big ones, then countries like Britain even nationalised but so many new industries came along but that basically did not matter very much.

The debate about policy in IT about further competition in the market has been replaced by competition for the market. Some people argue that it is OK that we get monopolies arising because so many new markets come along and so many old markets disappear or are transformed by technological change that stuff is contestable nonetheless. Now, I do not have a crystal ball which enables me to see where we will be in two hundred years time, whether we will still have Microsoft, Google and

Facebook around, but I do observe that many of the big companies formed in previous ways of innovation are still with us.

MF: You mean like Coca-Cola, Nestle etcetera.

RA: I am not so much a student of such firms but of engineering firms. IBM is about a century old and slightly older than that are the big German chemical companies and then of course there were a whole lot of car companies that started about a hundred years as well that consolidated into a dozen worldwide which are still with us. So when companies of consequence come out of technological innovation, they do tend to stick around. There is always a worry at the back of my mind that maybe we will come to a time when there is no obvious space for more big information companies just as by the 1930s we had perhaps come to the point that there was no room for more big chemical companies.

MF: You said politicians either don't know how to deal with these new technologies or they are reluctant to intrude on a market that is still developing. On the other hand, this notion of involuntary participation of the public. Your average person signs up to Facebook - no-one ever reads the terms and conditions, they want to talk to their friends and family, they want to be invited to parties, they want to know what their niece looks like now that their brother lives in another country and so they just click 'agree' and sign up; whoever has access to Facebook's database now knows everything that they put online.

Likewise, here in the UK we have the most CCTV of any country in the world. The statistic I heard was that the UK has 25% of the world's CCTV.[3] Only today I read an article coming out of the US that there is now evidence that the federal government has been using a system called Trapwire[4] to access civilian CCTV and run it through facial recognition software to keep tabs on people without their knowledge.

There is again this ongoing concern about involuntary participation. How much of this is us needing to embrace new technologies as they arise while being wary of abuses and how much of it is a panopticon being constructed around us either without our knowledge or without us having the power to stop it?

73

RA: I get the impression that Trapwire is some crap program on which the US government wasted a ton of money, now being talked up as some sort of civil liberties threat. DARPA spends all sorts of money on strange things and most of them don't work.

MF: So you'd argue that a lot of this infringement on civil liberty concern is actually due to very successful marketing by the security companies themselves rather than a genuine encroachment.

RA: We know that facial recognition in public spaces doesn't really work very well except as a placebo. There was a trial in Newham in London some five or ten years ago where the council put up some CCTV cameras and said "these can pick known offenders out of a crowd"; they can do nothing of the kind but crime actually went down.

MF: So on the one hand we have the willingness of government to encroach on liberties in the name of safety and on the other hand we have the very successful lobbying by the security-industrial complex to encourage the power structure to purchase their goods and services.

RA: There's a constant push by the people who want to sell stuff to change the terms of public debate. When the medical research establishment wants to get access to everybody's medical records, they do various things to change the terms of the debate on privacy. This is nothing new, this is how lobbying has worked since God was a boy.

There has been a huge amount of scaremongering used to build the security-industrial complex, particularly since 9/11. Many tens of billions of dollars are wasted on security as theatre, providing jobs in some constituency or congressional district. It was ridiculous in America, for example, to see the tower of bucks being spread out over fifty states when as a matter of practice only three or four states are actually at risk.

Similarly, it is ridiculous to see the amount of CCTV used in Britain. In fact, someone who is now a minister remarked at a private meeting before the election - Chatham House rules so I can't quote - ' Look, everybody in parliament knows two things: the first thing they know is that CCTV doesn't work and the second thing they know is that the voters think it works. Therefore, whoever wins the election, you must expect that hundreds of millions more will be wasted on CCTV and there is nothing you can do about it so stop wasting your breath.'

That is the view from a political insider, who is now a minister, about CCTV. That is the level of cynicism with which public policy debate is conducted in Westminster and Whitehall. Now NGO groups, and I am associated with a couple of them, of course try and push back on the scaremongering but of course we have nothing like the budgets or the incentive that the salesman or the security vendors have. When I speak to civil servants about this they say 'Look, thanks for coming to speak to us and we know that what you say makes sense but we might see you one or twice a year and meanwhile, in Whitehall, anytime I want something explained by a person from Microsoft or IBM, their government affairs people will have somebody in my office within half an hour.'

The difference in lobbying muscle between the NGO sector and the greedies is absolutely stupendous.

MF: That cynical attitude where it is not about informing the public of what the case is but rather manipulating the public's perception of the case to the financial benefit of an inner group of special interests seems to be a very dangerous way to go about "ensuring" our security or "protecting" our privacy.

RA: Well that is how the world works. Democracy is cheaper than dictatorship and for a number of reasons. When dictatorships go wrong, it is extraordinarily expensive. Having a civil war to remove the dictator can be ruinously destructive, but democracy does have its costs. Twenty or twenty-five percent of GNP simply gets wasted on jobs for the boys, on bureaucrats, on all the other things that the public choice economists have written about.

MF: So if we have that degree of cynicism in our so-called "democracy", would you make the argument that democracy as it is practised is more of a power-maintaining exercise than a real qualitative difference between the milder forms of dictatorship that have existed in the past?

RA: Well, that is a philosophical problem outside my main area of expertise and there is a whole lot that has been written about the essence of democracy and its value. It is of some interest to computer scientists because of course many security problems are ultimately government's problems and we see in different online systems different forms of governance from primitive tribal societies through to chieftain societies to Confucianism etcetera.

From the point of view of a systems guy, the main feature of a democratic system is that the system is contestable and particularly, important parts of it are fairly easily contestable. Now, in the UK for example, the constitution changes only slowly and so things like the civil service and the legal system have enormous inertia. A change of the party in power for the other party in power is fairly straightforward and happens regularly. Changing policy to suit our favoured pressure or lobby group is unfortunately easier still. It is not entirely clear how you can get to throw the bums out and replace them with a new bunch of bums without getting at the same time the ability for the bums to be persuaded by people with money to cut them sweetheart laws.

MF: What you said about democracy being contestable is one of the concerns I definitely see in the new ways of communicating with one another through social media. There is far more scope for interference, for control, for interception, for surveillance. If you are under 25 now, everything that you have ever done is a photograph online, a status update. Every view that you have held that you subsequently discarded is recorded somewhere on some database. When I was young at school, you were always under threat of something going on your 'permanent record' and it was pretty much a joke because everyone knew that if you moved school or went to university, nobody really kept those records. They were just in a file somewhere, there was no 'permanent record'. Now it seems that, for each individual that is 'plugged in', there is a permanent record that is accessible to people who take an interest in you. This has, or could have, a very chilling effect on people who are trying to contest the very democracy that we are trying to maintain.

RA: The real involvement that I have had in political lobbying tends to have been around digital rights issues. I was involved in the key escrow business in the crypto-wars during the 90s,[5] then in export control in the early 2000s and at various times in privacy of medical records. The big issue now at least in the UK is the Communications Data Bill[6] and the attempts by intelligence agencies to greatly increase their power and scope by doing wholesale data mining of the internet against domestic surveillance targets.

Previously we had tolerated GCHQ because they busied themselves with worthy and relatively harmless activities like deciphering Hitler's telegrams or tapping Chairman Mao's phone. They have been short of business since the end of the Cold War and would now like to become a super-police agency listening to everybody's emails, texts and status updates. I think there is a real hazard in this. It is the sort of thing that you find being done in places like Syria, Iran and the UAE. It is not the sort of thing that other democracies are doing with the unfortunate exception of the USA where the NSA turned its dishes inward after 9/11.[7]

So, in terms of a threat to democracy, I am concerned that we may be heading from being a state that can watch anybody to being a state that can watch everybody, as the old German Democratic Republic tried to do and as governments such as Egypt and Tunisia were found to be trying to do at the recent upsets in the Arab Spring.

The problem is, how does one push back on the desire of the government for total surveillance when people happily accede to almost total surveillance by Google, Facebook and others? Well, perhaps the sticking point will come if governments decide that they need to have access to everybody's Facebook account and everybody's Gmail. Maybe that will be a bridge too far.

MF: But in a functional sense, given their ability to make demands on ISPs and to demand access to the servers that hold that data, don't they already have that access? Is it just implicit rather than explicit?

RA: At present the government does of course have wiretapping facilities at phone companies but they may be able to tap about 1% of lines. Building that out to the point that they could wiretap 100% is simply a matter of engineering. It is simply a matter of giving a few billion dollars to the Chinese for the black boxes, but there is a policy issue which we are in the middle of debating now with the Communications Data Bill.

MF: Is there a way of reconciling a need for preserving people's privacy, their control over who has access to their data and how that data is used, with genuine security concerns or do you see it as being more of the same continuing indefinitely?

RA: I suspect that we'll see more of the same continuing until there's some shock to the system that causes people to sit up and take notice. In the case of medical privacy, for example, we're about to start next month making essentially everybody's medical records available to all interested researchers. It's surely going to happen that some dim-witted professor of psychiatry is going to leave a laptop on a train containing the records of all ten million people in Britain who have had a diagnosis of anxiety or depression. They're not prepared to anonymise stuff more thoroughly than removing names and addresses because every other piece of data that you could remove from a record is used for something or other in the research community. It's an inevitability that sooner or later a laptop's contents, sensitive personal information on millions of people, are going to pitch up on Pastebin. When it happens, there will be a public outcry and stuff might change, but not by much.

MF: There was a very similar question raised when genetics became a viable technology a decade ago, that you could have designer babies or spot when there was a congenital defect in a foetus before it was born and either fix it or abort. This raised the spectre that in the future, insurance companies wouldn't insure you if you had a heart defect because it was preventable in the embryonic stage or only people with the purest of genes would be able to get certain jobs or certain perks. Do you think there's the possibility that people might find their viability for an insurance policy or even employment affected by a medical record that is available to the people that are looking into giving them a policy or hiring them?

RA: It depends. In America this is a big deal because employers pay for medical insurance. In Europe, it's usually the government that pays for medical insurance and the government insures everybody.

MF: In the concentration of personal information into gigantic databases there's function creep, where we allow one thing to come in for a specific purpose but then it is put to other uses.

RA: This happens all the time. It's one of the ways that bureaucracies grow. Bureaucracies set out to monitor the relative performance of schools and end up monitoring the relative performance of all school children in the country, and then want to take over and build a system that will host definitive copies of all school certificates. It's just a question of people bidding for more power and money.

Ultimately, technologies get adopted only if they bring some benefit; we do live in a capitalist society after all. The question is "who's benefiting?" The current model of advertising-supported services means that it isn't necessarily the users of these systems who are always getting the greatest benefit from them. In the long run you'd expect the market to sort this out, where markets are contestable. The problem is that information goods and services markets often aren't, because of two-sided market effects and other externalities which lead there to be monopolies.

So the big question I suppose is what happens once we no longer have each wave of big firms being replaced by another: IBM replaced by Microsoft, Microsoft replaced by Google, Google replaced by Apple and so on. We're nowhere near equilibrium and we have no idea what equilibrium in technology policy would look like.

MF: That's also shown in the issues with copyright. Technology has allowed for something which bypasses the typical ways that companies protected their revenues and intellectual property. It raises a very valid question about how much a work of art, say a song or a film or a book, is owned by the person who assigned themselves copyright in it and how much over time it is actually owned by the culture it contributes to.

You could make the argument that a famous song by Led Zeppelin, for example, has been such a part of our culture for 40 years now that it's perfectly valid for people to feel entitled to use it in a way Led Zeppelin might not want it used or their management company might want it protected for revenue reasons.

Obviously people who create art have a much less reliable way of supporting themselves, and so when it hits they tend to be some of the strictest in protecting their investment, which has been weeks or months or even years of pain writing a novel or an album or a film.

RA: The emergent problem is that in the old days all the stuff we used to do was local and involved interacting with other people or things we could understand, but increasingly what's happening is that the interactions we do are with machines, with large systems which are often based a long way away and are thoroughly impersonal, so the individual is more and more isolated and alienated and there's very little reciprocity in most transactions.

We also see an erosion of the ability of courts to provide any neutral arbitration in disputes between someone and a big software or services firm or bank - the firm simply doesn't make enough information available for the courts to make a reasonable decision and the typical individual doesn't have the resources to make a fight of it. If they did, the firm would immediately give up. So we see, in effect, a creeping transformation of the world into one of walled gardens, where it's take it or leave it.

MF: There are deeper philosophical ramifications to this concept of walls. There's mutually assured destruction. The technology allows for the eradication of these walls but at the same time, if the power lies solely with the corporate or moneyed interests that want those walls preserved, they can use that technology to keep those walls there indefinitely, which is also unhealthy. It's a very important question. What really belongs to the individual? What belongs to our society at large? What role does technology play in drawing the line?

RA: My colleague Bruce Schneier[8] has described this as feudal security. In the 1200s or 1300s, if you lived in the Scottish Borders, you had to give your allegiance to one of the clans there in return for protection. This was a great deal if you were a farmer with two or three sheep who wanted protection from being raided by other clans and having your sheep stolen, but from the point of view of the middle classes it wasn't a good deal. Medieval societies were hollowed out as a result and the only middle class people you found tended to be in those towns that had some kind of Royal Charter or other means of protection from the predation of the barons. So there are long term questions about what is public space, what is contestable space and what sort of spaces there are for people to develop as professionals, entrepreneurs and so on.

No Free Lunch
with Robert Rapier

"We are all hypocrites. We think oil companies are keeping us addicted when it is really our demand for low oil prices that keeps them doing what they are doing."

I met Robert when we were filming Critical Mass at the Global Footprint Network's Footprint Forum in Siena, Italy. He was generous enough to give us an interview for the film and we stayed in touch from that point. It was on his suggestion that I read "The Long Emergency" by James Howard Kunstler, the first full book on the topic of peak oil that I was exposed to.

At the time, he was Chief Technology Officer and Executive Vice President at Merica International, a forestry and renewable energy company. He is also the author of "Power Plays: Energy Options in the Age of Peak Oil" as well as the R-Squared Energy Column at Consumer Energy Report, where he is Managing Editor. His articles on energy and sustainability have appeared in The Washington Post, Christian Science Monitor and Forbes.

Robert was born and raised on a farm in Oklahoma. He speaks in a soothing drawl, with the directness one would expect from a Midwestern farm boy. It is a source of frustration to me that on those occasions when we have been able to speak, it has not been over a beer.

Mike Freedman: When we spoke whilst working on the film, we talked about peak oil and input shortages that affect a hugely diverse range of products and services. One of the things I find difficult to reconcile is how far we have to go just to access energy, be it subsea drilling for oil, hydraulic fracking. We are doing things of which we do not know the consequences, with much greater frequency. It seems that we have to keep doing more drastic things.

Robert Rapier: You are exactly right. We are not drilling five miles deep in the ocean if there is easy oil still to be found. They are building floating cities out in the ocean to get at oil and then pipe it all the way back to shore to get it refined. We are pushing into the Arctic. We do not do that if the easy oil is still there. This was the amazing thing about this Maugeri guy.[1] He was a former executive with ENI, the Italian oil company. He came out and said we will be producing a hundred and ten million barrels of oil come 2020. In fact, I don't know if you saw George Monbiot come out and write in one of those UK newspapers "I am convinced now that peak oil is not a problem; it is global warming that is going to get us."[2] He based that on that Maugeri paper. I have taken a look at that and for it to be true, it would require oil production growth rates that we have not seen in decades.

At the same time we're pushing into all these unknown frontiers, he expects oil production to happen at a faster rate than when the oil was much easier to get. For that very reason, I think that is absolutely impossible. This new oil is going to be more difficult to produce and come online at a slower rate.

On the other hand, you have to be very careful not to pin down a date on peak oil. This is where peak oil people have lost a lot of credibility. In 2005 they said this is it, this is peak and it is doomsday - in a few years we'll be living in the Stone Age.[3] I said even then, you do not know. Oil production is somewhat a function of price. If oil prices tomorrow went to five hundred dollars and it did not totally wreck the economy, which it would, but if they went there, oil production would rise substantially in the next few years. That is a fact.

Now the downside of that is we are going to deplete at a much faster rate because we are using up what is there now. When the oil price goes up, more investments are made.

Here is an ironic fact that I think I was the first person to note: people generally do not view Obama as a friendly president to oil. He is going to be the first president since LBJ to be in office during four straight years of rising US oil production.[4] The reason is high oil prices since 2005. The oil companies have invested more and more money. Oil production actually fell for eight straight years under Bush but it fell at a slower and slower rate by the time he left office. It just happened to turn upwards in Obama's first year in office. It is just a function of the oil price. The companies out there are fracking in the Bakken, the Eagle Ford shale in Texas, so our oil production is on the rise.

It will not rise to the 1970 peak level. Nixon approved a pipeline, then Carter gets the benefit of the rising oil production in the US because it turned upwards his first year in office, went up for a few years before starting to decline again. I think that is what is going to happen here. We will tap out the Barnett and we will get that easy, fast oil and then production will start to decline again.

But there are a lot of countries that have not experienced a fracking revolution yet. So I would say production can rise maybe a little bit from here but then the scenario that I think becomes important is the one that I call 'peak-light'. It does not matter if oil production is rising if demand is rising as fast or faster than that. You have very high oil prices, crippling for economies. In the US in the last five years, we have dropped almost two million barrels a day of demand. Why are oil prices still a hundred dollars? Because China and India increased their consumption by more than that. Developing countries, and I wrote about this at length in my book, are almost immune because their level of consumption is so low that even a hundred dollar oil does not affect their consumption at all. Their consumption is almost a straight line up right along with oil prices. That happens because they are only using one or two barrels of oil per person, per year. We are using twenty-two in the US. So when oil prices go up a little bit it hurts us a lot more than it hurts them and we are able to cut back. We drive twelve thousand miles a year so we cut back five hundred miles a year; we do not take as many discretionary trips and the next car we get is a little more fuel efficient.

For them they are putting seven people on a moped and driving across town for the first time ever. So that is new consumption that has never been there before. When we are doing renewable energy in the US and looking at our carbon emissions in the US, they pale in comparison to the situation over in China and India. If our carbon emissions in the US completely disappeared tomorrow it won't take us back to 1995 global levels of emissions and they would be very rapidly rising.

83

US-based emissions is not the right problem. We have to set an example. The analogy I use is somebody who is very obese loses five pounds and then tells a starving person in India 'this is how you get by with less food'. Well, they are already getting by with a fraction of the food that we eat. We do not have the moral authority to tell them they can develop on a fraction of the energy that we use. There is no road map. We can't show them how to do it. We can say 'in theory, you can do it' but they say 'well, why aren't you doing it?' The reason we are not doing it is because it is still cheaper to consume fossil fuels.

As far as global warming goes, there was a survey done in India a few years ago where I think only thirty percent of Indians even knew what it was.[5] So if they do not even know what it is, whether it is hotter tomorrow or next year or ten years from now is of less importance to them than whether they can slightly improve their standard of living. There are a lot of people at a very low standard of living and very little energy consumption. A little energy consumption can improve their standard of living by a lot. So that is why their energy consumption is going up even in the face of hundred dollar oil. That has profound implications for the rest of the world.

MF: You are talking about a difference between developmental and discretionary consumption of energy. We have very high discretionary use because the developmental use is already embedded in the system, whereas they have a certain amount of developmental use that should be required, that should happen in order to amend the inequity in lifestyle. It is definitely a consumption problem in that sense because ultimately it is going to be our discretionary energy 'budget' that takes the hit rather than the developmental one, because discretion is elastic and development is not.

RR: There is a very good TED presentation called The Magic Washing Machine.[6] It explains very clearly why their consumption is going up. This guy talks about his mother or grandmother getting her first washing machine and how much of her days that freed up and how liberating that was. Every woman in the world aspires to have a washing machine. That really hits home. You think 'wow, their consumption is going to keep going up a lot from here'.

If you ask the average person in the US "could you cut your oil consumption in half?", a lot of people can't. They live far from from work and they have a certain amount of commuting

84

that they have to do, but even if you could do that, you are still at five times the per capita consumption of China. We cut by two-thirds, we still are two or three times what China is. China is going to consume more because they have seen the Western lifestyles. They want things that consume energy. They are selling more cars now than the US and building all these coal plants. They are going to be consuming coal for the next forty or fifty years in these coal plants, so they are locking in a lot of coal consumption.

To the extent that global warming is a really serious issue, that is ground zero. That is where the real problem is. A lot of environmentalists in the US give the impression that it's really a US problem and it is true that the historical emissions, a lot of that is from the United States. I have calculated that the emissions from the US over the last forty-five years would have contributed about 6 ppm to a 70 ppm rise in the global CO_2 concentration in the atmosphere. We contributed the most but there are still a whole lot of people contributing. We are not contributing the most now. CO_2 emissions in the EU and in the US have fallen in the last ten years. The graph in Asia-Pacific is just straight up with no end in sight.

MF: So we are in a position where the way that the environmental movement wants to switch people on to issues of scarcity and of limitation is to place the locus of control or blame, whichever you want to call it, with us in the country that we are in. You can't reach the British public by telling them what is wrong in Uganda. You need to tell them about what is wrong in the UK so that they feel empowered, that they can do something. At the same time there are a thousand people standing in line for every litre of petrol I do not burn.

Into the future, how do you see this simultaneous demand/destruction in the West because of high prices and maybe environmentally conscious lifestyles being paired with this inexorably rising demand from the East and from the global South because they simply need to develop to a certain standard that we reached a long time ago? How is this going to play out?

RR: It is going to mean oil prices are going to stay high. All the fracked oil that has come online has prevented oil prices from going to a hundred and fifty or two hundred dollars a barrel. You probably will not see that in a couple or three years. Demand is keeping oil prices from falling below seventy dollars or so. Also, the fracking is not competitive below that price.

85

Newt Gingrich campaigned on 'two dollar gasoline' - that is both foolish and naïve. We are past those days. Barring a total collapse of the economy, there is going to be no two dollar gasoline ever again.

If oil prices are sustained at these levels or if they go a little higher, we will in the West continue to decrease our consumption. There are still gas guzzlers all over the roads here. Over time, people will decide this is the new norm, these high prices, and fuel efficiency will become more important to them. At the same time they cannot understand if we are becoming more fuel efficient and using less oil, why we are still paying ninety dollars a barrel for oil. It is explained by the consumption patterns in the developing world and if you have seen their consumption you know that it can only go up.

MF: You said that barring some kind of catastrophic economic collapse in the West, oil prices will stay high. Well, what if there is a catastrophic economic collapse in the West? That seems to be the major narrative playing out in the media these days.

RR: Yeah, I know a lot of people who believe that. It is not really my area so I do not know. I do know that if it happens, demand is definitely going to go down, but how will it impact the people in the developing world? It probably will not cut their consumption. It will cut ours because we will not have jobs to drive to. Recession always causes slowdown in industrial activity so our oil consumption falls, emissions fall. That always happens. The situation we are in now though is that supply and demand are in such tight balance. Ten years ago we probably had five to ten million barrels of spare capacity in the world. Over the last ten years, new capacity was added at a much slower rate than demand increased. What that means is, as our demand falls, all it takes is a little bit of demand in developing countries to eat up what we do not use.

Ten years ago, 9/11 caused worldwide oil prices to fall because there was so much excess capacity out there that when our demand fell we really had a grossly oversupplied market. We do not have a grossly oversupplied market today. We cannot get into that situation without this massive demand destruction and I do not see that happening.

MF: On one hand, high oil price has a draining effect on the economy - it affects global GDP, it affects people's earnings. But on the other hand you have quotes from OPEC nations that now they cannot allow prices to fall below a certain level. Like you said, ten years ago forty dollar oil was a bonanza. Now, they are saying we cannot let it get below seventy-five dollars a barrel otherwise it is not worth it.

RR: OPEC was satisfied with twenty-five dollar oil ten years ago, that was fine and dandy with them. Historically, they liked that price band because as prices went up demand went down and alternatives became more competitive. I think they figured out that alternatives are further out there than they imagined and as governments make more money, they spend more money. So, these huge revenues that are coming in, their budgets blow up and they get accustomed to that.

Hugo Chavez has been pushing for hundred dollar oil for several years, saying that is a fair price. Iran says that is a fair price. Some of these other countries now need eighty to ninety dollar oil to balance their budgets. OPEC will slowly strangle us to death. They will continue to become accustomed to a higher and higher oil price and because of the price and power they have, if they can get together and agree and everybody does their quotas, they can keep oil prices quite high. They could, within a week, drive oil prices up to two hundred dollars a barrel, no problem. They have that kind of pricing power.

Saudi Arabia still is producing ten percent of the world's oil and if there was a revolution there and oil production fell dramatically, you would see really high oil prices very quickly. It would wreck economies, bankrupt airlines, as 2008 did. A lot of small airlines went bankrupt in 2008 when oil prices ran up so sharply. Worse than the sharp run-ups are the little run-up and retreat, which is what we have seen in the last few years. Prices run up, demand falls a little bit, they retreat a little bit but it is like a stair step. It goes up and down but over the long term it is climbing, just at a slow rate. We are becoming acclimated to those higher prices because it's not a straight line up. I think if price ran up quickly and stayed there people would really start to make some major changes, but when it runs up and retreats a little bit people feel much better about four dollar gasoline if they were just paying five dollars than if they were paying three dollars.

It is all relative to where you have just been. There was a Huffington Post article talking about ethanol impact on gasoline prices.[7] One person after another said 'Have you not noticed? This pattern happens again and again, year after year.' We are running up and then retreating but we are not retreating to the levels we were at before. People are just becoming acclimated to it.

MF: You raised two things that are really important. One is the issue of alternatives that I do want to get into with you in more depth. The other is a rhetorical issue that arises in every election cycle in the US or to a much lesser extent in the UK because we do not have the same direct link between a voter's preference and the price of gasoline. So, the guy comes out on the stump, rolls up his sleeves, picks up the microphone and tells everyone America is going to be energy-independent in two years, four years, six years. All you have to do is trust me - we will be producing everything we need. It seems to me this might be either a typical, cynical electioneering ploy or it might speak to a deeper truth; America might be energy-independent in ten years but not the way people prefer. They might only be able to afford to use the oil that is produced in America.

RR: I have said it again and again. I can make America energy-independent but you will not like it. The average person would not like how I would make America energy-independent. My proposal is: tax less of something that we want, which is people working and earning income, and more of something we don't want, which is people consuming much more than they need to. I propose to raise fossil fuel taxes in general sharply and offset that by either an income tax credit or just reducing income tax rates. I would do it in such a way that it was revenue-neutral but people in the US would start paying European prices for fuel.
Political opponents will immediately jump on that and say you want to raise gas taxes and ignore the fact that I am trying to keep this revenue-neutral, but even seven Republicans have come out and said they like that idea. Higher consumption hurts the US economy when all that money is flowing out. If you can raise that price, rein in consumption and the price for paying stays in the US economy because it is taxes now, having that would mean a chance for America being more energy-independent.
Basically what we would have to do is cut our oil consumption by about two-thirds. That is doable. Over the long haul, people cannot commute fifty miles to work and the cars on the roads would have to look very different to how they are now.

MF: People could commute fifty miles to work if America had anything remotely resembling a twenty-first century public transport system.

RR: Yes, but the population density here in most places does not warrant it. In certain population centres it does but we are still pretty spread out. The whole mid-section of the country is spread out.

MF: Lowering income taxes and amending that with essentially a consumption tax was mentioned here in the UK as well and it seems to be part of a new move in certain political circles to shift the tax burden from a progressive tax regime onto people buying things. It appears that this would disproportionately benefit people who are wealthy because if we go to a flat tax on everyone's income and then introduce progressive taxation across a range of consumer goods based on how few of them we want people to use, say starting with plastic forks and moving up to gallons of gas, then that still shifts the burden onto the consumer, who is not necessarily the person with the most money to contribute.

So, I totally agree with the thinking behind your proposal but I think one of the reasons it might have been attractive to Republicans and also why I have heard it mentioned here by a Conservative government is because it is closer to their goal of having a flat tax to benefit the wealthy and they can sell it by saying it balances itself out when really it just means that if you get chauffeured to work in a taxi then it does not cost you anything extra but if you have to drive your sedan to work at Walmart then it is going to cost you extra.

RR: Well, rich people consume far more energy than poor people do. A family of five, let us say they use 2500 gallons of gasoline a year. Over the next two years I am going to phase in a $2 a gallon gasoline tax and I am going to give them a tax credit of $5000. Even if they do not have enough income, even if they have no income, it will be like the earned income tax credit. I am giving you the same amount of money, if your consumption is average, that this is going to cost you. If you take steps to reduce your consumption, you are going to end up ahead because you are going to get $5000. If you cut your consumption from 2500 to 1500 gallons you are going to save money. For the very wealthy, maybe you have to give the same thing to everybody but you base it on the average consumption -

89

they consume far more than the average consumption. So they are going to get hit proportionately more than a poor person because they consume so much more.

That is the way I would structure that proposal. Like I said, I have seen Republicans float this a few times. Democrats are on board with this - they like higher gas taxes. Secretary Chu has said we have to make gasoline prices much higher, but that is politically unpalatable so he has backtracked from that.[8] You cannot sell a gas tax in the US. We have not increased gas taxes since Clinton's first year in office. It is just a political nightmare to go out there and talk about raising gas taxes. It is political suicide.

About the political rhetoric: when gas prices are falling going into an election, it is the oil companies manipulating price to help a certain candidate. When they are going up, and this is the case right now, the oil companies hate Obama and are trying to get him out of office by running up gasoline prices. Almost every single year, after summer driving season, gasoline prices fall going into November. Even when it is not an election year. It is just that when it is an election year they notice and they believe that oil companies are manipulating prices to impact the election.

MF: For an economy to flourish, for a country to do trade, for people to have a decent living requires a certain degree of stability, a legitimate authority protecting rights on the one hand, revenue on the other. The profile of a world in which energy is limited, expensive and subject to inelastic demand points to greater instability as countries either take advantage of these new economic circumstances or try to shift the scales in their favour by securing oil supplies through military adventure. It seems we could be trying to preserve stability because it is healthy for the functioning of a nation whilst inducing instability in those places that might have an advantage over us. Do you think that would be a reasonable assessment of the future ahead of us, energy-wise?

RR: I do not know that we will intentionally induce instability in places like Iran because the impact is going to be global. We would probably do it inadvertently. We like to meddle in countries that have oil - we have done this in Venezuela. That is definitely a possibility.

The larger issue is growth is going to be very difficult in the years ahead because of the headwinds from the high and increasing oil prices and energy prices in general. If you look across all countries, the GDP efficiency per energy consumption varies greatly. China is about an order of magnitude lower than we are, Sweden is much higher than we are. That argues you could grow without increasing your energy consumption. You could effectively grow even whilst decreasing your energy consumption if you become more and more efficient. Beyond that, as oil prices go higher, growth is going to be very sluggish. It is my 'long recession' scenario where any time economic activity tries to heat up, it drives energy prices up and energy prices are a brake on economic activity. I think that will become more important as oil prices go higher, to learn and grow without increasing our oil consumption.

MF: I wanted to get into the issue of alternatives because you are very sharp on pointing out where alternatives are oversold or their possible future role is inflated. You are in favour of them, you are just in favour of them being based on sound science. I was wondering if you could give me a 'bullshit/no bullshit' tour of the alternatives landscape that we might see in the next twenty to forty years?

RR: Ultimately any species that does not live sustainably, they either go extinct or their numbers are reduced till they do live sustainably. Everything has to live sustainably in their environment and that includes us, but with a lot of oil resources that we could utilise and draw down, we have gotten away with living unsustainably for quite some time. At some point we have to consume energy within the annual solar budget, and ecological budget, of the planet.

Oil is plant matter. It grew without any human inputs, it was harvested without any human inputs. The earth put it under pressure and heat and converted it into oil without any human inputs. We are trying to replicate that on an annual basis. It is definitely going to be more expensive in every single case to do that than to go drill a hole and pull oil out of the ground. We are pulling out years and years of grown biomass where Mother Nature already did all the heavy lifting. Trying to replicate that on an annual basis is just going to be more expensive.

This is why renewable energy creates more jobs. It takes a lot more people to make the same amount of energy, so it is more expensive. We have to understand that. The energy sector employing a lot more people going forward is a consequence of declining 'energy returned on energy invested'.

A lot of the renewable guys will tell the tale and spin the story that the reason they cannot compete is the oil companies get subsidies. That is maybe a politically attractive argument to make for them to continue to receive subsidies, but they already get the same subsidies that an oil company gets. They get the same tax deductions.

In the world right now there are a couple of renewable energy options that can compete head to head with oil. One is sugarcane ethanol but even over the last few years sugar prices have gone high and it has made that less competitive. The other is palm oil. Palm oil can be produced at a price very competitive with oil but is rife with environmental issues. Indonesia is cutting down the rainforest to put in palm oil plantations and so it is endangering a lot of habitat and so forth. The question is not simply renewables, it is trying to do renewables right. What is going to prevent Indonesia from cutting down the rest of the rainforest? I was in Malaysia a couple of years ago. I see all these forests being cut down and the European Union is putting pressure on them to produce this sustainably. I said "what do you think about that?" The answer I received was "China will buy everything we can make and they don't care". That is very telling. I think we risk destroying and harming the environment in the pursuit of renewables.

MF: Which is ironic.

RR: It is ironic but it is happening, no question. Indonesia is now draining their peat bogs in the pursuit of palm oil. There are tremendous CO2 emissions as they drain and burn these ancient peat bogs. It is like digging up a bunch of coal and burning it so you can plant palm oil. There is just not enough land area for us to replace oil with biofuels. It is a calculation I have done several times. If you look at all the arable land that you could reasonably devote to biofuels, I do not see us ever replacing more than ten or twenty percent of our current oil consumption with biofuels. Even that may, environmentally, be very detrimental to do.

The bigger question is, are renewables ready yet? Certain renewables are, certain renewables are still too far out there but we will continue to fund them, governments will continue to fund them until hopefully they are competitive. So far, the government has done a very poor job of figuring out what is right around the corner and what is far down the road.

Issues have come up about contracts that the US Navy has

paid for fuel made from algae. They are paying twenty to thirty dollars a gallon for this stuff. That is not competitive right around the corner. There are a lot of options that are a lot closer than that. A distinction needs to made: what could stand on its own in ten years and what cannot. I think that algae is one that cannot stand on its own in ten years.

That is my metric : how long before you can get off the subsidies? Some of these, there is no transition off the subsidies. They are going to be an order of magnitude higher than the price of gasoline now. In ten years they are still going to be four or five times higher, definitely double the price. In that case these things are not really going to be economical unless we constantly transfuse them with government money. That is the only way these things can keep going.

I have called bankruptcy on several of these companies. I have said they do not have a viable business plan, they cannot produce cheap fuel and they have gone bankrupt. Range Fuels made ridiculous promises but it got them money. They ultimately went bankrupt and did not produce anything. They supposedly produced a little bit and then shut down. They were out of money.

MF: We are seeing the marks of a bubble in natural gas in the US, particularly shale. Through various media outlets I have heard at least one member of every major political party, from the US and the UK, say that we have got a thousand years of oil, a thousand years of natural gas, of coal. There is no problem, renewables are never going to be economical so we do not need to worry about it.

The major argument at the moment is that fossil fuel consumption is damaging to the environment through CO2 emissions. The extraction of fossil fuels is damaging to the environment on the ground but a huge number of renewable technologies may not have the clean footprint that we want them to have. How do we balance out the oversold nature of our fossil fuel reserves and the uneconomical, ironically environmentally damaging nature of the renewables that are on the table at the moment?

RR: In the energy business there is no free lunch. There are consequences for every energy option you can think of. Nuclear power is a fantastic base load power that occasionally demolishes landscapes. There is always something. Wind power is killing birds and endangered species and people do not like the sound near their house. In the UK there has been a lot of protest against wind power. That is really the first time I ever saw it. I was living in Scotland and I saw people rising up against wind power and you think 'what is the problem with wind power?'

Here in Hawaii, geothermal is under attack from people who think that living near a geothermal plant is killing them. "Hydrogen sulphide is coming out, I can smell it. It is killing me, making me sick, sending me to the hospital". Nobody wants energy production in their backyard. Solar panels may be an exception, people do not mind solar panels on their house, but for most energy production, they want it far away. It does not matter if it is renewable, non-renewable, they do not want that activity close.

The problem is we do not have these isolated places where we can go and produce all of our energy. This is what is happening with shale gas in Pennsylvania and the big debate in New York. New Yorkers would rather import their gas from Oklahoma and not worry if they can continue to enjoy their lifestyle without any implications. It is not in their backyard; they consume energy without really having to deal with it and think about the consequences.

That is generally the case when we fuel up with gasoline. We do not think about all of the implications of the gasoline we just put in our vehicle and the wars that are fought, environments that are damaged. That is never a consideration when we pull in and fill up. We think about what the price is and if it is available. There is a great disconnect. When BP has an accident in the Gulf of Mexico we think that's BP's problem. Why is BP doing what they are doing? BP may have made mistakes and they may have been careless, but we are the reason they are doing what they are doing. We point to the oil company and say 'you are polluting'. We are polluting. We are buying and burning what they are producing.

You will see environmentalists flying around the world lecturing on how bad fossil fuel consumption is. I saw Bill McKibben interviewed on The Colbert Report and Stephen Colbert asked him "How did you get down here? Did you ride a bike, did you walk?" and he said "No, I am a hypocrite. I flew."[9]

That is the problem. We are all hypocrites. We think oil companies are keeping us addicted when it is really our demand for low oil prices that keeps them doing what they are doing. I think that the average person really does not appreciate what oil does for them in their daily lives. We take it for granted. If you want to see people really change the way they think about the oil companies, just have them all stop producing oil for a month. The whole world would come to a grinding halt. You would have no mobility then. You will not have airline flights, ships going across the ocean or cars running around without oil. You will not have goods coming to the grocery store. The oil companies are enabling all of this and when they have an accident we blame them, we do not blame ourselves. We do not recognise our own complicity in this.

MF: When you get down to these issues of consumption and environmental destruction, real fundamental issues of behaviour, it becomes a much more philosophical conversation. What kind of people are we? Who do we want to be and how do we want to live? How do we perceive our relationship to one another and to the natural environment? That is a much harder conversation to have.

RR: We are all environmentalists until we are impacted by being environmentalists, financially impacted. I will give you a perfect example of this. There was a survey done in Canada a few years ago and they asked Canadians "Are you concerned about global warming?" Something like seventy percent said yes. Then, the question was "would you pay an additional ten cents a litre for gasoline to combat global warming?" The majority said no. So they're concerned but suddenly, if it impacts their pocket, they are not as concerned.
We could be renewable in the US at a much higher fuel price than we pay now. Most people would like to be renewable, we would like to have clean energy, but I think if they knew the price, most people would say no, that is too much to pay. Even Democrats, even liberals, they love the fossil fuel subsidies. The reason is because of the impact on poor people. They expect to have clean energy and they expect for that price to be cheap or competitive with fossil fuels and that is not really reasonable. These guys who are all screaming about fossil fuel subsidies, they were saying a trillion dollars a year in subsidies. About ninety percent of those were consumption subsidies in developing countries. These handouts to big oil they are talking about is Hugo Chavez keeping gasoline at ten cents a gallon for the people of Venezuela. That is presented as a handout to big oil. It is the Low Income Heating Assistance programme in the North East. Ed Markey[10] is one of the biggest anti-oil guys around and he has defended that programme and said it would

be inhuman not to continue it. There he is defending a programme that increases our fossil fuel consumption because of the impact it has on poor people.

You cannot have it all. You cannot have cheap energy and clean energy. It is going to impact on poor people. I am liberal in many if not most of my political views, but I think liberals in general do not understand energy very well. They think we will go tap our strategic petroleum reserve. This is one of the great inconsistencies in their position: we must use less oil, we have to get off of oil and as soon as oil prices go up, they want to tap the strategic petroleum reserve to get oil prices back down, which means higher consumption. You are screaming about CO2 emissions while trying to keep gasoline prices low? It is an inconsistent position, it cannot be reconciled. Yet it is a position they take.

MF: It's cognitive dissonance. You have views of yourself or of your own behaviour, they clash and then either you continue as a hypocrite until you have some kind of breakdown or one of these views has to be discarded:

"I am a good person who cares about the environment."

"I like being able to take my wife out to dinner and a movie twice a week and to drive down to the beach a couple of times a year."

So these two things go to war with one another and then either you stop going out to dinner and a movie in order to use energy that isn't destructive or you discard the opinion of yourself as caring about the environment.

RR: There is another option. You rationalise it away. You say 'the problem is not really me so much as it is the oil companies'. This is what Ed Markey does. He says "Well, that is not the kind of subsidy I am concerned about. That is not the kind of subsidy I am talking about. This is helping poor people and that is different than the handouts we are giving to the oil companies." He does not recognise his position on global warming, on CO2, is totally inconsistent with trying to make gasoline cheaper.

I confronted people about this:

"Do you think we should have oil subsidies?" No.

"Did you support Bill McKibben's Twitter storm talking about the trillion dollars a year we spend on oil subsidies?" Absolutely.

"Did you know that one of those subsidies is the Low Income Heating Assistance program?" No, that is not an oil subsidy, that is not what I am talking about.

It is an oil subsidy, it is listed as an oil subsidy in the database that he cited for these oil subsidies. So you are for and against something at the same time, you just do not know it.

MF: Within the environmental movement, this is something that causes problems time and again. On the one hand we want certain things to be true. We want to believe that we can have the pleasant standard of living that we enjoy without the impact on the environment. We say the only way to do that is to reengineer our priorities and our expenditures, all towards making people want what we want, but then what we want has its own flaws and its own limitations. It is not something that is real, it is something we want to be real.

We have talked before about how certain aspects of the truth are misrepresented to shore up an ideological bias and other aspects are completely jettisoned as they contradict.

Josh Fox is an example you gave me. He has been accused of misrepresenting facts in his film "Gasland"[11] but at the same time, on a philosophical level, he makes certain very compelling points about the fact that if you are splitting open the Earth like a delicious Christmas cracker filled with goodness in order to shore up a notional quality of life consideration then you may be up to something that is bad for yourself and for the planet. Sometimes there is the perception from the environmental side that there is a higher truth being served by the misrepresentation. There is an equally valid argument that the misrepresentation is what constantly undermines the environmental cause by allowing people to poke holes in their essentially philosophical arguments.

RR: That is the issue. He has brought wide, public attention to something that is well-known in the oil and gas industry. We know people can screw things up and we know water can be contaminated. All these things are known within the industry and it is something he has called broad attention to. At the same time he has undermined himself horribly by making factually incorrect statements. He cites cancer statistics that, in Texas, areas that have been fracked have higher cancer incidence rates. That is factually incorrect. It has been contradicted by a number of cancer researchers in the area who have said no, there are high cancer rates all across Texas. I have seen the math. There are high cancer rates in areas with no fracking. So he has been contradicted. The American Medical Association came out and

97

said 'we would know about a cluster associated with fracking, we follow this stuff'. Yet you bring this up to one of his supporters as I have and the first thing somebody said is 'you are a mouthpiece for the oil and gas industry'.

New York is considering allowing fracking in some counties right now. He sent a letter to the governor saying cancer rates are much higher in Texas. Somebody on the other side is going to point out this is not accurate and it will undermine his whole argument.

MF: I am a big fan of people getting their facts straight because I think that is always going to be the most compelling way of formulating an argument that sticks. You can prove someone has a vested interest or an emotional bias but if someone says 'under these conditions, the sky is blue', it is very difficult to disprove that.

It is valid to point out that, to use the New York example, the Delaware River basin provides drinking water for fifteen million people. If there is a one percent chance that something happening in the Delaware River basin could despoil that watershed then it seems grossly negligent to do that thing. What are we willing to do to our environment to extract the things that we think we need or want?

That is a discussion that really needs to be had. If we are willing to do something to a clean water source for fifteen million people, we need to think about that thing that we are doing very long and hard.

RR: I agree completely with that. It all comes down to choices. What are your options? If you do not produce this gas, what are you doing for energy? I think if we were fracking Nigeria and bringing the gas across we would not give it a second thought. Right there, in people's backyards, they are a lot more concerned about it. What are your options? Obviously no one wants their water contaminated but I think the issue then becomes 'what is the realistic probability here?'

The president's science advisor was called to testify on Capitol Hill. One of the senators asked him "Is there a single case of water contamination in the United States as a result of fracking?" and he said no. He said "I have two million frack jobs, not one case". If you listen to the film "Gasland", they are everywhere. They are all over the place. Every time there is fracking there is contamination.

Fracking has been going on for sixty years in Kansas,

Oklahoma and Texas. They used to drill straight down and frack an area. Now they drill down, go horizontal and frack a very long, horizontal area. I think it causes earthquakes - maybe it is the re-injecting of the fluids. There was never an earthquake in my life in Oklahoma.

Oklahoma last year had a pretty serious earthquake. Some geologists will say that is preventing worse earthquakes down the road. The buildup in the pressure on the plates is there anyway and the fracking releases that pressure before it builds up to a horrendous earthquake. I do not know if that is true or not but I do know I have seen that explanation.

MF: It is a neat way of playing it off as a minor concern: "Oh well, it's either a series of small ones now or one big one later".

RR: This was the case with deep geothermal. Deep geothermal, you got lava below the ground, you inject water, create steam and you run a turbine. If you go down far enough you can get into lava anywhere. So deep geothermal can take place in Europe. There was a site in Italy where they were drilling deeply and they caused an earthquake in one of those historic Italian towns and damaged a fifteenth century church and that was it, they said no more.

MF: We had the first UK government-approved fracking exploratory operation in Lancashire a couple of years back. Literally within weeks we had the first earthquake recorded in that part of the country.

RR: One of the problems is it really has to be well regulated. If you get a lot of operators, small operators, people whose safety standards are not the same, all it takes is one real bad screw up.

MF: As there are more of us in the world, as more of us aspire to or actually have a certain standard of living that utilises a certain chain of resources, a certain chain of extraction, the types of things that went unnoticed when there were three billion people in the world would naturally begin to happen where there are more people because there are more people everywhere.

Not necessarily that we are a bull in a china shop, but if there is one guy in a china shop he is less likely to knock something over than if there are fifteen people and he has to squeeze through the crowd and brush up against the shelves. It seems that we are getting crowded in that shop to the point that, with no malice whatsoever, stuff is going to get knocked over and the consequences are going to be proportionately worse for proportionately more people.

RR: The phrase is 'not in my backyard'. As more people are on the earth, every place is somebody's backyard. You do not want it in your backyard but the other person does not want it in theirs and ultimately, it is going to be in somebody's.

If we build more nuclear plants, we cannot build in the middle of nowhere. There are going to be people living around those nuclear plants. Fukushima had people living all around it. Those people have been displaced from their homes forever. They will never go back to their homes. I generally favour nuclear power but we cannot afford the kind of learning curves of Chernobyl and Fukushima where occasionally we ruin, for all eternity, thousands and thousands of acres and have people displaced permanently from their homes.

Nuclear has to be fail-safe. It may not be fail-proof but it has to be fail-safe so if it does fail, it fails in a safe position. That is the only way that you can do nuclear. Fukushima was not fail-safe, Chernobyl was not fail-safe.

MF: The greatest moral clarity that I have ever heard about nuclear power was E.F. Schumacher who said that if the only way you can supply your society with what it needs is to generate waste which is absolutely toxic to all living things for up to a million years, your society is doing the wrong thing.

That is the line. I cannot poke a hole in that statement. Looking at thorium technology rather than U238 technology, it is a perfectly valid argument to point out that thorium, if it had been developed over the past sixty years instead of U238, would be a cleaner or clean form of nuclear power. You would only have the resource use and footprint of the actual construction of the plant. The throughput is sand, water and the radioactivity decays in a matter of days or weeks rather than thousands of years. The argument being put forward is we never focussed on thorium because at the time that nuclear power was in its nascency, uranium enrichment created plutonium as a byproduct and we wanted plutonium for the arms race.

We emphasised that particular angle of nuclear and we completely ignored thorium even thought we knew that it could be cleaner. So I do not write nuclear off myself but I do not like

100

the idea that the argument is about the functioning of the plant. To me it is the waste more than anything else. It is like Schumacher said - if the byproduct is deadly to all life for longer than any generation's or bloodline's lifetime, into the foreseeable future, then you are doing the wrong thing.

RR: Inside the earth there are all kinds of radioactive things that would kill us in seconds, so it could be stored inside the earth if not for political issues. There are places where it could be stored and sealed up. It could be reprocessed. There are options for reprocessing that fuel on site and in the long run that is what they will end up doing.

I was kind of curious about the thorium thing myself because some countries should have developed thorium. I finally talked to a nuclear scientist and he said the biggest problem with thorium is it cannot sustain a chain reaction. You have to have some uranium in there to help keep the chain reaction going. Pure thorium just does not emit enough neutrons to keep that reaction going.

MF: Clean nuclear is like clean coal. There are always consequences. It is oxymoronic to argue that you can do something that is fundamentally extractive in a way that has no impact.

If there was a particular alternative that you saw being 'the thing', what would it be?

RR: The single most important technology that would enable all sorts of things is storage. The problem with solar and wind power is they are intermittent. If you had a way to store solar power cost effectively at night, you could run society on solar power. We could all have electric cars but we do not have effective storage and that is the problem.

That to me is the single most important problem, not only for renewables. Fossil fuel plants that would have adequate storage can run without coming up and down and oscillating. They could respond instantly to demand changes without changing the plant, which hurts the efficiency. Effective storage would be the most important enabling technology.

I like solar a lot. I know people who have solar systems who have batteries run at night. Those batteries do not store a whole lot of energy. They have to be very careful about how much electricity they use at night if they are off the grid. So there are a lot of options out there for storage but what we need is super batteries that are cheap that can store a lot of energy.

Work on storage. Find cost effective ways to store and suddenly you will be an enabler of solar and wind power. They will never be the majority of our energy unless we can figure out a way to store them cost effectively.

MF: In terms of the technologies I have seen developing recently, the one that I found most striking was graphene. If our problem is we have an overage of CO_2, if there was a way of carbon capturing in order to create the input to manufacture graphene, and it would be the tensile surface material we could use for a lot of the materials that we now use fossil fuels to create because we need plastics, that might be something that we could focus on.

Since the guys won a Nobel Prize for chemistry, since the initial graphene findings came out, I have not heard much about it. I do not know if, being an insider, you have heard anything about plans to work with that material?

RR: I can tell you from the thermodynamics of the situation. CO_2 is the lowest form of carbon and to turn it into anything requires energy inputs. So, it will require copious amounts of energy to turn that CO_2 into graphene.

It is the same thing with a water car. You hear people saying they are going to run their car on water. Technically you could do that but you are going to have to have another energy source to break down the water into hydrogen and oxygen. The laws of thermodynamics say that energy input is always going to be greater than the hydrogen that you are going to get out of the system. So you cannot run a car on water without having a substantial energy source that could have powered the car in the first place.

If you capture CO_2 from a coal-fired power plant, you do have a very concentrated source of CO_2. Carbon sequestration is never going to work because the power required to pump that CO_2 in the ground is about a third of the output of the power plant.

You get the same thing with CO_2 to methanol. You can take CO_2 and convert it into methanol but you are going to input more energy into doing that than the methanol contains. If you produced power to take CO_2 and convert it into methanol, you just back up all the way to the beginning and use that power to do whatever you were going to have the methanol do. Eliminate all those steps and directly use that power to perform the function of the methanol.

One of the criticisms I have had of some biofuels is, if you look at the steps, you can see they will consume more than one barrel of oil to produce one barrel's worth of oil products. In that case, why don't you just use the oil directly? There are so many schemes that are like this, driven by subsidies and ignorance, where we actually destroy energy. You can drive stuff by subsidies that make absolutely no ecological sense and that is the kind of thing you want to avoid.

You never want to take a barrel of oil and produce less than a barrel's worth of oil products.

MF: You said that at some point we are going to have to live within the solar budget that falls on the earth. Humans did that for thousands of years. That is what we did up until we got fossil fuels. We got up to a billion people and that was just about as far as we could have gone with that.

Technology might allow us to extract electricity from that solar rather than photosynthesis but it will still be within a budget.

RR: If everybody lives like the average Indian lives, the earth will support a lot more people. They are vegetarians, they are not fat. They do not get a whole lot of excess calories. You live like that, you can support a lot more people. You eat hamburgers all the time, the world will support a lot less people.

The Three Dimensions of Power
with Michael Marmot

"I do find it a bit bizarre that people are resistant to the idea that psycho-social processes, how the social influences the psyche, could be a cause of disease."

I met Professor Sir Michael Marmot in his office at UCL in central London. It took me almost twenty minutes to get past an incredibly suspicious security guard, then through three sets of swipe card-controlled doors thanks to the help of an adjunct professor. You would have thought I was entering a biological weapons facility for all the efforts taken to keep me out. It's interesting that we feel the need to lock down educational institutions in much the same way that we do the factories of war.

I saw Michael speak at the UCL Population Footprints forum in May 2011. He delivered a keynote speech on the huge disparities in life expectancy and health which are present in the UK but are either simply ignored or hidden by averages. I immediately filed him at the back of my mind as a man I would like to talk to.

In the current climate of dissatisfaction with the delivery of basic human requirements and the tremendous inequalities in life expectancy, mortality and financial well-being, he seemed like the right man to walk me through the relationship between health and wealth, especially the often-overlooked issue of power, or perceived power, being much more in need of redistribution than anything else.

He is a very soft-spoken man, exuding a gentle kindness which you can't help but be disarmed by. However, when he talks about the problems facing human society, especially the readily soluble ones, the firmness and intensity in his eyes show the passion and forethought that go into every carefully chosen word.

Mike Freedman: In your area of expertise, how would you describe the role of what you study in understanding the situations we face at the societal level now for health and for equity?

Michael Marmot: I had done most of my research in developed countries or looking at immigrants from somewhat less developed to developed countries. So I had not really looked at global health, but when I got involved in chairing the World Health Organisation Commission on Social Determinants in Health,[1] the starting point was a greater than forty year spread of life expectancy between countries across the world.

I made an assumption and the assumption was 'there is no good biological reason why that should be the case'. The women in Zimbabwe, could have the same life expectancy of the women in Japan if their social conditions were equivalent to that of the women of Japan. One in ten women in Afghanistan will lose their life of a maternal-related cause and in the best-off part of Europe it is one in forty-six thousand.

So I start with the assumption that if women of Afghanistan were exposed to the same conditions as women in the best-off part of Europe, they too would have a lifetime maternal mortality of one in forty-six thousand rather than one in ten.

MF: So health is determined most predominantly by context then, rather than biological factors?

MM: That is the starting position. That is between-country differences. The reason why Woman A may have different health from Woman B in Afghanistan may well have a biological basis, a genetic basis, and the reason why Woman A in Japan has a different lifespan to Woman B may have a genetic basis. Conceptually, if everybody had perfect environmental conditions, the individual differences would all be genetic because there would be no environmental effect left to have.

MF: Purely nature rather than nurture.

MM: Purely nature rather than nurture. What else is there if everybody has got a perfect environment? Indeed some people have argued that way, that our environment, relatively speaking, is so perfect now that the differences we see are largely nature rather than nurture. I do not argue that way. I think people who argue that, Americans for example, ought to go for a walk from the Museum District of Manhattan to Harlem, not the gentrified part of Harlem. Do they really think that everybody is living in the same environment? Is it less than two miles from the Guggenheim Museum to the northern reaches of Harlem? Look at the differences. People speeding out to the Olympics in London, if they had managed to get off the train at Newham, would see what life is like in Newham.

MF: One of the lowest life expectancies in the UK.[2]

MM: Absolutely right. The famous statistic that everybody keeps citing about the Jubilee line - somebody at UCL did it much more generally and for each stop east, you are going to lose a year of life expectancy.[3]

As a cyclist, I talk about the fact that I could cycle from home in the London borough of Camden to Tottenham Green in about half an hour and life expectancy for men there is about seventy-one. If I got out of there alive and got home, I could cycle from home to Kensington and Chelsea and life expectancy for men there is eighty-eight. So a sixty-minute cycle ride - seventeen year gap in life expectancy.

Anybody who thinks the environment of Kensington & Chelsea is the same as the environment of Tottenham Green has not been to either place. I am talking about social environment more than the physical environment. The starting position for the social determinants of health and my starting assumption, but I may be wrong, is that in these country differences, these national differences, is no good biological reason why they should be there and that arises because of our socio-economic arrangements.

If you say what about dirty water? Isn't that social as well as biological? That is not a very difficult intellectual problem, how to get clean water to people. It may be something of an engineering problem, a financial problem, but it is not some basic biological problem. What about biting insects? OK, sure, that makes a difference and there are tropical diseases that women of Japan do not get but women in Zimbabwe or Afghanistan do get.

MF: But there are also immunities that people in Japan do not have, that people in Africa do have.

MM: Well, that is right, but as we know a lot of those tropical diseases can be controlled by the social.

MF: By applying capital or effort.

MM: I mean how did we eliminate smallpox? When I say 'we' I mean the global community. I might be out of my depth here but I think the biological insight that was used was probably equivalent to what Jenner had when in the eighteenth century he first inoculated some milkmaid or whomever it was with cowpox. It was technical, about having freeze-dried vaccine; it was sociological, about understanding people flows, and it was organisational in getting a huge army of people vaccinating people to eliminate smallpox.

So, the biological insight was fundamentally necessary but we have not made all that much progress in two hundred years. It was not the progress in biological understanding over the two hundred years that led to the elimination of smallpox, it was applying human ingenuity to studying people.

MF: People's genes did not develop the immunity. We applied the effort, time, money and the political will and social effort to resolve the problem which we are manifestly either not doing or not doing enough of in parts of the world now.

One question I had about this WHO commission was the way that you explain your thesis. It sounds as if you ran into some kind of resistance to that as a self-explanatory condition in the world.

MM: I do not think I did actually. I do in general - there are a lot of people within medicine who think this social stuff is complete and utter nonsense.

MF: Really?

MM: They either think public health should not be doing it or why would you be fussing with this social stuff when we can get at the causes. What they mean by the causes is that biological alteration that increases your risk. If you think about non-communicable disease, they might say the cause is a raised plasma cholesterol level or a raised LDL cholesterol level and the line I took on the commission is 'what about the causes of the causes?'

What about asking why LDL cholesterol is raised or why blood pressure is raised? Ah, that is because people eat too

107

much saturated fat.

Why do people eat too much saturated fat? Why does heart disease follow the social gradient? Why is it that the lower you are in the hierarchy the higher the risk? They are smoking.

OK. Why do low-status people smoke more than high-status people?

I am exaggerating now: there is not a person left in Britain who fails to understand that smoking is bad for health. It is not ignorance. Everybody knows that smoking is bad for health. You would be hard-pushed to find anybody who fails to understand that. Smoking follows the social gradient. The lower people are in the hierarchy the more likely they are to smoke. So we know smoking is a hugely powerful, remediable cause of premature morbidity and mortality. Then we got to look at the causes of that cause, why it follows the social gradient. What is leading people to continue to smoke despite the fact they know it is bad for them?

MF: Did you find any kind of answer there?

MM: Well, we were not looking particularly at that question but in general what we know is people of low status tend to feel, rightly, that they have less control over their lives, there is less they can do to influence their risk of health and disease. Less self-esteem, less stake in the future. To give you an example, when we published the result of the Commission on the Social Determinants of Health, a bit like these differences I have been talking about in London, I highlighted the fact that the life expectancy difference in Glasgow for men was twenty-eight years between the worst-off and the best-off.[4]

In Calton life expectancy was fifty-four, in Lenzie it was eighty-two. Twenty eight years. So, for men in the worst-off part of Glasgow, their life expectancy at fifty-four was eight years shorter than the average for men in India. Three-quarters of the Indian population live on two dollars a day or less. That is not the case in Glasgow. In India they have unsafe water, unclean food, not enough food and poor shelter. Everybody in Glasgow has shelter, access to clean water and the food is absolutely ghastly but it does not kill you in the short term, it is microbiologically sound.

They have this ghastly health record in the poorest part. The causes that carry them off are psychosocial in the sense that they are poisonings: alcohol, drugs and external causes of death, violence and injury. Then lung cancer, which is behavioural -

smoking - cardiovascular disease. Somebody came up to me at a European meeting and said "I am from Lenzie and I drink in a pub with a friend from Calton. I was talking to him the other day and he said he had not made arrangements for his retirement, he had no pension arrangements. I said to him why not? He said, I'm fifty-four. Not going to need it."

Talk about a self-fulfilling prophecy. If I went to the fifty-four year old and said 'give up smoking' and he said to me 'why should I, I am going to die' and then you try and explain 'if you gave up smoking you might last a bit longer'. He has got the course of direction wrong. He thinks there is no point giving up smoking because 'I am going to die young anyway'. In other words he feels he has got no stake in the future. He has made no pension arrangements, he drinks to excess, he smokes and he thinks 'well, I am not going to live anyway'.

MF: It is almost as if you are not solely talking about social or economic factors. You are also talking about the psychological context. You are talking about the way in which, to use this man as an example, believing the "facts" about his own situation that he has been told by external, more privileged sources, his propensity to believe those as gospel is both instrumental in his own illness but also in a sense manufactured. If someone believes what you tell them and you tell them they are going to die at X years of age, then you have a direct relationship to their mortality.

MM: I do not think it is as simple as that. I do not think people believe just what they are told. I do not think, if I went up to him and said 'I think you are going to die at fifty-four', I will not try to reproduce his Glaswegian accent or the four-letter words he would use to offer me his considered opinion of what I have just said. I do not think that would affect him very much.

What I think would affect him is that everybody he knows is behaving like he does. All around him, his dad died in his fifties and his granddad died in his fifties and people all around him are unhealthy. He does not expect to be healthy. The fact that he was fifty-four, I do not think he read the report of the WHO commission and said 'Oh my gosh' or words to that effect.

MF: He was just thinking 'my father died at this age, my grandfather dies at this age' -

MM: And the chap who lives around the corner or the people

109

I drink with in the pub, unless they come from Lenzie, the good bit. I would not say it is psychological rather than social or economic, I would say the social and economic influences the psychological. That is part of how it works. In the end lifestyle is psychological. Your choice of whether you drink, do not drink or how you drink, your choice of whether you smoke, do not smoke or how you smoke, what you eat, whether you exercise, whether you are unemployed or unemployed at some level is psychological but that is influenced by the environment.

For example, still sticking with this country for the moment, the higher the deprivation of the neighbourhood, the greater the density of fast food outlets.

MF: I live in South East London, I can definitely confirm that.

MM: OK. So if you say I would like a low-cost meal, you are going to have to work pretty hard to find one that is healthy. Your choice of food is influenced by your environment. If we now look at a more global scale, if you are in an Indian village you are most unlikely to think 'well, Indians are doing remarkably well in Silicon Valley therefore if I keep my nose clean and work at it I can be a computer programmer and go off to California or even Bangalore and make my fortune.' You are a low-caste Indian, you have too many barriers to overcome to get there. We know there are more educated Indians than probably anybody else in the world but that is still a tiny sliver.

So my starting assumption is probably a billion Indians have the capacity to be educated to secondary or tertiary level but it is a tiny sliver that are now educated to that level. A billion could be, that would be my assumption. They have the intellectual capacity, or would have if they had good nutrition and good early child development.

MF: So the limitation in that respect has nothing to do with their aptitude, it has got to do with opportunity.

MM: That would be my assumption. If everybody had perfect nutrition and caring, doting parents then you would see differences in aptitude and achievement. There would be a huge genetic basis for that because everybody has a decent opportunity to start in life, that would be a huge genetic basis for the remaining variation.

Given the way we organise the world, a few people would go to Delhi University or some other elite university and because

110

there are only so many places, even if we gave everybody in India perfect nutrition there would still only be a very limited number that get to the very top because that is the size of the very top. There would be pressure to enlarge the size of the top because there would be so many people coming up but my assumption would be that there is not a genetic or biological limitation on Indians getting to university. The limitation is the environmental conditions which are nutritional and parental.

An educated parent is going to be much more likely to have a daughter or a son who is capable of an education than an uneducated parent. Not because they are genetically predisposed to a lack of education but we know that is what the data shows us. The literacy levels, the performance levels of children are related to the education of parents.

That is true everywhere. What is really interesting is the steepness of that relation between education of parents and educational performance of children varies depending on where you are. In the United States it varies by state. It is steeper in Texas than it is in Massachusetts.[5]

MF: What do you mean by steeper?

MM: Imagine on the X axis we have got 'education of parents' and on the Y axis we have 'literacy of fifteen to sixteen year olds'. The more educated the parents, the higher the literacy levels of their fifteen year old offspring. In the United States, that is a very steep relation - for each step of parental education, literacy level of a fifteen year old goes up quite sharply.

In Sweden that relationship is nearly flat. It does not matter very much how educated your parents are, your literacy levels are going to be nearly uniformly high.

The relation between parents' education and the educational performance of their kids is dependant on the environment that conditions that relationship. Your guess is as good as mine as to why that might be the case.

In a place like Finland they have a very uniform educational system and the Finns always come top or nearly top of the international league when they measure maths, literacy and science. The Finns are right up there and they have very shallow inequalities, a very shallow gradient. In other words it matters much less who your parents are to your own educational performance. That is probably because the schools are uniformly good whereas what we have managed to do in Britain, and what they managed to do in the United States, is

111

that if you live in a poor neighbourhood, everybody going to your school is likely to be poor and it is going to be just much tougher.

This has been studied in terms of school performance. The determinants of school performance are parental background, parental input, general socioeconomic environment and peer performance. For an individual there will be a genetic component as well but I am talking about 'why does this school do better than that school?' Well it depends on what kids are getting from their parents in terms of psychological input, caring, nurturing and interest, the general socioeconomic environment and what they get from their peers.

Imagine you are in a poor neighbourhood. Parents are ground down by poverty, misery, depression and they are not giving much to their kids, shoved up in front of the television. That is what the evidence shows. I am not making this up. That is what the evidence shows very clearly. That is influenced by the socioeconomic environment so the bigger the inequalities, the bigger the inequalities in parental input.

They go to school with very little peer pressure to succeed. If everybody is acting up, the kids are more likely to act up. The teachers lose interest because it is harder. In a school where everybody is chaotic, the teachers do not care. Everybody is chaotic, they are just trying to get through the day. They do not care.

Now, you can see in a well-run school they can deal with kids from deprived backgrounds and improve things, but it is much harder.

MF: What you are describing in essence is a self-fulfilling prophecy whereby you can point to a poor neighbourhood and say 'look at the poor people, they do not educate themselves, they do not do well in school, they are condemning themselves to a life of poverty because they are stupid'. On the other hand you have, even before colonialism, in the origins of most class systems worldwide before there was a biological discipline to justify it, this argument that some people were born fundamentally different than others, whether that was because they were white, black, lighter, darker. Whatever the distinction is, the justification of social division has always been that those on the lower end have some innate disability or failing that cannot be made up for by environmental factors and therefore must just be left alone.

112

MM: Of course I would never use the language, even by illustration, to say 'people in poor neighbourhoods are stupid, that is why they are poor'. Bear with me for the moment and accept my general thesis that improvements in health are due to improvements in social conditions. You could argue, no, it is because we have got better medical care and we can treat diseases but put that aside for one moment.

So here we are in Britain, a blink of an eye away in time: the 1960s. You said to me rhetorically what you just said to me a moment ago: "Well, those people in those poor neighbourhoods, they behave so badly, they do not educate their children, it is hardly surprising that they should have poor health."

Now roll the clock forward forty years from 1961 to 2001. Those people that you said "what do you expect from people who behave and live like that, they could not possibly have good health", life expectancy of those people in 2001 is longer than the rich people in 1961. That is how much things improved. It is amazing!

So those poor, miserable benighted people who have condemned themselves to a nasty, brutish and short life have had this fantastic improvement in life expectancy. So much so that if you could somehow mix the top grade people from 1961 with the bottom grade people from 2001, you would have trouble figuring out who were the healthy and who were the unhealthy because these ones at the bottom had improved so much.

In 2001 of course the top grade people have had an even bigger improvement in health, so the inequalities if anything have gotten steeper. That is because everybody has improved but the top grade people improved more rapidly.

I look at that and I asked you to bear with with me a moment and assume that the kind of social conditions that I am talking about are responsible for the improvement right across society, so I look at that and say "Those people are not condemned. They are not condemned. Look at how rapidly their health could improve and by how much, that they could be healthier than the rich people who were their contemporaries forty years ago".

The fact that the rich people improved more rapidly - I am assuming for the moment that it is not just about access to medical care, it is not just that the rich people get the clot-busting drugs or leukaemia drugs more quickly than the poor. We have a National Health Service in Britain which is not bad.

It is probably better than any system in the whole world for getting equitable access. That is what the data from the Commonwealth Fund shows. We have got more equitable access.

MF: For now.

MM: For now. That is why many of us did not want the changes because we can see the equitable access that had been achieved. A major societal achievement is under threat. That is why we did not want the Health and Social Care Act.[6] It is why the Royal College of Nursing, the British Medical Association and the Royal College of General Practitioners, The Lancet, The British Medical Journal, everybody was against the changes.

So, when I look at those kinds of trends, the improvement in health for everybody across the social spectrum, the fact that we still have a social gradient in health that may even have got steeper - the lower you are, the worse your health - it means people are not condemned by their position in the hierarchy. I think what has happened is that the nature of being poor has changed dramatically. Being poor in India still means doing without food, shelter and clean water. Being poor in Britain today means your kids doing without the latest set of trainers, not being able to afford a ticket to your football club, not being able to entertain children's friends for birthday parties, not having a set of smart clothes to go for a job interview.

That is real deprivation. People who do not have those things really feel deprived but that is quite different from not having enough food to eat or not having a place to live in. We all worry about the homeless but there are not very many of them in Britain. It is really a tiny number. It is ghastly that there are any but it is a tiny number. That is not a major cause of inequality in health in Britain, being homeless.

So the ways of 'doing without' have changed. The problem is in India they have both. They have lack of food, shelter, clean water and they have lack of aspirations for the future, conditioned by their environment. They have the stress of not knowing where their next meal will come from. They have the disaster of a daughter getting married and not being able to put on a wedding party for her. Can you imagine what that means to a poor person? It means the same thing to a poor person as it would to a rich person. If a rich person could not put on a wedding feast for his daughter's marriage, he would feel terrible. So does a poor person.

114

There is this wonderful book that got published last year, "Poor Economics" by Banerjee and Duflo. They whole fundamental premise is 'poor people are just like other people'. They want the same things. They want what makes a meaningful life and they will give up food in order to celebrate a daughter's wedding.

Rich people will look from the outside and say "How can they be so stupid?!"

Banerjee and Duflo's point is "How can you be so stupid?!", you the observer.

Poor people want the same things that everybody wants. They want to have a good life and a good life includes celebrating your daughter's wedding, singing and dancing or doing things that are "stupid".

MF: In one sense you are describing socioeconomic forces and socioeconomic factors but on the other, this is where the psychology comes in. When you mentioned hierarchy and your use earlier of the word 'status', I do not know if you are familiar with the work of Thorsten Veblen, "The Theory of the Leisure Class"?

MM: Yes.

MF: He coined the phrase 'conspicuous consumption', that entire concept of a social pecking order that distinguishes membership in various strata of society through visible consumption. You could almost make the argument that poor people are more susceptible to economic factors because in order to compensate for the poverty, they have to spend what money there is on those outward factors of status that allow them to save face.

Like you said, "we will not have rice this week but our daughter will be able to walk to school in a pair of shoes that she otherwise would not have". This is a completely inconceivable balance of priorities for wealthy people because those are not choices they would ever conceivably have to make. So they would think 'of course you feed your children first and put shoes on their feet second' but those are not mutually exclusive decisions if you come from a background that is already deprived.

So there are socioeconomic forces but likewise these psychological ones.

MM: The ways of doing without have changed. People are still doing without, but they are doing without relative to the standards of the society in which they live.

MF: Not having Air Jordans is similar to not having beans in some sense.

MM: In rich countries you have got disempowerment which may lead people to behave in risky ways, smoking, drinking, but it may have more direct neuro-endocrine effects on health. The fact that you are suffering from material deprivation does not mean that you do not also have disempowerment.

Banerjee and Duflo say the poor are no more or less than rational than the rest of us. That is how we all behave because your daughter's wedding, what could be more important than that? You make all sorts of "irrational" decisions because spending it on your daughter's wedding is such an important thing. It is what makes life LIFE. If you could not do that, that is an intolerable stress. Just because you are destitute in terms of having clean water, enough healthy food or shelter, that does not mean you do not want these other things in your life, does not mean that you do not want to feel that life is meaningful and you can celebrate the important things of life.

So what I was trying to do in putting the rich and poor together is saying yes, destitution is absolute terms is obviously very important in low-income countries, but in both cases disempowerment, not being able to lead a life of dignity, is actually crucial.

Underpinning this, which is problematic for some medical scientists, is the idea that an important gateway to health and health inequalities is the mind. The way the social environment influences health and health inequalities, an important gateway is the mind. There may be other pathways as well, biological and physical exposures. Whether the mind is making decisions about smoking, drinking, lifestyle or in a poor country making the decision to spend money on a daughter's shoes rather than a daughter's rice, it is still the mind which is influenced by socioeconomic conditions.

I have the view that stress pathways are important. It is not just that it is stressful and difficult to have to make the decision "shall I spend the money on shoes or rice?" but that very stress can damage your health. It can get internalised not just because you are more likely to smoke or eat bad food but the stress itself can damage your health. For some people that is problematic.

They do not believe that.

MF: It is the same way that there is an overarching problem in psychology which they call the problem of consciousness. They know something is up but they do not know how to address or quantify it so they do not discuss it. It seems that what you are talking about with health issues and self perception, these psychological aspects being fundamental to our health, is also tied up with secular science and medicine not recognising the 'I', for lack of a better word. That there is something present that is not of a quantifiable nature.

MM: There certainly is a sense among lots of people within medicine and medical research that there is something a bit spooky and 'soft round the edges' about the mind-body question. You think 'What?', this late in the history of Western science people are still disputing, wrestling with the mind-body question? It takes various forms.

One is 'what goes on psychologically is not the cause of illness. We know the cause of illness. That is what happens to arteries, cells, molecules and DNA, that is the cause of illness'. And you think 'what has one thing have to do with another?' Just because there are biological mechanisms does not mean something is not triggering those biological mechanisms. What about behaviour? Once you think about behaviour like diet, obesity, alcohol consumption, where does behaviour come from? It comes from the mind. So one obvious way that the social environment impacts on health is through the mind and the mind then determines whether you eat, drink, smoke, have unsafe sex, a sedentary lifestyle etcetera.

Once you acknowledge the mind is important in that way, why would you fail to appreciate that there are more direct influences of higher centres on your endocrine processes? We know in early childhood that abusing children sculpts the brain. Depriving children influences brain function. We know there are critical periods. If children are not exposed to vision at a certain time, they never get it. Deaf children, if they have their hearing corrected early, they learn to speak. If they do not, they do not. If they are not exposed to arithmetic at a certain time then they never learn to manipulate numbers. There are these critical periods

There are social and emotional effects on the brain. There is actually quite a good scientific basis for how psychological processes influence physiology. Quite apart from the fact that

117

every week somebody publishes a thing that some part of the brain lights up when you are happy and some part when you are miserable. Well, of course! I do not think it is a ghost in the machine. Of course there is a biological counterpart to what we think and feel.

So, I do find it a bit bizarre that people are resistant to the idea that psycho-social processes, how the social influences the psyche, could be a cause of disease. Then when you get on to what you were saying about the concept of 'I', well yes, I think there is evidence that people lacking control over the lives, lacking in self-esteem, that is some intersection between who you are and the environment within which you find yourself. They shape each other.

MF: It is often said that this separation of mind and body is part of the problem, the secular sciences being formed in a way that takes components in isolation, studies them, the very concept that you can understand someone's psychology without looking at their physical environment, lifestyle habits or emotional background and likewise that you can understand someone's physiognomy, their biological issues, without looking at the mind.

We have a tendency towards Maslow's hierarchy of needs. The argument goes that once the body is OK, then you can start looking at the mind. Then once the mind is OK, then you start looking at these more nebulous factors but surely as you are saying, it is all of a whole. It is not mind and body, it is an organism. A human.

MM: I do not think of it in terms of a hierarchy. I think you need them all at the same time. You do not say well, we will wait until everyone in a low income country has got enough to eat, then we will think about how they can lead lives of dignity and meaning. It has got to happen at the same time.

MF: Then you are inviting us to look at things in almost revolutionary terms, because what we are talking about are issues that are not as simple as giving people some food aid, income assistance. We are talking about emotional, psychological, socio-environmental facets of a power condition. In one way or another, as you said before, people are disempowered. In that sense we are not talking about food distribution or income distribution, we are talking about the distribution of power.

MM: Inequities in power, money and resources drive the conditions of daily life. The conditions of daily life include food and water, but also education, parental input, all of that. The social, emotional, psychological as well as the physical.

When we talk about child development we talk about physical, psychological, linguistic, social and emotional development. They are all key to early child development and through the life course. So, we talk about inequities in power, money and resources that drive inequities in the conditions of daily life that in turn drive inequities in health.

Then I say, the way we think about this positively is empowerment. Empowerment in my view has three dimensions:

Material: coming back to what we were saying before, if you cannot feed your children you cannot be empowered. So that is pretty immediate. How am I going to feed my child today? It is hard to be more disempowered than that. The child is starving and I have no way to feed the child. That is disempowering.

Psychosocial: having control over your life, being able to lead a life of dignity where you can affect the decisions that are important. You may have enough food to eat but you still want to be able to to control your life circumstances.

Political: having a voice.

All three of those could apply at the individual, community, city, region and national level. If a country is disempowered in the World Trade Organisation agreements then it is disempowered; things are rigged for that country. It would not be a bad way to describe Greece to say that it is disempowered as a country, with devastating effects on its population. I would not for one minute try and allege that Greece was not an architect of its own misfortune but we are making it very much worse for Greece because we have disempowered them. We have said sorry, it may cause intense hardship on your population but the bankers require you to screw things down, maybe killing your economy, but that is what you have go to do! That is disempowering a whole country.

MF: We have seen that before, in the not too distant past, have devastating effects on the surrounding countries as well.

MM: Yes. War, invasion is pretty disempowering. There are a lot of other ways to disempower countries but even in peacetime we see that we are doing this. I can imagine the people of Portugal and Spain feeling a bit twitchy.

MF: This idea of three dimensions of power raises two avenues of inquiry. What you are pointing out is that we have a centralising, hierarchical principle: we centralise power, we organise upwards,we have top-down authority, drawing boundaries and circles, including some, excluding others.

This really speaks to how our society is organised and you could even argue that that is the basis of most civilisations that we have ever known. You could then see that your three dimensions of power are on some level inherently violated by that centralised, hierarchical principle. In that sense, could you make the case that civilisation itself is a terminal condition?

MM: No, I would not at all. I started disagreeing with where you were going early on. I take health as a measure of how well we are doing. It correlates quite highly with other measures of well-being. Let us take Western Europe at the end of the twentieth century and the beginning of the twenty first century. I do not think there has ever been a population in the history of humankind that has even been so well-off in terms of good health, democracy, freedom in a real sense.

So the idea that civilisation is disempowering people, no, it is not. Education is very empowering. We have never had better education. Relief of poverty is very empowering. We have never had as few poor people. Living in safe neighbourhoods is very empowering. Well, it has been a mixture of how safe they are but it's a good deal safer now to walk London's streets than when Jack The Ripper was stalking the streets.

When politicians in this country were talking about "broken Britain", I thought 'what "broken Britain"?' Crime rates are going down, life expectancy is increasing, people can exercise their democratic rights - I mean, it is fantastic. I do not think we are controlled by some terrible central power structure. I think there are some dangerous signs and they are related to erosions of civil liberties in the interest of security. This is always a trade-off for any society, to get that dividing line right, but I think most people in Western European countries have been amazingly privileged.

Europe contains some of the healthiest countries in the world, increasingly affluent, high levels of education, democratic functioning, good social safety nets, that is great. I think the problem after the global financial crisis is that that is under threat.

Somebody who wants to get rid of all that in some libertarian notion is going to find that people slip through the safety nets and there is no social structure to pick them up when they fall down.

All those good things are part of what we want civilisation to do and I take the level of health and health inequity, the unequal distribution of health, as quite a good measure of how our civilisation is doing. We are doing pretty well; average health has been improving in Western Europe. We have not done quite so well in the fair distribution of health. The gap has not narrowed between the less well-off and the well-off in the way that we might have liked. We would like everybody to improve more.

MF: We have not necessarily had the gains that we would have liked to have seen and there are numerous data sets that come out on an almost daily basis pointing out how there seem to have been two periods, the 'great prosperity' and the 'great stagnation'. We made great gains after the second world war in the Western social democracies of the world and then after the seventies some combination of neo-libertarianism and malaise set in and there has been a decoupling of how the wealthiest have done whilst the rest of us have made really no great strides since then.

We could argue that there is greater wealth inequality and greater wealth concentration now than there was thirty, forty years ago and that it looks like a trend that is not likely to stop anytime soon. If equality in those three dimensions of power is central to our health at all levels, what are the implications of that for global health and is there a way of ameliorating that trend?

MM: I think it is a matter of great concern. Let me start with the UK. The British Social Attitudes Survey[7] asked people what they think unskilled factory workers and the heads of large corporations earned? On average, people thought that heads of large corporations earned thirteen times as much as unskilled factory workers. Could you imagine a head of a British corporation getting out of bed if he only earned thirteen times as much? He probably earns thirteen times as much in a week to what the other guy gets in a year!

So, people have no idea how big the income inequalities are in this country. It is probably four or five hundred, not thirteen. Then they were asked what should it be? They said six. Ten years ago they thought it was ten times the ratio and that it should be five. If you believe in democracy, and I do, the British

121

population is not egalitarian. When it comes to income, they do not think that everybody should earn the same. They think there should be five or six-fold differentials but not four hundred-fold.

Who benefits from four hundred-fold? What you do is you get tame economists arguing that everybody benefits because the wealth produces...you know the argument. Garbage! Self-serving garbage. You do not need me to rehearse the arguments that actually giving these obscene bonuses to the bankers caused the problems we are suffering now. It may not just be a phenomenon, it may have been a cause of the global financial crisis.

Nobody would argue, unless you are one of these overpaid bankers, that there are any benefits of having the differentials that we have. They have gone far too far but in Britain, and my guess is probably in most other countries, the population is not egalitarian. They do not think everybody should earn the same, so do not assume that what I was saying was 'everybody should be the same'. I could not imagine a society where that was the case.

The idea is to get much closer to egalitarianism, the kind of things that are in my three dimensions of disempowerment, making sure everybody has enough money to live on, the minimum necessary for a healthy life. Everybody has that minimum. Everybody has a modicum of control over their lives; whether they are a relatively low paid factory worker or a globe-trotting superstar, within their domain they have a modicum of control over their lives. They have some political voice. Their opinion counts for something.

Egalitarianism along these dimensions of power are very important but that is not the same as saying everyone should have the same in terms of income.

When it comes to countries, there is a real challenge here. Let me divert from income to global warming, greenhouse gases. There is a case, a moral case, for contraction and convergence, saying 'why should we in rich countries have greater rights to heat up the planet than people in low income countries?' The idea that there should be some convergence for CO2 output per capita, there should be overall global contraction.

China has the same rights to pump out CO2 per capita as North America or Australia. One should not be more privileged than the other. So we should be thinking about contraction and convergence in terms of some of the important dimensions that I am concerned with and that I have laid out, which is not the same as saying we should all have the same.

MF: I call it the circus problem. Everyone likes going to the circus but nobody likes shovelling the elephant dung. It needs doing but you cannot have slavery. You cannot horse-whip the guy into doing it. You cannot threaten his family and hold them hostage. Whoever ends up shovelling the elephant dung needs to feel that, within reason, they are looked after at the circus; they do not need to make as much as the ringmaster or the acrobats but they are an inherent part of the process.

If nobody shovels the elephant dung the whole circus will fail. It is this real problem, as you said. There is surely some kind of wiggle room in terms of incentive, people feeling there is a prospect of advancement in their own lives, but within reason.

MM: The elephant dung has to be swept up and most people would argue, and I do not disagree, that the circus master should get paid more than the elephant dung sweeper. It is also the case that automation, machines have abolished some of the worst jobs.

In India there are women whose job is to remove human excrement with their hands. Can you imagine anything more degrading, dehumanising? We do not do that in most countries because we have flush toilets. I heard someone developed a company, they were providing toilets to villages, people had to pay for the privilege to use them, run them and then they retrained these women as hairdressers.

So one day they were handling shit and the next day they were handling hair. That is terrific! So what are you doing for these women? You are giving them dignity. They know that it is the lowest of the low to be scavenging human excrement with their bare hands. Then you give these women some self-esteem, training and they become beauticians. You need some technology to allow that to happen because you have got to have toilets. OK, they do not have enough money for toilets in every house so they have communal toilets and people have to use them, but then it liberates these women.

Yes, someone has got to shovel the elephant dung, but you can change things. We get rid of more and more of these demeaning tasks and give people the opportunity, however humble they might be, to lead a life with a modicum of dignity.

MF: So to try and sum up the world view that you have brought to the conversation looking forward.

On the one hand we have this crucial issue of disempowerment which is multidimensional and can be dealt with. There are steps that can be taken and it does not require some kind of communist utopia in order to make sure that people are looked after and feel that they have control over their lives.

We have issues in power distribution, wealth and material deprivation and we are pressed to make sure everyone has a seat at the table and at the very least the opportunity to have what everyone else has. We are simultaneously looking at a future, in the next thirty or forty years, of resource limitations or even shortages and growing populations.

So at the exact same time that we need to make sure that people today have more, there is going to be something in the region of thirty percent more people over the next fifty years and a possible cap on certain crucial inputs, such as oil, that we use as the tools for the types of advancement that we were saying is the solution to a lot of problems that we have.

With these critical inequalities, with the impact that these social power issues have on our health, with a burgeoning population and a likely future of contraction and convergence as well, how would you pave the way towards the future with these factors taken into account?

MM: It has come up many times: people listen to me and they say 'This is really interesting Professor, what is the one thing you would recommend to President Obama or the Prime Minister?' One thing? I say 'read my report'. If I thought there was one thing, I would not have written a whole report.

But if I had to answer, I would say put fairness at the heart of all policy-making. Now, you say all governments claim they are doing that. OK. Then I come back to what I said about health and the fair distribution of health. Put health equity at the heart of all policy-making.

A former minister of finance from Brazil said 'When I was minister of finance, people like you came and argued that they had the right answer, in your case put health equity at the heart of all policy-making and I had nineteen other ministers who came and said put my thing at the heart of all policy-making'. I would say ignore them. If they get it right, health will improve and health equity will be promoted and health inequalities will diminish.

Looking across Europe, this economic debate, 'should we go for policies in favour of growth or austerity, what is the right way out of the mess we are in?' The economists cannot seem to make their minds up about that one. My criteria would be 'what is the likely effect on the lives people are able to lead?' Hence on their health and the fair distribution of health.

If policies of austerity throw people on the scrapheap, lead to high unemployment rates which in turn lead people to commit suicide and homicide and have increased mental illness, that is bad. I would not do that. I would go with the other lot of economists who argue that we should go for growth rather than go for austerity.

When I have said this to some people, they say 'Yes, but what about the next generation? What if austerity was the way to improve conditions for the next generation?' Well, John Maynard Keynes said in the long run we are all dead. So, one needs to be a bit careful about arguing that, although from the point of view of the environment we do argue that. We do worry about the next generation.

The reason I cannot answer your utopian question is because I think utopia is the wrong way to go about it because that implies having one model that you impose on everybody. I would impose a democratic process and a set of criteria by which we judge the likely outcome.

MF: I like the idea because it requires such a restructuring of the way I am used to thinking about this. If we strove for everyone on the planet to have the same life expectancy, the manner in which we achieve that would automatically require that we redress a huge amount of the imbalances that we have.

I cannot help but agree with you that surely if people's health and the inequality of health worldwide is a good barometer of how badly we are doing in some regards, then making health equality an absolute priority at the heart of any process of development makes perfect sense. By shooting for the right outcome, we dedicate ourselves to a process of eradicating inequality and disempowerment.

Contraction and convergence is a type of resource austerity. It is not austerity of money but it is still 'we need to consume less of this or emit less of that and other people should have more of it.' We are talking about an austerity of things, of which there is a finite supply, as opposed to austerity of money which is created out of thin air anyway.

If we are looking to a future that will require some types of contraction that people might not like, but might require certain expansion of the rarefied air of elitism to include people who are currently disempowered, where is the balance in the individual so that we can reconcile these two things? We can accept less in certain respects but also hope for more.

MM: When I talk about inequalities in health I am talking about systematic differences between groups. If we equalise the environment there will still be differences in health. Some people will live to a hundred and ten and other people will die at fifty or sixty. That will always happen but everybody's health would improve.

So I am not talking about abolishing all human variation, nothing of the sort, but it is a reasonable vision to have that if you took somebody from sub-saharan Africa and put him in Norway, within a relatively short time he or his children would have as good health as the Norwegians. There is nothing about being a Sub-Saharan African that condemns you to a short life. It is the fact that you are poor, subject to famines and tropical diseases.

It is certainly the case that we get much more unhappy if people take things away from us than if they are given to us. When you get air conditioning, if you live in Florida, you think 'wow, this is terrific.' You get a quantum increase in your happiness. Once you have air conditioning, if somebody takes it away from you, the decrement in your happiness is probably twice as big as the increment when you got it in the first place.

So, taking things away from people is not a good thing to do. If we are saying to people in rich countries 'You know the way you live now, there is a lot of stuff you do not need', that is politically very challenging and politicians really do not like to do that.

If you look at people in a place like London, with congestion charging and so on, in an equivalent-sized city in the United States everyone would be driving to work. In London they do not. Is that a big hardship? Do you feel somehow disempowered because you do not drive to work? I do not feel disempowered because I do not drive to work. I feel empowered because I go on my bicycle. So, giving up the combustion engine, living in London, is not disempowering. I could probably get to the tennis court on Saturday morning without the car but I use it on Saturday morning occasionally to go and do a family shop. The amount of time I use a motorcar, I can afford a motorcar and the petrol despite the prices of the petrol. We could run our cities without motorcars, they would probably be better places to live in general.

So taking the car away from people forcibly is politically a terribly difficult thing to do. People get very unhappy if you try and take things away from them. They get moderately happy if you give them things and get terrible unhappy if you take them away. I am not suggesting we have got an easy political road yet.

In Copenhagen, thirty-eight percent of journeys to work are on a bicycle. They have tumbled to the fact that life is better. My guess is if you stopped some of those cyclists randomly and said 'Would you rather be coming in by car?' they would think you were crackers. Why would they want to do that? For a whole set of reasons they would not want to do that. Probably in Copenhagen they are fairly socially conscious, they will give you a good environmental reason as well as a personal reason. Having said it is politically difficult, it is not a difficult thought experiment to see that we could change our dependence on the combustion engine very easily. It would not be difficult.

That is quite apart from electric cars, technology and the hydrogen economy. Some of it is technical, we could make technical changes, engineering software so people do not need to travel so they can work in hubs in villages and communicate via wireless. Some of it is technical, some of it is social. Getting there politically would be very difficult but it is not theoretically difficult to have a low carbon economy, for example.

That would allow a more carbon intensive economy in low income countries, more industrial development. We already know a majority of the world live in cities. Problem is one billion of those people live in slums. That will take a bit of carbon, to improve the lot of those who live in shanty towns. It is not scientifically difficult to figure out how to do that, is it? It is not even economically difficult to figure out how to do it.

MF: It is your three dimensions of power.

MM: But it is getting the politics and the social together with the science and economics to sort that out. That is complicated but it is a different sort of complication. The reason that I am optimistic is I figure that we have or we will develop good scientific solutions for a lot of our problems.

Our problem with money is its maldistribution, it is not about not having enough. We have got lots of it, huge amounts of it sloshing about, but it is how we use it. It is getting the social right which is what I do. I talk about the social determinants of health but I am optimistic because I figure we know a lot and it is a matter of taking that forward.

Redefining the Situation
with Professor John Darley

"Getting people to mobilise to prevent harms in the future is terribly tricky because of the stories that 'they are not really harms' or 'yes, there are harms but scientific miracles will come along and solve the problems in the future so we can let them ride a little now.'"

In my research for Critical Mass, I came across the Kitty Genovese case[1] and by extension John Darley's work on the Bystander Effect,[2] which I felt would be relevant both to the psychological effect of urban crowding and to the larger environmental problems we see unfolding around us.

My original intention was to have a segment on the Bystander Effect in the film, which ended up not fitting into the structure we had. I met John Darley at Princeton University, where he is a professor of psychology.

I had also hoped to speak with Kitty Genovese's murderer Winston Moseley, who is still alive and incarcerated in upstate New York, but navigating press access to the prison system in the short amount of time I was in New York was beyond the possibilities allowed by our schedule and budget. As an interesting aside, Winston Moseley took a B.A. in Sociology while in prison in the 1970s.

John works out of a fair-sized office at Princeton which is piled high with paper, stacks upon stacks covering every available surface. As we were filming, he asked if we could do it in an adjoining classroom which gave off a less chaotic impression.

He has a soft grandfatherly voice and speaks quietly but firmly, making eye contact with me repeatedly over the top of his glasses. His answers are insightful and he takes care to speak to the question rather than deliver well-rehearsed talking points. His replies are peppered with anecdotal examples that seem to be drawn from his own life rather than a text book. I am surprised by the way in which he genuinely listens and responds to me when I offer my opinion on what he has said. Grandfatherly may seem like a condescending way to describe him; I use it not just in the sense that he is in his seventies but also that I feel an emotional gratification when he is impressed or interested by something I have said.

Mike Freedman: Do you want to be briefly give us an overview of what led you to your research and what you found?

John Darley: Sure. I had moved to New York and a friend of mine was teaching at Columbia when a terrible incident happened. A young woman, Kitty Genovese, got stabbed to death in the courtyard of her apartment building. She was stabbed to death by a random, somewhat crazy person but the incident took quite a while, it took about fifty minutes.

She was stabbed, he ran away, he came back, she called for help but nobody helped. Nobody had immediately called the police. All the calls came in slowly to the police later. So, we have the discovery that in a courtyard of an apartment building surrounded by other people, a woman was stabbed to death and nobody intervened.

That shocked the city. That shocked the state. That shocked the country. There were articles about it and people began to talk about the hostility, alienation and the ignoring of other people that people developed in New York City and that those were the reasons that she received no assistance. People living in cities were people alienated, hostile, apathetic, all those things.

My friend Bibb Latane[3] and I thought the story might be different. We got together for dinner and worked out on a tablecloth what could go on in terms of our particular science which was social psychology.

Social psychology is about the ways in which we are all alike and affected by the groups within which we exist. We thought perhaps two things happened. First, the people surrounding the courtyard, lights went on in the windows, they knew other people were noticing the incident as well so we reasoned that their own responsibility to do anything about it was diffused.

If you are alone and you see a disaster, you know that if it is going to be reported it will be reported by you, but if there are many other people around, some of whom might know first aid, ' I know, there is a retired policeman in the building across the way, he will do something, I am sure', you feel less responsibility to intervene.

Also, the fact that no other people were doing anything suggests they thought that there is something not wrong going on. 'There is some other explanation for this. I bet there is a film crew, I bet they are making a movie. I bet it is a lover's quarrel.' People afterwards said all those things, that is what they thought it was because nobody else did anything.

'Diffusion of responsibility' and 'definition of the situation' were the two principles we suggested were at work.

Then we did some experimental research where we staged incidents and watched who would react and it turned out that indeed both those principles made a difference. If you knew a lot of people were available and one person seemed to be in need of help, you did not help. If you thought you were the only person who heard the person in distress, you helped. So diffusion makes a difference.

Learning the meaning of a situation from others is something we all do. That is how we get socialised as we grow up. We learn that when we go into a church we act in certain ways. We learn when you go to school you act with a certain deference towards those large people in the front of the room. We learn by watching others do. To watch what others do is quite a normal thing to do.

So when I walk my daughter to kindergarten, suddenly she sits on the kerb and cries. She says 'Daddy, I am not going to know what to do. I won't know what to do' and I would cry too if I did not know what to do.

The way we solve the problem is we observe what others do. So we walk into a class and we see what the more experienced students do. On the very first day at the new school you were very quiet, watchful, and you did what the other people did. You were not sure why they were doing it the way they were doing it but you were sure it was the right thing to do.

If you surround a person by two other people and the two other people are going to be confederates and their act is going to be to sit still when strange things happen, then the person on whom we focus is going to sit still also and think that nothing really bad is going on, so sitting still when smoke comes into the room through the corner is a perfectly good thing to do.

Sometimes that leads us astray. Instead of realising that the other people are equally shocked, we think 'Hey, they know there is nothing really wrong' and go about ordinary business. Pluralistic ignorance. They are acting from the same motives that I am, confusion, but I misinterpret their motives and I do what they do. Research has been done since and those findings hold up pretty well. So the notions of diffusion and definition of the situation have a lot to do with how people react in urban situations.

MF: Now, you found out that the size of the group also plays a role?

JD: Yes. The larger the group that you perceive as being available, the more diffusion you feel, but that does not necessarily mean that you will not get help from a larger group. If there are a hundred possible respondents, even though each of them feels less responsibility than a person alone, there are enough people around that somebody is going to help. That is a fact about probabilities.

When you pair that with the definition of the situation - you also see those other people not doing anything and you think there is nothing wrong - then you do get crowds frozen in place. The classic examples were the fires that used to occur in theatres, where smoke would start to billow out from behind the screen or up on the stage and if you read the descriptions, for half a minute, maybe longer, everybody sat frozen in place. The whole theatre crowd was frozen into an anti-panic mob. They did not intervene, they did not do anything. They did not get out even to save themselves.

Then, somebody yells fire or you see a blaze, then everybody runs out. Now you have a panic mob but notice the half minute when you had an anti-panic mob. That is the inhibitory effect of crowds on people responding to other people in difficulties.

Diffusion of responsibility can be corrected by very clear evidence that there is something going wrong and somebody really needs help.

Definition of the situation has some of the same characteristics - when fire follows the smoke, then the fire is an unambiguous signal of something wrong and people are wise enough to exit the situation.

MF: Is it possible that that kind of moment of suspended animation can increase depending on the size and inaction of the group?

JD: Certainly. That result would be stronger when you have larger groups if they are diffusing the responsibility to each other and picking up the definition of the situation from other people surrounding them.

Let us take a more unpleasant example. During the later Roman empire thousands of people would go sit in a stadium and watch people kill each other. This was all regarded as reasonably interesting to watch, perhaps a little amusing as the lions ate the various convicts. We would not find that amusing today but back then that was what everybody did so it was marked as a reasonable thing to do. People would go out to the gladiators and watch. The way in which a society defines normality and accepts it as an appropriate spectacle is a very strong guide to behaviour.

MF: If we were to view environmental concerns, increased environmental damage. In essence, to the average guy going about his business to New York City, abstract danger. The tendency to respond would not just be based on whether or not he is a long term thinker, it is not just about the evolution of the physical brain as a short or long term gauge. It is also about how the people he associates with are responding as well?

JD: We now have managed our societies so that we can inflict long term significant harm on the environment that will have its effects years in the future. The asbestos dust that I breathe now can kill me thirty years from now. Things we do to our environment apparently will raise the carbon dioxide level in a way that may make the supporting of life much harder for us to do but we have certainly a diffusion of responsibility about that.
"I would be willing," some people say, "to reduce what I do but I do not see other people willing to reduce the activities they do that generate the carbon dioxide, so why should I do that? Maybe it is not real."
So, if you examine actual polling results, certain groups in the United States that used to believe that indeed climate change and warming was a significant social problem are reducing.[4] Fewer and fewer of them believe it anymore. There are enough people providing communications that say we can ignore it safely. They are beginning to convince people, because to not ignore it means we have to make uncomfortable changes and that is very difficult for people to contemplate.

MF: Is there a normalcy bias in there as well? You look out your window and it is a deer eating an apple from your tree, the crickets are going and the kids are playing in the front yard and you switch on the news and they are telling you about what you can buy this Christmas and you figure, what disaster? What is the problem?
There is the prevailing norm not just in the behaviour of the people around you but also in your perception. Does that play a role?

JD: I suppose it does. The idea as you say that you see the deer at play, the children skipping through the meadow, it does

132

give you a feeling that this is normal and this is right. I guess, I think that is not going to change. You do get that process, I agree.

We now have collected enough people on the planet so their normal activities or their activities which are giving them a better standard of life are having some dangerous secondary effects. At least that is what I believe.

MF: A hundred people in the theatre will take a split second before someone says fire but six hundred people may take a little longer because overcoming that perception of inaction takes longer since there are more people waiting for a reaction.

Do you think as our population has got bigger, that diffusion of responsibility has spread? With seven billion people on the planet you would think someone would have figured out a way to do something if there was a problem.

JD: As our societies have gotten bigger, really quite large numbers, people develop roles, they interact with each other in role terms and that creates distances between us. Given that we then get more crowded, we systematically disattend to the actions of others. We do not pry. We need to leave each other a little distance to get on with our lives, so we have contracted in some way not to pay too much attention to all these teeming people as we go by.

That requires all sorts of changes that make us very different from what we think of as the original societies, the small hunter-gatherer societies that the anthropologists talk about.

The other thing we have done is retreated behind barriers, literally walls. The walls of houses, community centres. We see less of others. We apprehend what they are doing not only because we disattend but because we put a wall between us because we disattend. That too creates distances that are hard to transgress, to invade, even when it is time to be helping others.

Human populations agree to walls that they can find private spaces behind. They agree to relate to each other in roles - if I see you and you are carrying a nightstick and wearing a blue uniform, I know your role: you are a policeman. So I know when to approach you, when not to approach you and what I can approach you for.

MF: Does anything stand out from the experiments you made? A human moment where you saw a human being respond a certain way or you saw some subjects do something

133

that was expected or unexpected? What parts of your research stick out for you?

JD: Observing the subjects, watching their faces, their actions, I realised how normal people could do what I continue to be surprised by: ignore people in distress or sit together when smoke is coming into a room.

They genuinely are still thinking about what is the right thing to do. That is the problem. They cannot solve what is the right thing to do. If they are alone and somebody is yelling for help, the right thing to do is instantly clear: help. But if they think a lot of other people could help and are not, it is not clear what the right thing to do is.

These are forces that act on normal people but watching them respond to these forces, watching them look to the behaviour of others and see the inaction, I finally understood what we were seeing and that is what ordinary people do in complicated situations of the sort where they had very little preparation for what is happening and they had very little explanation of why it is happening.

MF: We find ourselves today with a surfeit of information, and yet there is still very much that diffusion of responsibility.

Do you think we have progressed? Or do you think that by there being more people now it takes even more effort for people to find the right thing to do, to define their moral compass internally rather than from the reactions of others?

JD: I think people by and large respond similarly to social forces and the magnitude of those forces has changed. That is the difference. Now we have people in cities constantly surrounded by others, more people than we are used to. We know that.

We now have gained enough scientific knowledge so that we know how to be pretty destructive to the future of our environment. We have run the number of people up and people are seeking to increase their standard of living enough so that we are having more impact on the environment in ways that are dangerous, but to future generations. Getting people to mobilise to prevent harms in the future is terribly tricky because of the stories that 'they are not really harms' or 'yes, there are harms but scientific miracles will come along and solve the problems in the future so we can let them ride a little now.'

When we have this set of problems where the consequences

134

are in the future and not visible in the present, it is really difficult to see how we are going to be sufficiently persuasive about the existence of these problems so we mobilise action.

Our thought processes, which are generally quite good, have developed under environmental pressures and we think very well about most things that occur in our natural environments. They occur and the change they produce can be observed quite quickly. Effect follows cause pretty quickly.

Now we have a world in which our inventions have made some effects very slow to develop. That is hard for us to think about.

Back in the 1950s, nuclear energy was to be an essentially clean, safe and free source of electrical power. If that were the case we could simply wait for the nuclear plants to become perfected and we could burn coal while we waited because science was going to come to our rescue. I think we moved away from that thinking a bit. We realised that all processes have byproducts and it is the unintended accumulation of those byproducts that is causing us climate change.

We have people who make quite good livings by telling us that there are no problems because people will have to really change their activity patterns if we agree that climate change is a problem. Years and years ago, we saw the presidents of cigarette companies stand up in front of a Senate committee, under oath, and swear that tobacco smoking did no harm. It is easy to say that they did not believe it. It is maybe more realistic to think that they did believe it because they could not do anything else. It would have required such changes in their millionaire lifestyles that they simply could not make it part of their beliefs.

MF: If we look at the aspects that I think obtain to the situation right now then.

You have the diffusion of responsibility which, if you were going to be general for the sake of argument, you could say 'more people means more diffusion' - if there is some kind of round that the inaction has to take before we all -

JD: The round is slower.

MF: The round is slower. The definition of a situation - our perception of the situation relies on how useful, unbiased and direct the definitions we receive are. If we get used to defining the situation by mass media, politicians giving speeches, NGOs and think tanks publishing reports, then the definitions we are receiving are either biased, slanted, inefficient or incomplete - that again adds to the problem.

Then you have the normalcy bias.[5] "The way it is now is the way it is going to be because that is the way it has always been." Then what you were saying about the tobacco guys, it is kind of a cognitive dissonance. You cannot accept the blow to your sense of self, that you would be that type of person. Like the Baskin-Robbins guy: he was a guy who just wanted to make a dessert that people liked. He did not want to kill people. When it became blindingly obvious that people had heart attacks because of ice cream, he could not accept it.

JD: We have got a lot of factors in play, many of which are mental ones. One of the things we are asking is that people face up to the fact that they have been doing things that they thought were rather innocent but which in fact are inflicting really quite terrible harm. That is very hard to do. That is like admitting to your children that their dad has been a bad man. Difficult.

Second, there may be a quiet despair here. If we ask people 'look, just between the two of us, do you think there is enough of a case for climate change so we ought to be prudential and try and stop what might be changing the climate? Do we think we should do that? That would be prudent would it not?' The person may say 'I think so but I am helpless. There are billions of people; I am one person so I do not see what I can do.'

Then, given that that would be an exceedingly uncomfortable thing to feel, I may say 'you know, I take it back, I do not think there is climate change after all.'

So you get that kind of thinking, I agree, where many elements go together.

You can have two cognitions at war with each other but until something casts a spotlight on their war, you do not notice them. So I think people drop back and do not spend much time noticing the problems in what we are doing . Perhaps that describes us. I do think the climate is a real problem. I very much want us to do things about it but I also spend quite a lot of time getting on with my ordinary life in which I do ordinary things.

MF: Therefore the cognitive dissonance takes hold in the sense that:

> 'I am the kind of guy that provides for my
> family and looks after my children and loves

my country.'

versus

'I am also someone who works at the Ministry of Defence and my task is to choose targets that occasionally kill women and children.'

Then you put this together and you get 'I am a good man' and 'I do things that are morally repugnant in isolation' and they never get reconciled until one of them stops happening or until the person has a kind of breakdown.

JD: Yes. You put that rather well. That makes a good deal of sense. One might say the almost existential tension between our actions and the consequences they have can make us exceedingly uncomfortable.

We pay taxes that support a military system that is on the offence more than on the defence these days. That can be disturbing but we make these social constructions of 'that is decided far above my head and my task is to be the best citizen I can be, realistically acting in ways that do keep me and my own immediate family afloat'.

Think about climate change: we know that there are some scientists who think there is reasonable evidence that our climate is changing in ways that will have severely negative consequences for life on the planet. We also know that we are going about our day-to-day activities, doing whatever we do regularly. We do not think about climate change much, so there is an inconsistency between those two ideas and in some way I have to neutralise that inconsistency.

The way I do it is complicated. I do not exactly deny that climate change is happening but I avoid thinking about the question. I get a lot of help in avoiding thinking about the question because there are lots of people who say we do not have climate change problems. So I reduce the importance of the climate change idea and once it is reduced enough in importance and I look at it rarely enough, the dissonance has not been resolved but it has been avoided. Buried. Disappeared.

MF: I bought a car a while back and two miles down the road, after I bought it, the car packs up in the middle of the highway. I called the guy, no answer. We get it towed to my mechanic and he tries to get it fixed. In the meantime I finally

137

get the guy on the phone. I say "you sold me a lemon, what can we do about it?" and he said 'It's your problem now!' and then he hung up. I feel like that is what we are doing with our planet. We have defined a situation whereby personal responsibility is less important than personal gratification. So what we end up with is "I had fun with the planet, now it is your problem, see you later!"

JD: Yes. Climate change is disproportionately contributed to by whom? The well-to-do people in the well-to-do countries.

So we are saying to the developing countries "No burning of coal to create energy, we have got to stop."

They are saying to us "Wait, you did it for years and years and now that we are about to benefit you do not want us to do it? That seems to us deeply unfair."

MF: I think one of the problems we suffer from is a structural issue. In order to impose order from an external pressurising force, we diminish the role of the internal compass in people from the get-go.

We stop defining our own situation because we are taught that you abdicate responsibility and reaction to allow authority to deal with it. You do not get the other kid back, you go tell the teacher and the teacher deals with it. It is a consistent message all the way up to when we are adults.

I think that we are robbed of our ability to define our situation effectively because we have had the water muddied. How do you encourage a process that allows people to begin defining their situation in a proactive way? To begin to define it based on that internal compass?

JD: It is genuinely very hard to say what we are to do to move toward better uses of our planet. Perhaps we could make a deal so that if you see me, neighbour, stepping forward, working on insulating my house and doing some recycling, could you come along with me there? Then you could take the next step and maybe I could imitate you.

I do not know how else we are going to get toward where we need to get. We need to develop a sense that we are all moving in the same direction and therefore we would be very willing to move as long as we see that others are. As long as we define it as the right thing to do and as long as we see that nobody is free-riding, nobody is trying not to help. If we can do that as a collective, we have some hope.

138

Why Do The British Not Eat Horses?
with Iain Overton

*"As media becomes more keen to distill things
into a simple formula, you are getting these
worlds of science, law, academe and financial
markets that have become more complicated
and harder to explore."*

At the time that I spoke with him, Iain Overton was the
managing editor at the Bureau of Investigative Journalism,[1]
ensconced in an unglamorous block of offices on the premises
of City University in London. All of the Bureau's work takes
place at one long table at which four people sit facing each
other, working on computers. Branching off of this oblong
space are a kitchenette, a photocopier and the toilets.

His office has high ceilings and tall, thin windows set in brick
walls painted white. The room is so aggressively sterile that it
actually has personality. One could take the decorating choice
as an extension of a professional journalist's avoidance of
opinion.

Iain is informally dressed and he speaks quickly in sentences
heavy with a world-weariness just on the healthy side of bitter.
He makes himself a thermos of tea before we begin and pauses
in his disquisition only to refill his cup or listen to my responses.
I imagine that if we were in the pub he would be happier, and
something about his delivery and carriage makes me picture
him as a chainsmoker. In other words, he is every inch a
resident of the Fourth Estate and an Englishman.

I had sought Iain out to discuss the future of investigative
journalism in a time of news budgets being slashed and ever
more commercial pressures being applied to factual reporting.
Over the course of our conversation he proved not only
knowledgeable but passionate, and by no means dogmatic
about the interplay of economics and news-gathering.

I restrain a smile when he pronounces "chutzpah" with the
'ch' like "charity". Journalist enough to know the word, too
English to know the Yiddish pronunciation. I like him
immediately.

Iain Overton: When you are taught the ropes as a junior producer at the BBC, they send you on this storytelling course and they get this, I can't remember the guy -

Mike Freedman: Is it Bob McKee[2] by any chance?

IO: No, not Bob McKee. There is another Californian who comes over and tells you to read Bob McKee's work. Basically it is Alan Yentob's[3] long hand infecting every single aspect of storytelling. 'This is how you tell a story. Now children, we are going to take you on a hero's journey and everyone has to be a hero'.

On one hand I do buy into the idea that you need to engage with audiences and using the old structures of traditional storytelling are incredibly useful, Campbell's 'Hero With A Thousand Faces' and all these things are useful to read. The trouble is the essential impulse of storytelling has to be a leap of imagination. It cannot be prescribed. The moment you prescribe everything, the moment you say 'we will do it in this format', it ceases to be imaginative. It becomes quotidian.

That is the problem with BBC storytelling. It tries to make things formulaic and therefore lacks originality. That is fine if you are just sitting there eating a shit meal in front of your shit TV in your shit house and that is your aspiration for life, but if you are looking for greatness, something transformative, you are never going to get it on the BBC. There are only a few people in the BBC who have the chutzpah to stand up and say 'I want to do something that is truly revolutionary in terms of filmmaking' because you are going to be told 'get to the back of the queue, everyone wants to be the next Scorsese.'

It is a transplanting of the anti-intellectual sentiment that exists in British schooling into the BBC. If you try to intellectualise stuff too much and actually have these leaps of faith where you want to be truly creative, you are slammed down. There are lots of creative people in the BBC but they trim their mast accordingly or they go to America.

MF: I was talking to my dad several months ago about economics and he said that economics is the practice of looking at something that is happening and saying 'OK, so this is happening in reality, now does it work in theory?'

It seems to me that the process you are describing is like that: 'This is what you want to say but does it work in the format in which we are willing to say things?'

In a sense it does not just have an impact on what your audience sees and the relationship you have with them - it has a fundamental impact on what stories you tell.

IO: Absolutely. There is a fundamental challenge that exists within this. As the BBC tries to grapple with the fragmentation of media, it tries to find stories that are able to be translated onto different platforms. It is very conscious in its commissioning process of the multi-platform nature of its commissioning and in so doing it then falls into rather quotidian commissioning of things like the hero's journey - 'We will send Simon Reeve on a journey round the Pacific and in so doing he will find certain things.'

The problem within that is 'where does investigative journalism lie?' Investigative journalism does not necessarily have a natural journey. Sometimes it is data-driven, sometimes it is a forensic analysis of court reports, sometimes it is not going to have the actuality they demand as part of their commissioning process. 'Where is the drama? Where is the movement? What are we going to film?'

You are getting this from not only BBC commissioners but general television commissioners who then lead the way in terms of the mood and the tone of what we all consume.

As media becomes more keen to distill things into a simple formula, you are getting these worlds of science, law, academe and financial markets that have become more complicated and harder to explore. So, if you go to a commissioner and say 'I want to do a really in-depth analysis of how high frequency trading mechanisms are influencing the end cost of commodity prices and the impact that has on political processes in North Africa', they are going to look at you like you have grown another head.

If you look at the long term volatility of wheat prices, it is certainly in line with the rise in high frequency trading and also the liberalisation of markets.[4] Within this you get enormous companies like Glencore coming in, gaining the upper ground. They have greater intelligence than the regulators in this area and they end up buying up and selling lots of wheat. They can end up, I believe, influencing the overall market price.[5]

For instance, two years ago, Russia had a problem with their weather. Putin suspended Russian wheat exports.[6] Some people suspect that there was a meeting between Glencore and Putin that led to the suspension. Glencore had gone long on Russian wheat before the droughts had occurred, so it had exposed itself massively. By going long and then the exports being suspended, their position on Russian wheat was null and voided. So they did not make a massive loss. Who is the biggest importer of Russian wheat in the world? North Africa. Wheat was significantly expensive. This caused a political, inflammatory response, young men in the streets.[7] There are obviously other factors involved: Wikileaks, demographics and all the rest of the political process but underpinning all of this is, I think, the issue of trading mechanisms, commodity supply and its impact on political process, on human rights and profit.

Now, this is an incredibly complicated area. If I went through to a BBC commissioner and even began to explain that I wanted to do a thing about how the manipulation of commodity prices by bankers had effectively ruined the world's commodities supply and that is why there is increased likelihood of famine, water going to be commoditised[8] etcetera, they would look at you like you have grown another head and their shift would be 'why don't we just send someone on a holiday to Ghana because we can take pictures of starving children.'

The BBC response to complicated matters is often to localise it because it makes it much easier. You can take a picture of a starving child in Africa but the wider picture is that it might actually be some trader in Chicago who has a deal in Russia that has resulted in wheat prices in Africa that has a knock-on effect and causes a starving child.

These things are too complicated, in the commissioner's mind, for them to understand. Intellectualism in television was a high ideal in the 1960s and has swiftly gone out of fashion. I think it is a pity it has.

MF: How much of that is ideological in the sense that people, through what they have been told or what they believe, do not think audiences have the aptitude to grasp complexity? How much of it is a kind of economic imperative where budgets are cut or mergers happen? Not specifically the BBC but, for example, when GE bought NBC. Obviously there has got to be some kind of relationship there. One of the ways you can handle what gets reported is, just like a body, you can cut circulation off and lose a limb. You can strangle all funding for news work and that will prioritise stuff that gets the ratings in.

IO: I think it is very hard to disentangle those two concurrent issues. On the one hand you have this impetus for ratings, on the other hand a cultural shift has occurred. The standard response of virtually every single commissioner you speak to is 'That does not rate well'. They have it in their head that certain complicated matters do not rate well. They admittedly do have an evidence base that supports some of that. If you run a very complicated story about share prices and it is immediately inaccessible in the public's eyes, you are going to get lower ratings.

If I give my children ice cream every single day, as we did during the summer holidays, now that we have finished the summer holidays, they still want ice cream. Weaning them off ice cream is even harder.

I think you do need some sort of slightly avuncular process, paternalistic even. That phrase is considered so abhorrent because it immediately comes as a condescending, elitist, top-down type approach. Even though the BBC is packed full of people who probably are that, ex-public schoolboys who went to Oxbridge, they are so attuned to the fact that they are the antithesis to what their audience have expectations of that they immediately react to that and say 'That will not fly'.

So you can have very high brow conversations with people at the BBC but the output so often is something much lesser, not just the BBC but across broadcast as a whole, lesser than I think it could be. Ambition to some degree is sucked out. Of course, you have to temper this. The opposite of that is when you allow people free rein and you end up with just one person's vision that is too caught up in their own philosophy and then becomes impenetrable. You do need to find a balance. You cannot just have intellectualism for the sake of intellectualism on mass media.

I think the greatest storytellers are the ones who can take something really complicated like the financial crash or BP's actions in the Gulf of Mexico and translate it into something that is deeply accessible. The challenge that broadcast has, and print as well, is that finding those people and giving them the space and the opportunity to go investigate it. People just do not do that anymore, and the time and the money of course.

MF: On the one hand there is what people want or what people think they want and on the other hand there is what they need to know in order to be engaged, educated citizens of a broader society. Everyone is trying to come across as this decentralised, new media, 'accessible' conversation-based thing where it is all user-generated. It is all commentary but very little analysis. How much of this is 'people having ice cream' for a while and now still wanting it, how much is simply them being given something frequently enough that it is all they know? Particularly in the music industry you see the record labels saturate the market with a particular type of music and then when people buy it, they say that is what they want.

In a time of shrinking budgets, corporate consolidation and ownership, how do you balance what the gatekeepers think people want with what people need to know? Is there something tangible that you can point to and say 'in a democratic society, in an open society, this is what people need to know'? Do you have the right to say that?

IO: I am a fundamental believer in evidence-based journalism. Obviously all journalism ultimately should be evidence-based but frequently, in a time of budget cuts, it becomes based on what other people have stated elsewhere. Link-based journalism rather than evidence-based journalism.

Let me give you an example: Harriet Harman stood up in the House of Commons, I will probably get the figures wrong here, but she said something to the effect that there are 30,000 trafficked women in the UK. I began to look into that as did a journalist at The Guardian.[9] What had happened was that the 30,000 figure had been taken from a Home Office finding as to how many Albanian prostitutes were working in London. There was an extrapolation: London was a tenth of the British population, therefore if there were 3300 Albanian prostitutes working in London, you should times it by ten.

That evidence had come from a charity who relied on Home Office funding to provide a hospice for trafficked women. They had got their findings from a Telegraph piece that had estimated there were 3300 Albanians working in the sex industry. That had assumed that every single Albanian was therefore a trafficked woman. Then when I looked at the original article, it was not actually '3300 Albanians work in the sex industry'. The original journalist had estimated that there were something like 320 Albanians and the charity had multiplied that by ten because they said it only took a small portion.

So you have got this massive extrapolation that resulted in change. The change obviously was a political change in relation to prostitution but it was not evidence-based. The reason why no-one properly scrutinised it is because the idea of the white trafficked woman in the sex trade is attractive to politicians as

144

something to rail against. Police chiefs will always use it to say 'look, we are doing well now, fighting against trafficking and crime and we need more money because this is a major issue'. No editor in his right mind is going to turn down a headline that says there there are 33,000 trafficked women in the UK and you end up with this situation.

I first started in journalism working for Donal McIntyre who was an undercover journalist. I was given, as a junior researcher, the task to find a trafficked woman in London. I spent four months trying to find one. I spoke to dozens and dozens of prostitutes. I could not find any. All of them said 'I am here for the money, I am not trafficked at all'. Now, I am sure there are trafficked women and do not get me wrong, I think it is a pernicious trade that affects a significant minority, but the trouble is you end up transforming the story, which is not based on evidence.

If you then take something that has a weak evidential base, hold it up to scrutiny and present the world with strong evidence, you can have a major impact. Our work on drones is exemplary of this. The New America Foundation in the States has basically been tracking drone warfare but it is a neo-liberal organisation. Its representation of drone attacks, its coverage of drone attacks has been at times piecemeal and I would go so far as to say they have possibly been neglectful in reporting all of the evidence.

We have come along and taken a much more strident and encompassing approach.[10] We laid out all of our methodology in a detailed document. We said 'this is how we approach it', we put it up to peer review by academics, we presented our data and over time the number of hits on our website and media pick-up on our findings has been absolutely huge. For a tiny organisation, we have had major impact; front page of loads of papers. I think we will end up influencing American policy. We certainly have been instrumental in formulating the counter-debate to the issue of drones. At least our evidence has.

Take the idea of the digital 'long tail'[11]: there is a massive peak at the beginning when the news hits and then, if you maintain some sort of sizeable information-based evidence on the web, over time the cumulative number of hits is greater than the peak. In a new age, always pursuing the singular hit is, let's not say counter-productive, but there is more virtue in looking for depth in your stories with evidence which will attract people from a whole variety of mediums or sources to come in.

You can end up having a significant impact not by always

145

chasing the first hit of the day but by providing something much more detailed so people go and use that as a resource. This idea of investigative journalism being people in macs meeting under Waterloo Bridge being given a brown paper envelope, that certainly still exists and should exist, but given that we live in a world of so much information, there is a virtue in being a filter of that information into a central spot.

MF: Data-driven reporting being more of a resource than a form of media.

IO: In a sense, yes. I think the impulses of old media still dominate. You always want the headline, you want the exclusive, but even if you do get the exclusive, your exclusive window is going to be a minimal one. Somebody else will cut and paste it and get it up ten minutes later. If the exclusivity window is shortening then what else are you of value? I would say the next thing of value is in-depth work.

Over time you will build up a reputation for a 'go-to person' on a certain subject like health. There is a virtue in developing expertise in media and presenting your evidence in a very transparent way.

There is also this idea that investigative journalism and journalism per se has to be a process whereby you keep very quiet about what your story is until the day you go public with it in a big way. I think there is also a virtue, particularly if you have got a lot of followers, to be fairly transparent, in the right circumstances, as to what you want to investigate. We came out and said 'we are really interested in drone warfare' and we get tips and ideas about drone warfare all the time now. Obviously if you are investigating a particular person you probably do not want them to know or you start getting libel letters.

Paul Lewis at The Guardian is very good at this for instance. He uses Twitter[12] to tell his audience what he is interested in investigating and then they give him tips and hints. He has hundreds if not thousands of potential contacts in a certain area and I think he gets a lot of exclusives as a consequence of that and builds up his story. There is a virtue in your organisation saying 'we are going to be the repository of in-depth media, in-depth data'. The Guardian is one of the forefront media organisations doing that.

There is a virtue in you, as an individual journalist, developing your outreach amongst Twitter followers so you have more contacts and they follow you because they are interested in subject matters that you are an expert in. There is a virtue in papers not necessarily chasing the headline exclusives but showing they are offering in-depth focus on certain subject matters.

This is borne out by evidence. Svenska Dagbladet is a Swedish newspaper. Whilst the other newspapers in Sweden have shown a similar curtailment of sales as you have seen in the US and UK, Svenska Dagbladet has actually seen a rise of both market share and sales off the back of an editorial policy that says 'we are going to ensure that forty percent of our front pages are going to be pre-commissioned' and focuses on things we know are going to be of interest in the future.[13]

Of course you cannot do that do dogmatically. I think The Independent under its previous editor had a problem where everyone else would be running 'Osama bin Laden is dead' and they would run a story about water resources in Southern Africa. It just looked weird. Obviously if there was a big story you have to lead on it because that is what people want, but I think on quieter news days there is a virtue in saying 'we are going to put our flag in the ground and be the media organisation that properly scrutinises the banking sector' or this or that. Then hopefully, provided the quality of the journalism is maintained, you will attract audiences.

MF: Let us look at the issue of too much information. We have the explosion of social media for journalists who want to reach their audience and also a feedback loop where the audience can pass on tips and share stories.

You have got a huge proliferation of blogs of varying degrees of journalistic intent or integrity. You have also got in recent years a tremendous explosion in publicly visible policy think tanks of various murky origins in terms of their funding and on top of all of this you have the usual business of journalism and the day-to-day business of government.

One of the tactics of government both here and in the United States has been to release five thousand pages of documents when they are forced to release one. It takes so long that by the time you track down the nugget, everyone has forgotten what you were looking for. In this tremendously varied media landscape where everything is increasingly thin-sliced, your audiences are more niche, the number of people you can reach is smaller as you rely on that long tail. The money that goes into it is smaller because of all of these other factors and on top of that there's the amount of information that one needs to parse through in order to actually find the stories, do the investigation and to compile that data-driven analysis. What are the prospects for the future as this trend seems only likely to intensify? What is the future of investigative journalism in this kind of landscape?

IO: It is a very good question. Chairman Mao, when asked about the French Revolution, said 'It is too soon to tell'.[14] I feel that as well. Gaining a reputation and credibility is harder now in a crowded landscape. Whilst I think we are doing well, speaking frankly, just because you set up a website with great content does not mean people will come.

The Daily Mail is very clever. It basically looks at what is trending on Twitter, Yahoo and Google and then does stories about it so when you Google it you see a Daily Mail story at the top.

I think there is part of me that thinks that investigative journalism works best when it is part of a wider offering of goods. There is a struggle to be just an investigative unit on its own. I think if we were an investigative celebrity unit we would probably pour more people towards the investigative end of what we are doing but there is a problem in tone and reputation that comes with that. It is not something which I think I would do, but you have always got to attract people to what you are doing.

Traditionally I think people have said 'do something that is of relevance to people's lives' but increasingly, as we all become highly individualised because we are able to choose what we experience through siphoned media and not mass media, relevance to people in their lives is harder to obtain.

I go back to my original point about there being a virtue in having specialism as a journalist. You are never going to own the mass market in investigative journalism but you have got to ask 'what really is the purpose of investigative journalism?' Ultimately I think it is about trying to change things for the better.

We had, I believe, quite a reasonable success when we exposed how Bell Pottinger[15] was behaving badly in terms of its handling of PR clients, manipulating web facts and, as they said, 'utilising dirty tricks'. The outcome of that was they obviously used every single PR trick that they could find but we were exonerated in doing the investigation. It strengthened the fact that there is a public service justification for investigative journalism even if it does not mean the thing you are

148

investigating is a matter of life and death. There still is a moral imperative for investigative journalism.

Secondly, the outcome of our investigation meant that the companies that hitherto had gone to Bell Pottinger gave up their current work with Bell Pottinger and went somewhere else. We had a tangible impact on business for Bell Pottinger, which possibly meant that other people would have looked at the moral or financial consequences of accepting the sort of clients that Bell Pottinger were accepting and decide not to do that. You send out a strong message to others. A minority of people who are witnessing your story react to the story itself. Should investigative journalism be for the masses? It is an ideal but I do not think it is necessarily going to result in your end goal, which is influence.

MF: You said 'should it be for the masses?' Online and segmented mass media seems to be the future for most people. People have their search results optimised to their own tastes.[16] They will increasingly be presented with things that they are more likely to already know or want to hear. This in effect means that you fall into a trap where you end up preaching to the choir a lot of the time. My question then wouldn't be 'should investigative journalism be for the masses?', but rather, given the way technology and society seems to be headed, can it?

IO: If you hit the right scene that then fits into a zeitgeist. Wikileaks hit that scene and they had great content. I think it needs to be a combination of great content and something unique about what you are doing that makes you, as a website or a media organisation, interesting enough for other people to go to.

You probably do need, underpinning it, some sort of reputation. The reputation of Wikileaks was underpinned by the authenticity of the documents. In the absence of that, Julian Assange is an interesting character. I think he would quickly have diminished just as an interesting character. He delivered significant information.

There is no magical moment that you can create. There are magical moments that are created in the sense of the zeitgeist: Parliamentary expenses, Wikileaks.

MF: With those two examples, and I think it is very telling, both of those were not investigative pieces. Those were leaks.

IO: There are moments where investigative journalism can capture the national imagination but it requires the impetus of a large media organisation. 'The Secret Policeman' caused a national debate when the BBC went undercover as a policeman and showed racism within the police.[17] I think Panorama's 'Care Homes' again caused national debate.[18] The power of both of those was not that they necessarily told people what you could not already imagine, "bad things happen in cloistered institutions", but it was personalised.

There is something fundamentally problematic about that sort of 'impactful' investigative journalism. Yes, institutional racism in the police is a very important subject, as is the issue of caring for people with learning disabilities, but the approach of a lot of commissioners lies in exposing only those accessible human stories.

Whilst those can have a mass effect, I think more people know about Julian Assange than the contents of Wikileaks. I do not think the hard evidence revealed when we looked at the Iraq war logs[19] became that well-known. There are some pretty shocking things in there about US culpability, whether President Obama breached the Geneva convention on war crimes and things like this.

These things are lost in the noise of the human level. You have got the human level of Julian Assange, the human level of that moment where the policeman says something outrageous or when that person is slapped in care homes. These things are all visceral, media-reproducible events. The problem with that, in my view, is whilst they are all very important, the thing that really affects us is actually the moment when a trader in Credit Suisse double-clicks on a buy and has an impact on wheat, share prices or commodities. That then has an impact on pensions, government lending to banks, house prices and on all of our lives that results in cuts in the NHS, provision of social goods in the Western world and results ultimately in bankers being incredibly rich and lots of people with significant disabilities getting their £93 per week cut.

These are real consequences. The bankers or some sort of failure in the financial services has a real and lasting consequence on the running of a democratic society but this is not an easy thing to turn into something that you can grab in a media moment and tell people about. Therein lies the problem.

The secrecy of tax havens.[20] The lack of transparency that exists in our own banking system.[21] The lack of honesty that politicians have about the benefits of having a financial services sector in London as opposed to Frankfurt and us bailing out the banks.[22] All of these things are cumulatively, deeply hurtful to society, but to try to turn them into something people can immediately grasp and that therefore will be reproduced on YouTube is a virtual impossibility.

The reason why there has not been substantial reform of the banking system and the reason why we are seeing on a weekly basis more and more scandals in the banking system is a singular lack of engagement. Then you ask 'Why is there a lack of engagement?' Look at how the Tory party is funded. Our major political party is funded fifty percent by individuals who have exposure to the banking services sector.[23]

The logical consequence of how that has a deep anti-democratic effect is not really picked up. There are moments where investigative journalism peeks above the top. For example, The Sunday Times ran a very powerful story about cash for access,[24] but the truth of the matter was you do not need to go undercover to the Tory party treasurer to find out that for a certain amount of money you get to meet Cameron. It is on their website: for £50,000 you get to meet Cameron.[25] These things are stated boldly. It is more attractive to get that caught on secret camera because it is a media sound byte. Telling someone it already exists, well, where is the news line in that?

At the moment, quality of life for the future in Western Europe and the impact we have as a society by protecting the vulnerable, poor and elderly are going to be eroded by our inability to properly relay the complexities of these issues to a mass market.

MF: More than any other time we are obsessively concerned with a pre-packaged message. This seems to be true of media outlets like television stations or newspapers as well as brands and companies. Every mom & pop restaurant now has a head office where you need to speak to a press officer before you can film there. Everyone is absolutely obsessed with preserving and managing their image. This obviously is part of that story structure issue we spoke about. In investigative journalism, when you begin looking, you do not know what you are going to find and when you find what you are looking for, you then construct it in a way that can be understood. That is absolutely the opposite of beginning with the message then figuring out how to relay that message.

Marketing literature has created this reductive sensibility where we function in a binary landscape. You either buy it or you do not buy it. Someone is either a 'have-a-go hero' or a tragic terrible person. Usually it is the same person over the course of a few weeks. This binary marketing exercise that began with sales and now seems to have invaded media and storytelling is the nemesis of complexity.

We start with a pre-packaged idea - we are forced to by the commercial interests that give us money or because someone will not speak to you unless you allow them to only say the things that they are allowed say by their communication officer, which makes the interview or the "access" to them completely meaningless.

On the other hand, the very landscape you are trying to place the story within is one of reductive, binary marketing literature which eradicates complexity. So it seems that it is a combination of an economic drive to create these conditions on the one hand and also a more pervasive social, intellectual malaise on the other.

IO: I think you are very right. One of the things I have noticed, especially starting off with an unknown organisation and building up credibility over time, is that as a commissioner you tend to have a suspicion of a wrongdoing before you commission someone to look into something. Perhaps you veer towards a liberal sentiment by being a journalist in itself but you try to take on board both sides of the argument.

There is something inherently problematic in that. Quite often, even if ninety-nine percent of people believe in one side of the argument, you still give the neo-Nazi a voice to give his alternative view so it looks like there is an equal weighting, but it is not equal at all.

One of the virtues of our type of journalism is that if we do not present the evidence in a very meaningful, academic way that is argued thoroughly then people will dismiss it. Your story gains greater traction if it is rooted in substance, whereas if it is rooted in just political will, then it quickly disappears.

Look at The Daily Mail's health section[26]: if you type in cancer, Parkinson's, Alzheimer's or multiple sclerosis you see a succession of cures. None of these things have been properly cured. It would make you believe, if you were an alien landing on Earth and you took everything at face value, that all of these things were curable, but there is no cure. Celery will not cure you of Parkinson's, neither will red wine. The evidence base is not there. So, The Daily Mail discredits itself.

The people with the greatest at stake in the story will be the arbitrators of whether that story lives or dies in terms of reputation.

The other point about this binary problem: if you quote a press officer for something he says off the record, of course he will deny it. Another thing that they do now is 'do not address the story'. Attack the journalism. The first thing you say when you do not like the story is "This is ludicrous journalism. Rubbish. They are unethical. They are bad journalists."

We did an investigation into a very large company and we were working with a broadcaster. The company completely made up a list of total lies about the behaviour of my journalist out in the field, about how they were bullying, aggressive, sexist, threatening, saying 'you have to do this or you are going to regret it'. None of it was true; they could not provide evidence that any of it had ever happened, they just made it up. They sent a letter to the broadcaster complaining about our work - the broadcaster got cold feet and the story was partly shelved. These things happen all the time. This is a PR mechanism.

In this idea of trying to create balance, the mass of journalism often gets balanced against the ludicrous rantings and inaccuracies of a tiny minority, yet in the audience's mind these two have equal weighting. Therein lies a problem. You cannot ignore the fact that you have to give right to reply because right to reply sometimes can reveal that you have an inaccuracy in your story. It also protects you from the libel laws in this country to some degree.

The binary nature that you mentioned is not just a consequence of the financial nature of the market-driven response to the story. There is the BBC-led sense of balance that causes some sort of weird interaction, there are the libel issues that occur in our country. Also, there is this increasingly honed PR response to bad news. I think all of those fit into your very pointed and sensible remarks about there being a weird marketing play going on when it comes to stories.

MF: You mentioned the libel laws: as far as I am aware the UK is the only country that has a libel law where you can be guilty of libel even though what you said is true.[27]

IO: Yeah, it is quite remarkable. Hopefully the libel laws will change. The Times successfully won a case in court last year where they showed that the suspicion of something being in the public interest would cover them, even though the reporting they did was ultimately wrong.[28] They did not end up getting

153

sued for it.

We are totally hamstrung by our libel laws in this country. You know something is as you said but by stating it you open yourselves up to the burden of proof being on you rather than the individual. So if I wanted to report, as I did, on President Putin's wealth,[29] President Putin is not going to sue me but the people who may have benefited from President Putin's rise to power certainly were interested in suing me. I received quite a few letters from very influential and very wealthy Russians who accused me, via these London-based lawyers, and they are always London-based lawyers, with these outrageous claims of how offended their oligarch was by my article and how unless I took it down I was going to have to pay trillions of pounds in reparations.

A tiny organisation like us, I have to weigh that up against how much money we have in the kitty, which is virtually none because we live hand to mouth. It certainly does influence your editorial decisions on what you publish and what you do not. Therein lies the strength and the wonderfulness of organisations like Wikileaks. There are platforms where the truth might out eventually but the challenge then is: who highlights it if the moment you start reporting it you get a slap?

You would not be able to publish it in your book unless you want to get sued, but we reported on one case where, within a Wikileaks document, there was a name of a Russian oligarch who possibly benefited from Putin's wealth. Even being reported in Wikileaks was considered libellous by the individual - we were merely re-reporting what Wikileaks had already reported.

Why has there not been significant reform of our libel laws? Who benefits the most from tight libel laws? Obviously people with power and influence. Who have the capabilities to reform our libel laws? People with power and influence. So there is something inherently problematic as to why we have not reformed them.

Underpinning that is also this idea that we moved from being an empire of deeply dubious moral ethics but driven by some sort of profound philosophy to ultimately nowadays, London is the butler of the world. We are prepared to, excuse my French, wipe anyone's arse if they pay us enough. The greatest minds of our greatest universities are all snapped up by the accountants, lawyers, management consultants, tax consultants and banks, straight out of the doors of the top ten universities into their well paid graduate training schemes.

They all go in, they all work their silly socks off and their clients are Russian, Uzbek or Afghan-based, whatever it is. We end up laundering the world's reputations, finances, tax accounts etcetera and we do it in the name of professionalism. If you target the professional integrity of somebody's law firms, accountancy companies, their standard response is to say "how dare you, we are fine upstanding Englishmen with wonderful degrees and are part of the establishment." It would be ludicrous to assume that Deloitte, Price Waterhouse or Clifford Chance are somehow implicated in the human rights abuses of these emerging markets.

MF: "How very dare you."

IO: "How very dare you" and you "discredit journalism" by doing so, but we are implicated. I have got dozens of friends who work for these companies: you ask them what they truly do and they are quite willing to go to Myanmar and sign a deal with a Chinese trading company to buy up a water supply which ends up decimating the livelihood of a village. They are quite happy to send out angry letters for a Russian oligarch who has probably put bullets in the back of people's heads in Moscow. They are so distanced from reality.

This is the fundamental problem of this breakdown of the way that modern society works. Investigative journalists want to show this lawyer's letter is part of the wider problem. That is a very difficult story to tell, that we are all cogs in this wheel that ultimately impacts everyone else's quality of life. If you go through to a news commissioner and you say "I want to do a story about how we are washing the reputations of people around the world", it is a hard sell. The BBC and other organisations do not readily take these on because they see it as a value judgement. Their response is 'What's wrong? They are not doing anything illegal.' Of course they are not doing anything illegal. These individuals helped frame the laws that said what they could and could not do because they are lawyers and they end up writing the lobbying laws.

MF: Then the question is: if these things are legal why are they ashamed of having them publicised?

IO: They themselves would argue they are not ashamed of it. They would attack the journalism and say 'we are not doing anything illegal, we adhere to the structure and the codes'. Look

155

at our financial codes that dictate how the whole financial industry is run in the UK; most people do not realise that laws are not written by politicians. Laws are written by industry who give it to a politician and then it is pushed through.

Civil servants work very closely with lobbyists to write amendments and laws. They do it under the auspices of 'a dialogue with industry'. Of course you cannot deny that dialogue with industry must exist, but the lobbying is so pernicious that we have completely bankrupted our country and yet we will not reform the very institutions that have bankrupted us. I do not think the engine of the UK is The City. I think that if you look at the long term cost-benefit analysis of the financial services sector on the British economy, it has been a resounding loss.[30]

They have cost us tens of billions of pounds which will have consequences to our grandchildren. There is no proper transparency in place for our lobbying industry. We are not even allowed to know who is lobbying who. Even if you submit a Freedom Of Information request, the reply is ' We cannot reveal names of individuals'. You are always battering up against the very closed world of the upper elite in British society, which goes back to my original point about libel laws, regulation, banking and the regulation of a whole variety of sectors. It is a small elite who will do anything they can not to have their slice of the cake taken away from them.

MF: Or even diminished.

IO: Yeah.

MF: It seems to me the tendency of hierarchy trends towards totalitarianism in much the same way that the particular form of capitalism we have now trends towards monopoly. In a sense, totalitarianism is simply monopoly of political rather than financial power.

IO: I think it is the logical endgame of capitalism in many ways. I do not think you have to be a Marxist to agree with some of the principles that Marx lined out. The capitalist model, there is some sort of internal mechanism within it that will dictate that it will end up monopolistic, even if the Monopolies Commission is thrice set up to try and prevent that in a global environment. That is why we are all in the pocket of the Chinese at the moment, because we sent all of our business to China.

That is the logic of capitalism.

MF: It is the irony of corporate logic. As long as they can make a profit they will sell you the rope to hang them with.

Every generation feels that it is in a crucial place. I think it is a very common perception and emotional sensation that people alive today have, that we are at a crossroads, moving towards some sort of endgame.

You have explained about what investigative journalism feeds on and how it can best be used, where it is best placed and directed, the desire of power to keep its own secrets, the laws that allow those secrets to be kept and penalise people asking uncomfortable questions, the way in which those power structures that we see around us have managed to make themselves less accountable without changing the laws but simply by changing their policies - this trend does not seem to me to be in any way looking to reverse.

So, if these trends continue, how is investigative journalism, or that more askance take on the nature of our very society, how is that going to function if the oxygen is continuously sucked out of the room?

IO: We have, since the Second World War, lived in increasing comfort and quality. There is a real danger we are going to hit the buffers on comfort and quality, as we are already seeing. At the moment you go to Greece and people are still sitting around and enjoying life. Yes, things are pretty bleak, but they can still buy a coffee. If it comes to a point where they cannot buy a coffee, where things become like they were in 1930s Europe, I think you are going to get this issue where people become more politicised.

In the moment of politicisation there will be an emotional response and there will be an intellectual response. The intellectual response will be based on whatever evidence is available. In Greece, the evidence is compelling that a significant minority of people have benefited hugely from financial dealings and corruption[31]; there may be a transformation, an overthrow of existing structures.

The challenge of course is in Britain is underpinned by the question which I was asked when I was at university: why do the British not eat horses? The French eat horses because they effectively executed all of their landed aristocracy. We do not have a great tradition in Britain of overthrowing our hierarchies. We are quite comfortable with our highly organised

157

class system. We did not challenge hunting rights five hundred years ago, or our lords and leaders, as I do not think we properly challenged the rights of succession.

You have to ask yourself this fundamental question: in a post-financial crisis world, what did we do? We voted in an Old Etonian and we elected a mayor in London who is an Old Etonian. The English elite response has always been to maintain their elite position.

MF: To double down.

IO: Yes. The revolution will never really impact Britain as it can on the continent. I think in the next ten years we will see quite significant problems in continental Europe. I think that they will send a deep shiver down the spines of the elite of Britain. I hope that the role of investigative journalism within that is to expose where the fault lines and failures of the current system are and suggest that those elites reform in line with the recommendations of the people in the media who have exposed them.

So, I do not see a revolution happening in Britain in the near future. There never has been one. We are just not of a revolutionary nature. What will happen will hopefully be a reformist agenda led by evidence, and that is really what we and other investigative journalists should be led by. Evidence-based reform.

A Game of Shadows
with Sven Hughes

"I absolutely despair when people say that knowledge is power. What knowledge? Whose knowledge?"

I found myself at a preview screening of Fredrik Gertten's "Big Boys Gone Bananas", a documentary about his experience of being sued by the Dole Fruit Company because of his previous film, "Bananas", which they had not even seen at the time their injunction was filed against him.

After the film, there was a Q&A with the director and two experts in strategic communications, a field which perhaps best can be slotted between the more benign forms of public relations we are all most familiar with and the very murky world of perception management. Sven Hughes was one of those two experts.

Sven is an enthusiastic British guy with glasses and a cherubic aspect to his face. We spoke at the bar after the Q&A had ended and he alluded to a past as a reservist in psychological operations for the British military. Like many people engaged in a career viewed suspiciously by outsiders, Sven is often the first to criticise practitioners in his field. He gave me his card at the end of the evening and we agreed to talk again.

Sven is the founder and managing director of Talk Torque, a strategic communication firm specialising in 'verbal engineering'. They "help commercial and government clients to win the war of words". A screenplay written by Sven was made into the feature film Ghost Machine; the plot deals with shifting perceptions of the real world and the virtual world of a game.

Sven is a charming man, well-versed in how to establish rapport. He talks with passion and clearly has thought long and hard about the issues and implications embedded in his chosen field. As with so many of these conversations, what begins as a discussion about one subject quickly draws multiple seemingly disparate threads together. We speak over the phone for two hours, rarely stopping to breathe.

Mike Freedman: How did you get into strategic communication?

Sven Hughes: First of all, you want to set up what strat-comms is. Strat-comms is a trend that goes back to Genghis Khan and before that. It is something that Britain became extremely good at in the Second World War through the likes of people like Sefton Delmer,[1] the political warfare executive of managing information.

So how did I get into that? I worked in marketing for nearly twenty years, which is both tactical and strategic management of information. I was also working as a reserve soldier for British military psychological operations and British Special Forces as well. So I was working in the marketing industry but then also as a reservist in that capacity.

The combination of those two sets of skills projected me forward into political campaigning work, consultancy with big business, defence and political clients in terms of their information management. There is a hierarchy here. Is information management above strategic communications or is it below strategic communications? There are all sorts of buzzwords flying around the industry that are not necessarily extremely useful.

MF: Just to kind of sum up, what would you describe as the bread and butter work in your field? Have you seen a shift in the main focus of what you do since you got started?

SH: There is a savviness that has crept into the general public. The industrialisation of information has happened over the last ten years in a way that has not happened previously. New technologies are one part of that but also the skills of marketing have become so refined. What used to happen was basically a transfer of information between one party and another. Of course there was an agenda in that but really it was fairly transparent in terms of what was trying to be achieved.

Now, that information you are transferring is part of a much bigger strategic objective or information management exercise to achieve some entirely different aim from the seeming aim. That is the difference. Whereas before it was an objective to transfer information from one person or company to another, now it is to put the tactical information in the area of operation, if that is commercial, military or political, to achieve a behavioural change in line with a bigger strategic intent.

MF: Would you say that there has been an underlying agenda made more explicit in your field? Or do you mean it is more about protecting one's image or the image of a brand, company or government rather than actually communicating facts to the public?

SH: If you look at the layers of image-making that happen through a commercial organisation, it will show you the degree to which this has become a complex issue and goes from the boots on the ground of a military operation up to the geo-strategic. At every single level now there is image creation, information management taking place.

But let us keep a commercial context. Someone comes in and is interviewed. They are image-projecting and they are very aware of how they can control their image, not just by what they wear or what they say but what their profile is online, whether it is LinkedIn, Facebook, articles they may or may not have published etcetera.

If they are smart they will image-project using all of the various capabilities at their disposal to get a job in a company which has internal and external communications. Then the external communications are broken down to its shareholders, potential partners, potential clients, different strands of image creation both internally and externally. At each level of the company there is image creation between this layer and that layer, between the boardroom and the employees, between the boardroom and the press room, between the boardroom and the shareholders. Each of those is an image creation exercise in its own right.

Then that company works in a sector which probably has an oversight committee that is about information and image management of that sector within an industry, within a country which is then part of a region, within a trade group and that trade group may be part of a bigger international relationship between several countries and each of those areas again has image creation and image projection upwards and inwards and up and down the pipeline. Then you get to the geo-strategic level.

In every single level now there is, you could say image manipulation if you are going to be cynical about it, but certainly image and information sharing that is being controlled at each level and needs some sort of tactical capability but also a strategic oversight from top to bottom to ensure that everyone is pulling in the right direction to get to these shared strategic

161

aims, whatever they may be. That is different at each level of the grid.

That is no different from the military. Military would have exactly the same thing. If the geo-strategic ambition in Afghanistan is X, then that needs to be communicated and filtered down to every single layer of the organisation. To the world's media, to the boots on the ground, to Al-Jazeera, just as much to the Taliban Tier 1, Tier 2, Tier 3. To the women of Afghanistan as distinct from the children and the men. The core strategic idea will then need tactical execution. If you have been smart you have designed it on the strategic level to start with and then drilled it down through all your tactical applications.

MF: It is a very sweeping extension of the concept of a politician staying 'on message' when he gives his speech.

SH: That is right. However, a politician is actually nothing other than a hired hand now. The politician is really secondary; he or she is just one puppet for the message. For the real dealmakers in this environment, you follow the money.

Who is paying for the overall strat-comms objective? To then achieve that overall strat-comms objective they will hire in a strat-comms firm and where necessary they will hire in politicians and academics who will produce a conducive sound byte in line with their strategic intent. It is very rare to have the politician coming up with the strategic intent. They are much lower down on this ladder. The politicians basically are nothing more than puppets that you hire in or hire out according to what they are willing to say in line with your strategic intent. Suddenly they find they do not get the money to achieve all their political aims or they get voted out of power because of other forces that can be applied to ensure that only the voice that you want to be heard by your target audience is amplified.

MF: The very effective explanation you gave of how this concept of image perception and creation extends right from someone wearing a suit and tie to a job interview all the way up to the way armies drop flyers in foreign countries, it seems to me that there is a tool in play here that is harmless in some respects and quite reductively harmful in others. If a man or a woman goes into a job interview, dresses well, makes sure that they are groomed properly and that their Facebook profile does not have pictures of them firing a gun or pouring champagne into a minor's mouth then that is pretty sensible and in no way harmful because we are capable of distinguishing the human being who needs employment from someone wanting to cut loose now and again and having some opinions we might not agree with .

But when you extend the logic of that kind of selective presentation to the corporate, governmental or international geo-political level you end up with people wallowing indefinitely in Guantanamo Bay. You end up with people's fingernails being pulled out.

SH: Let us take China in Africa.[2] I think China would be absolutely right to say 'we want to put masses of investment in place for the people of Africa and build up their infrastructure so that we can give jobs to the local population, invest in the country and grow it economically, socially; we are the partners for progress they have been looking for. We have the money, people and resources to achieve it. What we are essentially doing is building a geo-strategic partner in the long term'.

I think they can perfectly well say that at the top level. That is the strategic ambition. When you drill down from that quite lofty positive ambition, each layer suddenly could potentially become quite gritty. The strat-comms is about covering up the rather aggressive way that business is done, to buy out certain local companies, which may still be achieving the overall happy strategic aim.

It is a bit like what Putin is facing at the moment. Putin just got Russia into the World Trade Organisation, he has opened up the telecommunications industry, brought down the price of the import of cars but the reality on the ground is that the same strat-comms strategy means the repression of people like Pussy Riot. He cannot then have this grand vision 'undermined', as he sees it, because he is trying to achieve a lofty strategic ambition. He has clearly not communicated that down to his people about where he is positively trying to take them.

This is the reality. The puppet masters above the politicians have lofty ambitions and when they set the strategic agenda it is sometimes with the most positive ambitions in mind but later in the process, the reality of achieving that means that you are going to have to sell arms to certain parts of Africa and not to other parts of Africa because to achieve a status quo in certain countries you need someone empowered and someone disenfranchised.

That is the nature of the reality of the rollout of their strategic ambitions. That is when it gets gritty. That is when it gets

163

difficult. People do not necessarily associate that gritty reality on the ground with the overarching strategic ambition that has been put in place five, ten years before. This is talking about a five, ten, fifteen, twenty year plan often.

MF: Then would you say that there is a very fine and in many places non-existent line between having a goal that one shoots for with conditions on the ground not necessarily reflecting the lofty ambitions and simply laundering the reputations of people by saying they 'mean well'?

SH: Absolutely. Like in Syria: a lot of the industry was asked to represent Assad. There is one British company that is working with him but pretty much everyone in the industry said no because there was no way you could look yourself in the mirror and say this is anything other than a white-washing campaign, cleansing his reputation of the horrors and atrocities that he and his side are carrying out. There is no question.

It comes to any individual firm to make a moral stand. Some people in the strategic industry say it is better to at least try and change a bad person rather than everyone walking away from them. Is it more morally acceptable to make a deal with the devil and try and turn them into a better person, try and lead them down a path towards democratic change or is it better to walk away and say I am not giving you any representation at all?

There is definitely a debate within the strategic communications industry as to those questions and there are definitely very big companies and individuals in London who will openly and publicly say it is not for the strategic communications industry to make that moral choice. It is a business and it services a need and whoever wants to buy that need, the other side can buy it too. I am certainly not one of those people, I do not believe that, but there are certainly very significant players in this industry who believe that. It is almost as if they have become the devil's advocate but what they would argue is that they are trying to change that person during the time in which they are working with them.

MF: It seems that that really is based on the lawyer's argument that everyone deserves a fair trial because it is the system itself that is just and therefore anyone deserves to be represented regardless of what they have actually done and on the other hand the quite nebulous idea that perception is reality and by changing the way people see someone who is doing something atrocious, you make them better because people do not see them that way rather than because they actually changed.

SH: Yes. I think your point is very valid, however in defence, and I am not normally a defender of these people, you can sit opposite someone who maybe in the West is considered a malignant force but we also have a compromised media in terms of its political standpoint. There is no way you are getting a fair representation of people on Fox, CNN or to a certain extent the BBC, who have been shown to be very flawed in this regard. Certainly News International, look at the Leveson inquiry. I think there is some argument to suggest that the way in which people are projected to us anywhere is a matter of question. To build up the bogeyman is often happening over a period of years.

Saddam was our friend one minute and then he is our enemy the next. The Mujahideen, are they our friend today or our enemy today? In Syria we are now on the side of the people that we were fighting against in Libya. The notion of who is right and who is wrong in a very muddled world is often extremely difficult to define and changes during the course of a month, a year, certainly a five year period. It is not quite as black and white as sometimes the skeptics, cynics, conspiracy theorists think. In fact, foreign relations, foreign policy, strategic communications exist in an environment where there are only shades of grey. There are no such things as black and white. The only black and white is text written in the newspaper but behind that black and white text it is all shade of grey.

There is no such thing as an objective newspaper that I have ever seen in my career in strat-comms. There is no such thing as a truly objective television or radio station that I have seen . Even ones that think they are objective are pushing a line of some kind and often the people who believe they are being objective are the most self-deluded people in the industry.

MF: Was it Kissinger who said 'Nations have no permanent allies, only permanent interests'?[3]

SH: Absolutely, that is exactly right. It is extremely unwise to be too dogmatic and defined because you really can affect the behaviour of your client by the strategic advice you give them. If you come from a moderate position and you start representing this person, over a period of time their position will soften by the very nature of the fact that they have chosen you to represent them and they are taking you strategic advice.

So, there is some sort of defence there. However, obviously, if you tried to defend the position of Assad at the moment you are going to be on quite shaky foundations. I am sure the people who are working with him will say that is the reason they are doing it.

MF: Just to finish that thought, I am struck by the fact that before this situation in Syria came to the world's attention, Assad still had a secret police, still limited access to social media and communications within the country and people were very happy to represent him. Once he is seen as being unrepresentable he becomes unrepresentable, which is a confirmation of the logic you are suggesting the industry cleaves to.

SH: Yes. That is right, but they move on. Probably the big strategic communication firms have made their money out of him. There is no question at all, Russia and Russian interests, China and Chinese interests are helping Assad with his strategic communications at the moment. It is pretty self-evident that is happening. Similarly it is pretty self-evident that Western information operations in some form, be that private, military, political, foreign policy, there is an information operations war happening around this subject in every country of the world pretty much, certainly any country with any interest in this.

Who is conducting that? Is it governmental or is private sector? That is definitely happening all around at the moment. The idea that people are saying we are not engaging with this in the strat-comms industry, you must be joking. Everyone is engaged in the conversation about Syria, so they are sourcing their information somewhere and because they are sourcing their information somewhere, someone has got a strategy in place to make them receive one piece of information versus another piece of information.

MF: It is crazy when it is explained that nudely simply because CNN themselves admitted they do not have reporters in country so they are relying on the reports of human rights organisations or the rebels -

SH: They have just said that they have not got reporters in there. If they somehow think that qualifies their objectiveness, no it does not. It just makes them an easier pawn to play in the game by the hidden hand that is playing them. That is now a much easier piece to move around the board because they are desperate for information. They have got to put product on the screen so they will take it from the people who supply it to them if they are not supplying it themselves.

So to that extent, as long as you can become a supplier for that information, be it through a cut out, two or three cut outs, you will get your opinion on CNN.

MF: Is there a metaphoric link here then between the way in which society moved into the industrial age of mass production with its attitude towards commodity -

SH: That is exactly what it is. I actually have a personal feeling on this and where it is has gone recently, it is only my particular opinion, history may prove me wrong.

The Mayfair Set, with David Stirling,[4] the former head of the SAS, basically commoditised and sold victory in the form of the arms trade. They rebuilt the British economy in part from commoditising war. Hard influence, land mines, selling mercenary soldiers into a country, fighting people's wars to affect geo-strategic aims that were favourable to Britain at the time. They commoditised and sold a different, mercenary style of warfare.

What happened then, in Britain, is that became quite unfashionable - the famous shot of Diana walking through a minefield being just one example. The Foreign and Commonwealth Office could not be seen to have a policy that was supporting this amount of death that was being exported. What happened at the same time was the emergence of the marketing industry, the likes of Lord Saatchi and Lord Bell, who were both working very closely with Margaret Thatcher at the time.

I think, knowingly or unknowingly, they created and commoditised soft power, still delivering victory to the clients but rather than selling them land mines, selling them information operations. That has been the growth industry in strat-comms. I cannot really speak on America's behalf but certainly in the UK I think that fine line between hard power, kinetic power or kinetic sales and soft information sales, that is where the transition has happened.

I think we still sell victory but we now sell victory in a

different way, a way the FCO will agree with, a way that our trade representatives can say 'it is jolly good, give him a Lordship'. We are going through an information revolution at the moment and I think we are one of the countries that has managed to commoditise it quicker and perhaps better than some other countries and make it easy for clients to buy, whether those clients are business, defence or political. There is an appetite for soft power, for information operations power or at least the power it gives by effective information operations.

MF: The language that you have used is, either intentionally or not, very telling. You said that the FCO cannot be seen to support certain policies, not that there is genuine moral repugnance to it.

SH: The FCO only has a certain amount of staff and budget. Let us not get too carried away with the amount of power that countries actually have. If you ever work with the government, even a big government, at the end of the day there is a limit to what a government can actually achieve. The private sector ambitions in a country will probably mirror the country's ambitions anyway.

Africa, a huge opportunity at the moment. Brazil, Russia, India. Any country in the world is looking for ways to gain influence in those countries. Foreign relations or commercial relations, they are both one and the same thing.

MF: This melding of political and financial interests leads us neatly into another very important question. In this age of the mass production of information, much as the industrial age was about the mass production of consumable commodities, how has that helped or hindered this field of perception management? How easy is it to get a story to stick or to disappear?

SH: This notion that you need a story to stick is not true. It's a bit like Muhammad Ali. The speed of Muhammad Ali, the constant repetition of quick jabs was what made him so phenomenal. It was the speed. What you get with the information age is speed of stories. This is what happened to the Tories under John Major. I cannot really remember a single exact example of why they were so murky, corrupt, dodgy and sleazy. Why do I know that they were the sleazy government? Because there were a hundred and one stories that came out. I cannot remember a single one of them but I can remember that they were the sleazy government and that was what got their arses kicked at the election.

You do not need stories to stick, you just need stories to be repeated regularly across all touch points. If you call someone a rapist enough times across enough touch points, it does not matter if they did it or not. I do not know if Strauss-Kahn is a rapist, I do not know if Julian Assange is a rapist, but I know there are a hell of a lot of people baying for their blood because they have heard that word associated with them so many times. It is most definitely the repetition of the word rather than any hard evidence that has the effect.

Ongoing repetition, the tsunami of story, story, story, that is how you effect the change. It is not necessarily that there is anything behind the stories but if you can say it enough times across enough touch points, if it is on CNN then it will be on the BBC, then Al-Jazeera, because they are competing for coverage. If you can just make them compete between themselves for coverage so it becomes a feeding frenzy on a story, then all the secondary and tertiary levels like blogs start talking about it. Before you know it, if you have managed to feed the word 'rape' or whatever it may be in relation to someone, the whole world is discussing their name in the context of being a rapist.

It does not matter if they come out and deny it because then they are still using the word. What you have done is put that meme and embedded it into them so that they are just constantly associated with that word, whatever that word may be. Rape is a very strong one. You look at that as the word of the moment because it is relevant to Julian Assange, Strauss-Kahn. I am not necessarily being a devil's advocate to suggest that this is part of a strategic communications campaign upon them but it would not surprise me if it it turned out that it was.

MF: I have a friend who works as a paparazzi photographer and he once told me that when he shoots his photographs, he will send a whole raft of them to the photo editors. Even if he has pictures of someone who is not famous, if enough pictures of this person show up on this editor's desk over a short amount of time they will start publishing them because they assume the person is famous.

SH: That is exactly right and that is what we are talking about. The speed and repetition is the fuel, the grease of strategic communications. It is what makes the wheels go round.

Everyone has to fulfil the requirement for content. They do not necessarily need true content, they need content. If CNN and Fox are on twenty-four hours a day, they have to dig up stories that are just emerging.

This is how you get online phenomenon. It becomes a story that someone's sung a funny song in a funny way on YouTube because it has been passed around a million times. They become an internet sensation. Well that is a new element of the story. Now, they have had a mental collapse since they became an internet sensation. That is another story. They have a girlfriend or a boyfriend, that is another story. One story has so many different dimensions to it because they are looking for the next way of fulfilling their content requirements.

They will take anything. People get this idea that strat-comms is having to work hard to push messages into the mainstream media. It is not that difficult to push messages into the mainstream media, be you government, company or the military, because they are bloody desperate for it. If they do not have content they do not survive. If they do not have more interesting content than the other person they will not sell as many papers the next day. Simple as that.

MF: John Calhoun, the scientist whose story and experiments form the backbone of the film that I made, described the number and frequency of contacts between the rodents that he studied using the term 'social velocity'. Simultaneously, certain economists describe the 'velocity of money' of being fundamental to the understanding of an economy. It is not just the volume of money but the speed with which the money circulates.

So what you are really talking about is part of this sensation many people have that society seems to be speeding up, the impatience with which we demand greater novelty, more colours, variations, options even if those are simply superficial options. It is a kind of informational velocity.

SH: I think people prefer it. I do not think people want the truth. Has anybody got the time to find out the truth? What is the truth in Syria? I have no damn idea what the truth is anymore, nor does anyone else. No one wants to be reminded of the truth. They are far too busy to deal with the truth.

Take the environmental issues that are being fought over at the moment. The moment someone comes out with absolute truth, the other one says it is an absolute untruth, or they have to apologise a month later that they got some of their figures wrong. So the absolute truth is no longer the absolute truth, it was a marginal truth, a qualified truth.

There is no such thing as truth. There is absolutely no such thing as truth. There are only different truths. So people do not have the time to believe in a truth anymore. They are not even looking for it anymore. They do not want the truth, they are not interested in the truth, they do not go out and search for the truth. They do not stop buying shit tittle-tattle in favour of the truth. They much prefer the shit tittle-tattle, sadly.

It is in that context, in that environment, that now politics and wars are all being fought. The savvy politicians and the savvy armies around the world realise that, to be honest with you, they do not even need to concern themselves with being held accountable for the truth. The Hague. Did The Hague establish the truth when they finally got someone in the dock? Did they establish the truth? No, and if they do it takes fifteen to twenty years to get there. If that is how long you have to wait for the truth then do not be surprised if your audience is not prepared to wait.

MF: When you were describing this lack of interest, or more specifically the social conditions that have made the patience required for truth almost impossible, it is akin to what some people would describe as a spiritual crisis.

SH: Fundamentally that is true. You can learn an awful lot from religion. One of the best ever viral campaigns is the Bible. My company is a verbalisation strategic communications company. Take the Bible as an example. You do not have to be Christian, you do not have to have read the Bible - I have not read the Bible from start to finish but that is not to say I do not know pretty much every single story, parable, name in there. The laws in this country are based on it. I see people every Sunday going and sitting quietly to be told, ingest and pass these stories amongst themselves peer to peer. It is a brilliant example of a verbalisation campaign.

It uses peer-to-peer networks. It uses high value individuals to push the stories. It uses multi-touchpoint campaigning. It uses advocates. Even the very notion of disciples is what brand advocacy is all about. It is a great example of a viral advertising campaign.

The Muslim faith. Fastest growing faith in the world and you are not even allowed to paint a picture of Muhammad. You cannot even depict Muhammad otherwise you get into trouble. All you have got is memes. All you have got is stories. All you have got is seeding something into a neural network and into a peer-to-peer network that is going to get passed around. A sticky story that is going to be told, retold, exaggerated, changed according to its local context and custom, manipulated by some people in their best interest versus your best interest, exploited for the sake of justifying a position that is unjustifiable.

Religion is nothing more than an example of a once-effective advertising campaign that is now being used to justify horrendous actions by people who understand the power of the assets they have at their disposal. These are people who have understood that actually this is an information operations tool that can be used to effect behavioural change in line with their strategic intent. So let us apply the layer of religion over the top of our strategic communications campaign and we might find that we get to where we want to go quicker; we make the people of this country subservient. We make women subjugated. We fracture the opposition.

You can say that to some extent that is what China is doing in Africa. The Muslim faith funnily enough is growing in Africa incrementally and China may well be seeing that as the front end of their strategic ambitions and aims. If one was a conspiracy theorist, one could say that those two agendas in Africa may collide very nicely for China.

MF: When you were talking about Christianity and Islam, all I could think of was very successful branding. One image, BAM!

SH: Absolutely. They are depicted a certain way. There are rules how you have to paint this and they have been around for centuries. The mother of Jesus must wear a blue cloak because that was at the time the most expensive colour. That was why it started. It was an homage to the expense. It was showing off how much you could spend on this religion, yet the fundamental thing that religion teaches you is that you are not meant to get into heaven if you are a rich man. It is so inherently fucked up, this whole entire thing.

It is a very good example of how to use messaging peer-to-peer, brand advocates, sticky stories, key verbals, sound bytes; it is a good lesson in that regard.

MF: There is another tactic that seems to be on the rise these days, which is that when an expose or an investigative piece comes out, the response by the "injured party" is to attack the journalist or the journalism rather than the veracity of the story. I was wondering if you could comment on that technique?

SH: Well, your PR company, your strategic communications company will go and essentially buy in expert council that supports your position. If you take it away from the individual and make it a corporation, if your corporation is accused of something or you as a political individual are accused of something, then you can out-trump the journalist by going and buying, off the shelf, an academic voice who will come in and say your side of the story or your client's side of the story, at a price.

They are paid to write a paper that is seemingly objective but you already know where they stand on the issue, so what you are doing is paying them a lot of money to enable them to have a voice. It just happens to be that their voice coincides with your strategic aim, which is to quash whatever is being said against your client.

MF: This dovetails quite neatly with the current vogue of experts on everything. Everyone is an expert. There is an expert on tomatoes. There is an expert on public policy. There is an expert on privatisation. Everyone is an expert and a lot of this is done through networks of so-called 'independent' think tanks that are presented as independent intellectual offerings rather than constructed mouthpieces and yet have murky sources of funding.

SH: A strategic campaign will already identify them at the very beginning of sitting with a client. If you go back to that original thing we were saying about top-level strategic planning, at that point you will be identifying with your client who the influential voices are.

Like you said, on tomatoes you will have people who say 'toh-may-toes' and people who say 'toh-mah-toes'. You will be able to hire either side to your argument depending on where you want your position to be. You will identify that very early on in a strategic communications campaign and make introductions to the people who are later going to become your amplifiers, your client's amplifiers.

This notion that people of their own volition stand up and have an expert opinion on something is a joke. Who is an 'independent' expert on something? Why would they possibly

173

want to go on the news that night and talk about it? Rubbish. The person who is going to be on the news that night talking about it as an 'independent' expert is going to be on someone's payroll. Even companies like the BBC or whatever news network think that that person seems independent but they just cannot see the levers of power that are being applied here.

They think the tactical story is the story when actually the tactical story is just one part of a much bigger strategic campaign. The dots may not even have joined up at that point. They would see no connection between the interview they are doing and the strategic aim that was designed two or three years ago in a dark room. They just do not see that they are a pawn. It is like CNN. They just do not see that they are a pawn but they are.

MF: Is there a case study that you have at your fingertips that you could give me as an example?

SH: It is a daily occurrence. If you take Afghanistan, the press are not allowed down south of the country to get to where the real war is being fought. If they are allowed down there, they are embedded within a team and only taken to certain areas. The reality of what is being done correctly or incorrectly in Afghanistan is not being projected to the world's media. I have got other examples but I cannot say because they are with clients or former clients.

MF: Well if there is a story that you definitely could not tell me about a prominent individual or corporate interest that you definitely did not represent, what type of machination definitely did not happen?

SH: When you get an op-ed piece in the newspapers or an academic profile piece on a person, country, organisation, seemingly objective, they have just come up with ten thousand words on this subject, highly researched with all the information that you could possibly imagine so that they give the final say on this issue - where do you think that person came from? Why is it that suddenly they are providing this information that is fully researched? They have been working on it for weeks. They were assured that it would get published and someone had to pay them for that.

If the person who paid them for that is a think tank that has just commissioned this from them, which way is that think tank leaning on this issue? You need to follow the money, but then probably the strat-comms firm is good enough that even if you follow the money you will never end up with them. It is amazing how academics can be incentivised to write pieces. They are skint, sitting around waiting for a paper to be commissioned because it increases their social standing if they have just written on North Africa, a big commercial project or environmental issues.

As I said, it is a bit like politicians. They are just the voices for hire to achieve strategic aims. If this person will not do it then the other person will and the moment one person does it then probably another two or three will also want to do it to make sure they are also seen at that level and stature within that academic world. It becomes a feeding frenzy where the news just perpetuates itself around an issue.

MF: Predominantly, we are told by the media and politicians that the citizenry of any given Western-style country are really consumers. That we are participants in an economy, that economics is the basic "science" we can use to understand our behaviour. Yet there is a very interesting quirk in economics: the fundamental assumption of economic models is what is called perfect information.

Now, what we have been talking about is the absolute opposite of perfect information. My question then is: how can a so-called free market based entirely on the presumption of perfect information function if the information that reaches the public is so heavily edited?

SH: It depends on how big the strategic brief is from the start. Is it beyond the realms of possibility to have the economists say that black is black and white is white and absolutely celebrate them by saying 'yes, that is absolutely right', when actually the overarching strategic intent may be to help them to come to that belief all along.

This notion that there is such a thing as perfect information is an absolute joke.

If you are suggesting that economics itself proves one thing or another, no it does not. Take North Africa as an example. Describe to me the economics of North Africa at the moment, with all the hidden hands, with all the cutouts where money is actually coming from? The Democratic Republic of Congo, the relationship with the mineral coltan and the way in which coltan has been exploited out of that country.[5] Economics never was involved in that because it was hidden. It was never admitted to be going on. Economics only gets involved when it can become measured. If you are dealing with the grey areas of genuine geo-strategic level strat-comms, they would not even know where to begin to measure it in an economic information sense. It would not be tangible enough to measure in that regard.

Perfect information is an absolute fallacy, an absolute farce.

MF: That raises a further, very pressing question. If on an economic level the explanations, models and framework we use to understand the behaviour of our own societies is built on quicksand because the two things that are presumed within those models and frameworks are perfect information and rational individuals maximising utility based purely on financial calculation, then what are the implications for not only society itself but for public discourse within society, if the very nuts and bolts of that discourse are pre-constructed, heavily managed and supplied by hidden interests that are not established or discussed openly?

SH: I think the model has changed. It is a very big mistake as either a company, politician or army to have a fixed position. To have a fixed position makes you very open to becoming a pawn for someone else. There are always multiple truths with multiple concurrent consequences in a constantly moving scenario. Just the very fact of the layer of the news networks means that a story can break and go around the world and will change everything.

Perception management is going on live, constantly. It is like a virus. It is constantly pulsing around the world. A fixed position is easy to beat. You should not ever try to have facts. If you stay in tune with a constantly moving position then you can constantly adapt your facts according to the new given context.

The question then is when do you make your move and stick and exploit the situation to drive the endgame narrative home? Look at the fight that they are having with the US election. It is a bit like boxing: they are both staying fluid, they are both moving round each other. There was almost a stick the other day with those inconvenient words that were said about rape by one of the Republicans. That almost became a moment that something was stuck firm and look at the way that worked against them. Suddenly there was something they could leverage on and go for the endgame narrative which is 'they are against women'. That will become endgame narrative through to the actual day of election if they can make that stick.

You do not want to stick today, in this world. It is what armies are learning. The clear objectives going into a conflict are less defined than they once were. Once it used to be 'We are going to beat Hitler and we are going to take down the Nazis and free this country'. With the Libyan narrative, the Syrian narrative, no one has really got a position on this. What they are doing is trying to get the other person into a position, box them in where they make a stand and then make that stand work against them, and then you have got your endgame narrative that you drive home. That is basically the new world reality. That is something that funnily enough applies just as much to someone going into an interview. They should be more ambiguous in their interview than they once used to be.

MF: In a sense of fluid dynamics you are talking about the principle of dilution. If you have a very thick, viscous fluid it moves very slowly and it does not shift over an area at a particularly fast pace. If that fluid is diluted, the thinner it gets the faster it moves and the wider it spreads. What you are talking about, these issues of dilution, velocity, inflation, mass production, these seem to echo other areas of our lifestyle and social framework in a very striking way.

SH: Different layers of the onion. You want to try not to commit. I fence a lot, I am a keen fencer. Half your time in fencing is dancing up and down the piste not attacking each other because the moment you lunge you are committed, your feet are rooted to one spot. You either better hit your mark or you are going to get a counter attack on you that you do not even see coming.

MF: When in motion, be like water.

SH: Exactly right.

MF: For the future of a meaningful public discourse or any kind of genuinely representative governance, what are the ramifications of a situation where no one holds a position, no one holds a principle?

SH: This is exactly what you have seen. This is why we have bland politicians, we have parties that do not stand for anything and certainly do not stand apart from each other. This is why everyone is crying out for a new model. This is why you go into super-federation alternatives in terms of European Union, but that does not work either. It is just becoming this grey mass of blandness.

That is where celebrity culture comes from. Everything else is just so dull these days. The only bit of excitement sometimes in people's lives is this celebrity culture of over-exaggerated people that have become manifestations of something that just is not real anymore. Look at the people that go onto Big Brother now. They are caricatures for a reason.

MF: You said earlier that strategic communications and perception management is a complete field of shades rather than of black and white, talking about shades of grey. When you discuss truth, you are talking about the fact that people just do not have the time to cultivate the patience necessary to find the truth or to wait for it or to really accept it or digest it when it is put in front of them. What you just said about this morass of moral and factual relativism where everything is just a wash of bland nothing, it seems to me that people are crying out for some sense of truth. That they are crying out for something that just puts a flag down, draws a line in the sand and says, OK, this is where we stand for better or for worse, whether you think we are wrong or not. This seems typical of social situations that give rise to extremism. They are the only people who stick to their position regardless of what is thrown at them.

SH: Let us take the austerity measures in Greece. 'I am going to do this for the sake of the country, it is going to be in the best interest of the country, we have to have these austerity measures' and they kick him out of power.

Osborne in this country: we are going to have austerity measures and the consequence of that is the economy has not grown for however many months now and everyone now has started to pinpoint Osborne as the man that maybe is going to go down.

Nick Clegg: in the interest of the country I have got to do a partnership with the Conservative Party. We are going to stand up for what is right in the country, we are going to push through policies, and today on the news they are already talking about the succession plans being put into place.

The problem is if you stick, the world moves on around you so quick, you will become yesterday's man or woman, yesterday's company. It is a dangerous game to play, to stick unless your enemy, your adversary has made a mistake and you can make events stick and you create your endgame narrative around their mistake and you exploit it and you ram it home.

MF: The example used of Nick Clegg, I do not know if I would entirely agree with that. The problem he had is that he did not stick. He said that they would form this partnership in order to let the additional coalition principles be Liberal Democrat rather than Labour because everyone knew no-one would tolerate the Labour government staying in power even in a coalition, but as soon as they got in they reneged on every single election pledge.

SH: You are absolutely right. Once he had backed down on the students' fees, that was game over for him, there was no way back from that moment. He did not stick on that issue.

MF: What you are describing is not an issue of genuine behaviour or genuine truth. If someone says they will stick and they go back on it they cannot be represented as defensible. So Nick Clegg cannot be defended because he said he was going to do one thing and then when he had the opportunity to do it he did exactly the opposite of the thing he said he would do and there is no way of spinning that.

So when you are describing the danger of sticking, it seems to me what you are really describing is the inability to spin someone who really made a point of saying what they would do and failed.

SH: Yes, it puts conditions in place. Sticking is a very stupid thing to do. If you say you are going to do this for the economy, well you cannot predict where the world economy is going to be in a year and then it makes you look like an immature person to have gobbed off too soon.

You have to be really careful as well. "As a company, we believe in this so we will do this." The moment you say you believe in this it means you do not believe in that and hold on, if you believe in this then why are you doing this? You set yourself up for the fall really.

This is why increasingly, my clients are going further and further into the shadows, be they commercial, political etcetera. It is actually them realising that the less they have to go public with what they believe, what they feel, what they want to or do

179

not want to do, the more they can stick to the shadows, the less they have to be accountable.

MF: Then the irony is that in this game of shadows, where we recede in order to disguise our motivations and our interests in order to not be caught out, the communication strategy is the person who communicates the least is the one who stays on top.

SH: Absolutely. Look at Russia. You do not know the ten people who really are the powerful men and women in Russia. You do not know them by name but they exist and they are more powerful than Putin. In most countries that is now true. There is the hidden hand. The politicians are not powerful. It is the people above them who are really powerful. The politicians come and go; they exist for four, eight or if they are really lucky twelve terms. The strategic intent is a much longer game than that and it will be run by people who are above the level of Prime Minister.

MF: From either personal experience or from encounters within your work, would you venture a comment on who those you describe as 'the hidden hand' or 'puppet masters' are?

SH: No. No I would not.

MF: You talked earlier about the way politicians go back and forth, circling each other without actually doing anything, like airplanes in a holding pattern between elections.

SH: That is a very good metaphor for it, and if suddenly one of them sees that they can land and get down quickly, that is exactly right. It is like they do the cycling in the Olympics. They just cycle round and round and then suddenly one of them breaks. Half of the race is watching them go round really slowly doing nothing.
It is a tactical game of getting the endgame strategy right. It comes down to explosive messaging very quickly and seeing if you can get the traction that you need.
You do not need the traction for long. You only need the traction until election day or until they trial and purchase a product. After that it is over. There is no more long term buy-in. How many card-carrying Labour Party people are there who believe in everything the Labour Party does? Not as many as there were, because you are not trying to win hearts and minds

over such a long period of time, you are trying to win them for election day.

MF: It is funny, that game of shadows, keeping your hand concealed for as long as possible before you break. In a sense it is almost tantric communication. You hold back for as long as possible because the longer you hold back the longer the explosion lasts for.

SH: That comes from the strat-comms people as well. The best they can do is to keep out. The best strat-comms companies are the ones where you do not know they are involved with a client. I certainly have gone into a country to work with a client and I will try not to raise my profile at all, to the point of not leaving a hotel room for months on end, not even being seen by the hotel staff.

It is not to say they are doing anything shady in their communications. It can be a completely transparent and accountable campaign, but it is sometimes just not good to have the questions and the narrative moved across to justifying the position of a strategic communications firm being involved in the first place, of which everyone has these preconceived ideas: shadowy, grey and dangerous. That is not true. It is information management, that is all it is. It is no different from a marketing firm in some respects.

MF: It is like Plato's allegory of The Cave. The people are in the cave looking at the wall and on the wall is a play that they assume is a play between real individuals and it turns out that not only is it not a play between real individuals, it is not even a play between the shadows of real individuals. They are actually puppets manipulated by people and the play is the shadows of puppets manipulated by people.

SH: Exactly. When people critique the strat-comms industry, they think they have hit their target but they do not even realise that the target is behind them.

This is what I am saying: politicians, people who have an agenda, they think they are doing a tactical thing and they think they have achieved their aims and they do not realise that their aims are actually someone else's aims, who are someone else's aims, who are someone else's aims. That is where the plan is struck. What they are doing is just fulfilling their part in a game that they do not even know is being played.

It is very easy to make this all sound very Machiavellian when it is not. It is just strategy and management. It is not rocket science. It is just taking the time to break down the strategy into its component parts with its consequences and its primary, secondary, tertiary deferred audience and messages. If you break it down, it is probably just the same selling ice cream as it is selling a message of peace in a country.

A marketing firm would give it just this much care and attention selling ice cream but we do not look at that so cynically. They would be choosing the exact pantone colour blue and they would be having conversations for hours about which exact colour blue and they would take it to focus groups. That care and attention they are putting into selling ice cream, we are saying there is an industry that puts that much care and attention into selling the messages for their clients into the mainstream.

MF: You mentioned Macchiavelli within this conversation about what is real, what is manufactured. There was a story recently, I think it was an academic, who basically uncovered new evidence that shows that Machiavelli actually wrote The Prince ironically as a satire of the Medicis rather than actually as a handbook for -

SH: This goes back to The Cave scenario. This is the point: it is a mistake to get fixed on the truth. This is what I hate with people in my own organisation. I do not let people say 'I think'. I like people to say 'I assess based on the evidence'. All you can do is repeatedly assess based on the evidence and the evidence will change and so your assessment must change.

You must not get fixed if you can avoid it. You must stay fluid and stay adaptable, the same way as a boxer or a judo expert's advantage is about dancing. It is only by adapting that you can give the most relevant content to a fast-changing target audience in a fast-changing media landscape in a fast-changing world.

MF: There is a very important issue here about the nature of the world, the way that society either progresses or believes that it is progressing. I wanted to ask you to what extent perception management is really expectation management? It does not just shape how people see the world, how they believe the world functions, but also how they think, feel and believe the world is going to be or could be or should be?

SH: I have a very cynical point of view on this sadly. The answer you probably want to hear and want to believe in is that it starts with local and grassroots. All you can know is your grassroots scenario around you. Your own experiences, you talk to your friends and your trusted networks and together you make an informed decision based on your own experience.

The thing is though, and this is what many grassroots campaigns with all the best intentions misunderstand, is that the moment they get to a certain amount of influence within either their peer-to-peer network or within the wider network, they will become attractive to a sponsor. That sponsor in the business sector is exactly as it sounds. McDonalds will recognise the huge influence within a grassroots group here and they will want to infiltrate and influence that grassroots by sponsoring them so they can bring them closer to their brand or product.

In a political environment, this is where it gets worrying. That grassroots that has started from their own experience, they will be looking to take their message to a larger audience. Sponsors will come into their orbit who can facilitate that, be it technologically to give them reach or politically to introduce them to another kind of Venn diagram of the circles connecting. That is a sponsor as well.

Maybe the sponsor is another military force. If they want to achieve some strategic objectives and to do some good in this region then the sponsor comes in the form of a bigger army that lends support. NATO jumps to mind or ISAF, twenty-three nations working together. What of course happens is they are immediately compromised by the addition of the sponsor.

They compromise commercially and politically. The sponsor inevitably erodes the power, sucks out the original intent and replaces it with their own intent and their own programming to the network that is now in place, but because it has existed peer-to-peer and has become a trusted network, that sponsor through their infiltration of that network will get their way. Their strategic intent and ambition will be achieved incredibly quickly before the network even realises what has happened to it.

I think that is what happened in certain instances in Libya, that is what is happening in certain instances in other countries and certainly it is happening in commercial and defense environments as well. It is not an answer to your question but the solution that is being presented to us at the moment is not the answer. What the answer is, I do not know yet, but what we are being told is the answer is not the answer.

183

MF: So in the game of shadows, exposure and success are actually destructive?

SH: They can be. Look at the Wikileaks relationship to Anonymous. It is ironic, is it not? Anonymous have tried to stay anonymous but by the very fact that they have become known, they now have websites, key visuals, key verbals, an advertising line and videos all over, that is not anonymous. Their brand is definitely not anonymous whereas once it was. Because of that, sponsors are being attracted, which is high value individuals speaking on their behalf, or security services around the world will be infiltrating them as pretend sponsors.

You can say the Occupy Movement to a certain extent was a sponsor. They would not see that in Anonymous. They would see themselves as the guiding force that created the universe in which the Occupy Movement could exist, but the Occupy Movement perhaps has done more harm to Anonymous than they could possibly ever realise. What they have become associated with now is a bunch of screaming people on the television making an anti-capitalist point, whereas what they started out as was a genuine anonymous force that had teeth and no-one understood it, no-one could deal with it, no-one could fight against it.

They have compromised themselves by allowing sponsors into their network.

MF: So you cannot fight what you cannot see?

SH: Exactly. Anonymous, they had the right intent, ambitions and starting point and they did it brilliantly to start with. My feeling now is that they are a busted flush. They are just becoming a whining group of people on the periphery of the big game. The big game has moved on. They got stuck and it has been turned against them.

MF: If I can press you on this morphing of perception management into expectation management then, if you were to look at the UK, US or the Western European-style nations more broadly, if you were to read the narrative, read these shades of grey the way that you have learned to by participating in the industry, where would you say our expectations are being guided? What are we subtly or not so subtly being told we should want or should look forward to?

SH: This goes back to the company where you have the MD talking to sales staff but at the same time talking shareholders and they think tactically they are doing one thing. What they do not realise is that they are part of a much bigger game that is ten levels up from them, a geo-strategic game which directly influences everything that they are doing. It affects their media, everything around them.

It is a matrix. They do not even recognise the boundaries of the world that they are in. They just perceive the world that they are in as their reality. I think you have to be very careful with England or some of the other countries in Western Europe. It is a matrix scenario. I can say 'in the world of the UK at the moment this is the perception management that is going on' and that is all quite tactical stuff. Actually the bigger question is the universe that exists behind it which we do not even see. Are we already playing China's game? Are we already being perception-managed as a country, as Europe?

There is a very good book that starts touching on some of these questions called 'The Next Hundred Years' by George Friedman. He is talking about the next hundred years in terms of America's influence and he talks about a very interesting strategic level game in the tactical consequences of the border between America and Mexico. You would think that the local politics of the border region has its own political reasons to be aggravated at the moment, to do with land ownership, rights of coming across the border etcetera.

What you are not seeing is the regional game, which is that America's population is getting older so they need more young people to come into the country to look after the old people as they get older. That will affect the local tactical conversations with Mexico and may mean more Mexicans can come into America. That will have an effect on what makes up and constitutes the United States. If you got a lot of Mexicans into the southern regions of America, maybe they will want some of those bits of land back that were originally taken away from the Mexicans. So the United States will therefore change.

If you are against America at a geo-strategic level, to achieve this weakening of America and start breaking up the United States of America and make them fight internal battles, you might want to help Mexico have a voice on the issue of the narcotics trade etcetera. It may be that the puppet master is always playing the puppet.

With a twenty, thirty, forty year geo-strategic narrative in place, I would not be surprised that that is already happening to

England or Western Europe too. Someone is designing that narrative now and is probably already influencing that narrative now. We are probably doing it in other countries too, let us be clear about that. We as England are doing that, France is probably doing that and Germany is probably doing that right across Africa, right across the Middle East, entire swathes of the globe.

These geo-strategic levels of the game are being played. The consequence of that is having an effect on our banking structures, trade relationships, where we put capital in terms of which industry we support, jobs which has an effect on our taxation, which has an effect on the amount of money we have to spend on our medical health service, whether or not that has to privatised, the staffing levels, the pay of nurses that needs to be taken into account which means the infrastructure of our travel system around certain hubs has to be taken into account.

The big game is being played in all these tactical little things which seem to have no direct relationship to the big strategic game that is already being played. Information operations and information management is happening at every single level of that to create the tactical and behavioural change in line with the overarching strategic intent.

MF: From my reading, research, meetings and conversations with people such as yourself, there does seem to be a common understanding that there is an underlying centralising principle at play here, whether it is the IMF pushing for the use of the SDR[6] as a global currency because they believe it will stabilise trade markets or the ways in which England became the United Kingdom and now is a part of the European Union and now as the European Union is going through some *sturm und drang* we are being told that the only solution is greater political and fiscal integration.

SH: Funny how that narrative has just popped up the way they want it.

MF: Well, this is exactly my point. Do you perceive as I do this underlying centralising principle to be in play? When you say that narrative has popped up the way they wanted, who are they?

SH: Basically the future relies, you hope, on good governance. The question is who are you asking to be the governor? It is not the politicians, it is not the prime minister. What the world is preconditioned to believe at the moment is good governance comes from their governments and it does not.

It is not an underlying structure, it is an overarching structure. Those are the hidden hands that are moving the tectonic plates of the world at the moment for sure.

MF: It is another observation of mine that the arc of government, of the state, curves towards authoritarianism. It is a broadly accepted trend that power wants more power and in that sense power is like a gas. It will expand to fill the space provided and we see consistently laws being brought in that we are told are innocuous, simply future hedges against possible events, but once they are in place it is very difficult to get them out of place and they can be used however the power structure wants them used.

Here in Britain we have very restrictive libel laws, we have these super-injunctions, excessive PR stunts, the game of shadows of perception management as we have been discussing, the embedded journalism within militaries and the corporate- or high net worth individual-funded think tanks masquerading as independent intelligentsia.

It seems that everywhere one looks is this reflection of puppets wielded by hidden hands. As you said, it is true that we are led to believe, programmed to accept, that the state is the best solution to these problems, the best way of regulating these various interests, to ward off chaos. Interesting, the way anarchy became described as synonymous with chaos during the Occupy Movement and the police were circulating literature about reporting people with anarchist sympathies. Yet again, this way of the number of impressions being the dictating factor of how sticky a story is.

In this almost entirely manufactured mental landscape that we seem to inhabit, particularly in the more so-called democratic countries, what is the future of genuine democracy, human relationships and liberty?

SH: Genuine democracy has not existed for centuries. I think you are being naive to suggest that genuine democracy exists now. It does not. There is no such thing as genuine democracy.

The battle is won several years before it is fought. The election is won several years before it is fought. The product is known to sell several years before it goes to market, if you do your job right. It is what the Mayfair Set were doing with selling victory. I think the good strategic communication firms in the world now would like to believe they sell victory and that is the assurance you get from them. Their track records prove that they do.

Is that a science? What is it? How do they do it? There are so many hidden hands in play, the strat-comms firms are holding so many of those hands when they go and take on the job by the very nature of the circles within which they move that basically it is fait accompli when they get involved.

They are the unifying element, the glue that sticks together all those various hidden hands. They are the friendly public face of those hidden hands, representing all those interests, so when they take on that job, it is a fait accompli. The notion that there is democracy is laughable.

MF: I think it is from Richard III when he says ' I can smile and murder while I smile'.[7]

SH: Exactly. I am not here in defence of the strat-comms industry. I am a big advocate of greater transparency, accountability. There are good and bad in the strat-comms industry but it is certainly the fulcrum of an awful lot of power because the world has changed and information is the sharp end of this. It is what you have to deal with every day.

It is the bit that sticks out of the surface, the tip of the iceberg. Beneath the surface it is the hidden agendas, the real power players that are there that you just do not see.

MF: If knowledge is power, if in the modern digital age data and information and the speed and ubiquity of messages constitutes the knowledge of the public, if we do not have a functioning democracy in a meaningful sense if we ever did, if this centralising principle, this move of power to fewer hands continues as we perceive it to be doing, then you can read my real question as, rather than being 'what is the future of democracy?', 'how does one take the power back?'

SH: I do not think you can. It has got so sophisticated now. It is like the hydra. If you cut off one of its heads, it grows back. Let us take News International as an example. The News of the World had to be closed down because of its behaviour with regards to Milly Dowler, phone hacking etcetera.

So they cut that head off the hydra and they put a new one

there which is The Sun on Sunday. Where were people going? They had the knowledge and the power then. Something very bad had happened. They could have all stopped buying News International publications and that place would have been out of business; Murdoch would have been completely out of business if everyone had just stopped and handed back their subscriptions to their TV services but they did not because they do not care.

They are still buying his bloody publications. They are buying The Times, The Sun on Sunday, The Sun. He did the customary thing, which is to cut off one of the heads of the hydra, and he put another one back on.

I absolutely despair when people say that knowledge is power. What knowledge? Whose knowledge? There is no truth. There is no pure truth. The pure truth in that instance was what was done by those journalists was unforgivable, immoral, disgusting, vile and should have had consequences for the business. The only consequence for the business was cosmetic - they closed down one newspaper and opened another one. There was no consequence to the business whatsoever, even when people had the knowledge and therefore the consequent power.

Everyone, even the academics, looks at it and says 'if you give them the knowledge they will do something about it'. No they will not.

The public will go back to what they have always done before, which is to move on from the story very quickly because as I have been saying all along, it moves so quick.

They do not want the truth. They cannot handle the truth. They do not know what to do with the truth and when you give them the truth they do not respond in the way they probably should do with the truth. That prime example of the News of the World situation, they had the truth. They had it in their hands and what did they do? They fucked it up.

A Society At War With Itself
with Dr. David Nutt

"Government is about perpetuating their own structures for their own benefit and whether it is good for people or not is irrelevant."

In 2009, Dr. David Nutt was controversially dismissed from his position as the chair of the Advisory Council on the Misuse of Drugs by then-Home Secretary Alan Johnson. His departure was followed by the resignation of several other senior members of the council, a body responsible for advising the British government on drug policy and legislation. In January 2010, Dr. Nutt launched the Independent Scientific Committee on Drugs, of which he is still the chair. Dr. Nutt is a Fellow of the Royal College of Physicians, the Royal College of Psychiatrists and the Academy of Medical Sciences; he is also the president of the British Neuroscience Association and vice-president of the European Brain Council.

When I began thinking about who I wanted to meet for this book, David was one of the first people that came to mind. I knew of his work from the media hubbub surrounding his statements on the relative harms of drugs and his subsequent abrupt dismissal by Alan Johnson, who was quoted as saying:

"He was asked to go because he cannot be both a government adviser and a campaigner against government policy."

190

I emailed David with the details of this book and my request for an interview. I received a one-word reply: "Delighted." We meet at the Chelsea & Westminster Hospital where David still sees patients regularly. He has a gentle handshake and a well-trimmed moustache. We walk the halls of the hospital looking for a quiet corner in which to talk. Unlike some other public figures I have met, he does not begrudge the conditions I require, nor does he seem rushed. We settle on a metal bench in the atrium of the hospital. As we talk, I am struck by a pragmatic humanity in his answers. He is not a starry-eyed idealist, but rather what I would like to think of as a proper scientist. He has not chosen a bias and then shored it up with selected facts - he has followed the evidence with a zeal that has frequently caused problems for him when profession and politics collided. He is generous with his time; he speaks unhurriedly and answers fully. Only at the end of our conversation do I find out that there is a taxi en route to take him to the BBC for another interview immediately afterwards.

At the end of our chat, I leave him outside on the pavement, patiently waiting for his cab.

Mike Freedman: Could you explain the role you played in government until 2009 and what you have been up to since? Maybe also a capsule background of neuropsychopharmacology?

David Nutt: Neuropsychopharmacology is the study of drugs as they affect the nervous system and the psyche. I am a psychiatrist. I am very interested in what drugs tell us about what might be wrong in disorders like schizophrenia, anxiety and addiction. Drugs are used to treat those disorders and therefore they presumably work on parts of the processes which are abnormal in those disorders. Of course, in the case of addiction, drugs are those disorders.

That is my field, that is my speciality: what drugs do in the brain. For that reason about twelve years ago I was brought into the government's advisory council on the misuse of drugs to take over as chair of what is known as the technical committee, the scientific committee looking at drug harms.

It became quite clear to me that the decision-making in relation to the Misuse of Drugs Act, which is the act which controls drugs in the UK but also determines the penalties for possession and supply, was less than ideal in the sense that there was no standardised template for assessing drug harms. In fact it was a sort of gestalt, amorphous decision-making process which I thought, as a scientist, was not very satisfactory.

So I developed a nine-point scale of drug harms. Three points relating to the damage drugs do to people, three points relating to addictiveness and three points relating to the social harms. I made everyone on the committee and quite a few people within government systematically work through a whole number of controlled drugs to see whether in fact their classification was justified by the evidence of harm.

That was a very interesting experience because it showed that you could do it. Also, it turned out that some drugs were in the wrong class. Drugs like mushrooms, LSD and ecstasy were Class A when in fact they were of lesser harm than some drugs in Class C. So it showed that the measures of drugs were wrong.

We had for a long time suspected that but we had not done a proper systematic assessment of many drugs. We did twenty drugs. That produced quite a lot of interest in the media. It was published in The Lancet.[1] It got a lot of discussion going and also created quite a bit of controversy because one of the things we did, which up until then government advisors had not really been allowed to do, was we put alcohol and tobacco in.

We thought that was absolutely critical because those provided yardsticks. So if something was more harmful than alcohol people would at least have a sense of what the harms were because they knew the harms of alcohol.

MF: It would also give a sense of proportion to the other drugs because you are putting it next to something that is considered socially and morally acceptable and legal.

DN: Absolutely. By and large many politicians do not like you doing that because there is a huge, strong alcohol and tobacco lobby. They would prefer them not to be drugs but foodstuffs or leisure activities.

We did it and we found to our surprise that alcohol came out as number five and tobacco came out as number ten. What was fascinating about that was that some people got very irate that tobacco was not number one because it kills more people than other drugs, but it is not number one because it tends just to kill the users and not other people, except for passive smoking. Alcohol scores higher because alcohol tends to kill other people: people get driven over by drunk drivers, they get beaten up by people who are drunk.

So, there were some people who thought we had got it wrong that way. There were other people who thought we got it wrong because how could alcohol ever be the fifth most harmful drug -

MF: Because gran likes her gin and that is not dangerous.

DN: Absolutely, because everyone drinks and if that was dangerous surely government would not let us drink a dangerous drug. So that was the beginning of that, but then people began to criticise the process. They said 'OK, nine points, well that is kind of arbitrary, that is just Nutt picking out from his experience what he thinks is appropriate, it is not good enough' and I agree. I did not think it was good enough.

I then went and, working with the Home Office, I developed a sixteen-point scale. That was from the bottom up. We had a conference, a whole weekend, we took forty experts and we said 'What are the harms of drugs?' Write on post-its every conceivable harm and there are hundreds of harms of drugs. Then you cluster them and it ended up there were sixteen clusters. Nine harms relate to the person and seven harms relate to society. Those harms to society, one of them is international damage, the wiping out of the Colombian rainforest by cocaine producers[2] or the Afghan War etcetera. Then there are harms like social damage to families, hospital costs. Seven harms to society.

The harms to the individual range from losing your job to dying when you take a heroin overdose, all systematised, standardised parameters defined in terms of how to assess it. Then we did it. Of course one of the challenges of doing that is you cannot compare dying on a drug, which is the harm to the individual, to what effect the drug has on the economy of Afghanistan[3] - those are completely different parameters.

MF: One is a human life, one is also human lives but more macro.

DN: Exactly. So the way you deal with these concepts that are in very different dimensions is to use a process called Multi Criteria Decision Analysis (MCDA). We worked with an expert from the London School of Economics, Larry Phillips, to do this. In fact he brought it to us. He wrote to me after we published the first Lancet paper saying 'This is fascinating but you could do it better. Use this technique, MCDA.'

We got funding and we did it through this new committee I set up, the Independent Scientific Committee on Drugs.[4] We funded the proper study and that was remarkable because from that very systematic analysis using this top-of-the-range technology, it turned out that actually alcohol was the most harmful. I have to say it was a bit of a surprise to us all but when you look into it the reason alcohol is the most harmful is because the social harms are so enormous.

The way MCDA works is that you can weight. The group weights the sixteen variables and ranks them according to which they think is most important. We rated the economic cost of drugs as the top and then we scaled everything to that. The economic costs of alcohol, it turned out, were enormous. It costs the UK economy about £30 billion a year.

MF: You mean spending on alcohol or you mean the cost of healthcare for people?

DN: In this country it is £3 billion healthcare costs, £6 billion policing, it is £12 billion from opportunity losses from people just not turning up to work.[5] But of course other groups could come up with a very different weighting. Some people might say the most important thing is that people should not die suddenly and they could rank drugs according to that. That could be their most important variable and others could be scaled down.

Other people might not care about the drugs' effects, just about what damage we are doing to international relations. So different groups could rate and weight these parameters differently and that is the power of this technique. People can use our data. We have scaled the harms of drugs in each of those dimensions and that is pretty incontrovertible. If you look at it, it is obvious that heroin is more likely to kill you by overdose than alcohol or mushrooms. Those scalings are generally accepted but the weightings can be done by anyone. It will be fascinating to see how other countries, people from other groups, schoolchildren, politicians, look at it. There are all sorts of interesting groups you could get.

MF: In society, like you said, you have a whole wealth of angles from which to assess the impact of drugs, the necessity for drugs or for their prohibition and what the right policies should be.

What is quite striking is that drug prohibition as a widespread and fairly draconian habit of the state is really fairly new. The UN conventions took place I believe in 1961, 1971,[6] Misuse of Drugs Act here in the UK was '71. So we are talking about something that is between forty to fifty years old in terms of the idea that drug prohibition as a blanket measure is the way to go.

DN: Well, I think historically prohibitionism, the concept of prohibiting drugs, has been around for longer than that. The concept of an international agreement prohibiting drugs definitely comes from the Hague conventions in 1912.[7] The idea that you might have prohibition of lots of drugs, that is a relatively new concept.

Up until that point, prohibition was religiously driven, like Muslim prohibition of alcohol, they tried to ban tobacco but they failed, cannabis they did.

MF: Like the Ladies Temperance Leagues in America.[8]

DN: That is true. I guess a lot of the drive to regulate drugs has come from a religious perspective. You have got to separate because the religious perspective from Islam is something different, it is not particularly a moral perspective but really a directive from the leader, whereas the Temperance Leagues were more moral: they do not believe that alcohol is evil as I presume they use it in their communions, but they believe the widespread use of it is immoral. So there are slightly different drivers but they were largely about individual drugs.

I suppose gradually there was an accumulation of concerns about different drugs and then the idea of a convention which bans everything became kind of appealing. I guess it sort of emerged after the Second World War with the sense that the United Nations was changing the world, let us change the world of drugs as well.

I think it is important to look at the history of drug prohibition in the USA, which really took a particularly evangelical approach in the 1930s. Alcohol prohibition was clearly an enormous problem in the USA, leading to a vast amount of crime and that led to a vast number of anti-crime enforcers.

When prohibition was repealed, that vast army of enforcers were going to be made unemployed. It was the Depression and the guy that ran them, Harry Anslinger, was a man that liked running his own private army in America. I think he concocted a fear of cannabis in order to justify keeping the enforcers together. Since then, all drug prohibition has to some extent been driven by this desire by the enforcers to continually justify getting funding.

MF: It occurs to me that there is a structural parallel with what some people see in the spread of anti-terrorism legislation. There is an increasing encroachment on civil liberties for the purpose of the 'war on terror' and one could argue that once the war on terror is no longer required, all of that armature of the state will need to be turned to some kind of purpose because they do not want to just scrap it.

The Department of Homeland Security is not going to say 'OK, we won, let's go home.'

DN: That is a very chilling thought. I have not had that thought. I would certainly agree with you that the vast increase in defensive protection against terrorism is driven by a similar kind of emotive fear generation that underpins a lot of the drug laws but the idea that it might actually turn inward, that is a very chilling thought. Thanks for that.

MF: Not just with politicians but with the enforcers who advise politicians, the idea is that power, like a gas, expands to fill the space provided. Power wants more power.

Another facet to that is this contradiction. On one hand the media, politicians and law enforcement have acclimatised people to the idea that drugs are dangerous and need to be controlled by the state, but then on the other hand whenever there is a survey or some kind of scientific basis to argue that drugs actually are not harmful and do not need to be state-controlled, the political excuse is 'people want it controlled.'

DN: Yes, and that analysis is quite correct. Certainly in the UK we know that, in relation to drugs that people know like cannabis, the majority of people do not want penalties. In fact half of the British public would prefer cannabis to be legal.[9]

Politicians do not go along with that part of the public because they think those are the people who do not vote. The last Labour government pursued a very hostile, anti-cannabis policy largely because it thought it would help them win the election, which it did not.[10] They actually flew in the face of good evidence that the public were discomforted by the way they were criminalising young people for using cannabis and it may have backfired in terms of the election.

I agree with you. Perhaps the biggest issue here is that the media see drugs as an entertainment. When a new drug comes along it is kind of a badge of honour to get it banned. Certain newspapers see this as a very good source of news. They effectively promote the drug by making a lot of headlines about it which increases use enormously. They generate the problem, if there is a problem in terms of harm with use, and then of course they force a solution on the government which is almost always banning because governments do not have the sophistication, competence, nous or courage to do anything else. It becomes a completely self-fulfilling little cycle and we have seen it happen in this country, in my lifetime with psychedelics in the 60s, MDMA in the 70s and 80s, mephedrone in the last few years.

It is a cycle. They are saying the same things now about mephedrone that they were saying about cocaine about a hundred years ago: evil drug killing our young people. Banning them has never solved anything as far as I can see.

MF: People will find a way, right? Prohibition did not work for alcohol.

DN: It is funny you say that. You say to people:

197

"Do you agree with prohibition for alcohol?"
"No, it was terrible," they say.
"So why are you doing the same with all the other drugs?"
"That's different."

MF: We know prohibition of alcohol caused the institutionalisation of organised crime. We know it made a whole bunch of very violent, unsavoury characters very wealthy and the exact same thing is happening now but "oh, it's different."

DN: There are a lot of things politicians can hide behind. You just talked about hiding behind so-called "public opinion", the right-wing press "public opinion" which is not all of the public. Also, they hide behind conventions:
"Oh, we cannot do anything, our hands are tied by the UN conventions."
Which is of course completely false because in the UN convention, signatories simply have agreed not to make drugs freely available, legal. There are lots of ways you can control drugs without making them legal.

MF: That is why there is that distinction of "decriminalisation" not being the same as "legal" in order to circumvent the conventions.

DN: Absolutely. The Dutch showed it categorically. They decriminalised cannabis use, set up cafes, for very good reasons. They wanted to essentially separate the hard drug market and the cannabis market. It worked.

MF: Don't they have the lowest per capita marijuana use in Europe?[11]

DN: Paradoxically yes, they also have less use. That is of course another argument. There is not so much incentive for people to see drugs if you can get drugs. The illicit drug market is a very cruel market. It wants to get people addicted because addicts provide the best, most reliable source of income. So the Dutch have a completely rational approach, fully within the UN conventions, and there is no reason why any other country in the world should not follow suit.

MF: You don't see guys in trench coats on street corners flogging a half of shandy.

DN: That's right, you do not.

MF: Another aspect of prohibition is a weird disproportionality weighted against a particular class of drug that speaks to me of the possibility of some kind of deeper motivation or attitude, specifically the categorically hostile attitude to hallucinogens.
Native American rituals and language were outlawed in America when they were crushing their culture. Naturally occurring psychoactive substances are a huge part of indigenous culture.

DN: Almost every indigenous culture. Wherever you go in the world it is hard to find a culture which did not use hallucinogens.

MF: So you have this political way of crushing alternative cultures that have a different way of expressing themselves and of navigating and describing the world. At the same time you have this widespread usage of something which is naturally occurring and that we have also synthesised ourselves. You could argue that LSD is simply a synthetic version of mushrooms -

DN: Of course it is.

MF: So the concept that these drugs are consciousness-expanding, that they allow you a certain quality of experience or introspection, might itself be the thing that is threatening to power.

DN: I am sure that is true. I am old enough to remember Flower Power and Haight-Ashbury and I am sure the US government was absolutely terrified that American youth would en bloc take LSD and refuse to fight in Vietnam. That would have completely changed the whole way in which US society works, which is about building bigger and better bombs and planes.

MF: You see it with the reaction to the Occupy Movement now.

DN: Yeah. Government is about perpetuating their own structures for their own benefit and whether it is good for people or not is irrelevant. It is about the establishment maintaining its own control and hallucinogens do give people sight of something which is very different and politicians are terrified of that.

MF: Or even just the concept that it *could* be different, you know?

DN: It is a proven. It is not a concept, it is a fact. People know that there are different ways of viewing the world. That is very threatening to many politicians because politics is about continuing the authoritative power structure you are currently in. There are not many politicians voting to get rid of politics.

MF: So this also then points to an interesting paradox within the logic of decriminalising and normalising the presence of drugs in society. You have Aldous Huxley's 'Brave New World' concept of a world where soma is used to medicate dissent and nonconformity -

DN: We have that now. It is called alcohol. Alcohol is soma. I have thought a lot about this. What is the best drug equivalent of soma? It is alcohol. People in this world have boring, tedious jobs and alcohol is the way they escape and they are in that cycle.

MF: So on the one hand a saner, more open-minded drug policy would allow for wider availability and more science-based analysis of what drugs are safe for whom in what context, but at the same time you do not want a situation where you have predatory medication, where a certain echelon of society is kept down by the fact that they are drugged.
There is a qualitative question of social good here that cannot simply be ignored. It needs to be faced head-on. You want freedom, but the tendency in the societies we have is for power structures to use the means they have at their disposal to perpetuate their own power and prevent challenges to that power. A tremendous swathe of the population experimenting with psychoactive consciousness-expanding drugs, exploring alternate ways of living, loving, feeling and communicating, this is not conducive to the type of throughput we are told that society is really about. There is the possibility that you'll simply

200

have Marlboro selling joints instead of cigarettes. You see what I mean? The machinery can stay in place but just push a different drug.

DN: That is of course true. One of the reasons I get attacked quite systematically by certain political opinion-makers is because they are scared the pharmaceutical industry will take over the selling of the mind-changing drugs rather than medicines and, because they have a very powerful and effective sales system, that could actually increase the use of these drugs in society.

MF: That is the point about freedom of choice. Something that struck me when you were describing this fear of psychoactive substances - we also have something present in our culture which is not a substance but it is psychoactive: the narrative we are presented with by the combination of political authority and media. That is psychoactive. It changes the way people think. It changes the neural pathways that are used to process emotion. It alters the way people feel, the way they think they should feel, what they think is possible. That narrative itself is psychoactive. So rather than having a wholesale prohibition of psychoactive substances, we have a monopoly of a particular psychoactive, the narrative..

DN: Absolutely. Since US prohibition, no Western society has even contemplated a drug-free life. It is never really discussed. The most interesting example is Iran. When Ayatollah Khomeini came in, he started imposing this very rigid Islamic attitude towards alcohol. Up to that point Iran was quite relaxed. He banned alcohol and then what happened? Iran now has this enormous heroin problem.[12] They do not treat it, they deny it and now they have a huge AIDS problem.
There are very few governments that want to go down an alcohol prohibition route. What we need to do is be very open to the benefits of other drugs reducing the harms of alcohol. I personally think if cannabis was available, in the Dutch way, in the UK, alcohol consumption would go down significantly. A significant proportion of people who now rely on alcohol as their intoxicant would prefer to go and smoke cannabis. That would reduce violence, liver disease and so forth significantly.

MF: Also, there is no way you can argue that people will drive stoned. We do not allow people to drive drunk now, so you can simply have testing for drugs rather than alcohol in police traffic stops. So the idea that legalising drugs is a threat to everyday life, well alcohol is exactly the same.

DN: Precisely. Probably more dangerous because it increases impulsivity, whereas cannabis probably decreases it. Some data came out from Colorado last year looking at changes in road traffic accidents since they had medical marijuana and there has been a fall in deaths on the roads because less people are drunk. Less drunks, less deaths.[13]

MF: Speaking about alcohol and other drugs, there is a correlation between addiction and depression. Eugene Marais called habitual drug use "a universal remedy for the pain of consciousness."[14]

DN: That is very true. I have come out of my clinic today and I have seen individuals fully congruent with that statement.

MF: We are not curing depression by legally penalising addiction. So it seems that society would be better off being geared towards curing the things that lead people towards habitual usage.

DN: I totally agree, and there are so many examples. A quarter of all young male alcoholics have social anxiety disorder. They drink because it is the only way they can get the courage and confidence to engage in social activities like parties. They are disabled by it, they become alcoholics and they lose their lives as a consequence. There are remedial solutions, treatments for social anxiety disorder.
Another really good example is the use of stimulants for ADHD. A lot of people use stimulants because they have ADHD and they function better on stimulants. They do not get diagnosed, they get arrested for stimulant use, they get put in prison. About 25 percent of all prisoners in the UK have ADHD.[15] It is absurd. We should be treating them, not punishing them.

MF: A phrase that you have used that I am quite fond of is that "a war on drugs means a society at war with itself". What I would like you to do, if you could, would be to cast an eye down the road. Over the next twenty, thirty, forty years, give me a picture of what the future looks like on the path where society continues being at war with itself, ignoring science as it applies to drug policy, and then what a sane drug policy would look like.

DN: If we carry on doing what we are doing at present, we end up in the UK with a cost of alcohol-related health harm that we cannot sustain. If we do it in the USA you end up with so many people in prison that you cannot afford to run anything other than prisons.

So the economic costs of doing what we are currently doing will eventually destroy societies like ours and the US. That does not mean we will not do it - humanity is quite capable of being stupid. A rational policy would be to say "OK, let's work out a policy that will minimise harms, social costs and facilitate the value of drugs". Drugs like MDMA were used for psychotherapy before they were banned. Drugs like psilocybin are being researched as possible treatments for depression.

So let us look at drugs in the round. Let us look at the good side, the bad side and let us just have a rational policy that will involve regulation of some sort that minimises the harms and maximises the benefits.

I do not suppose it will happen in my lifetime, but we could be using science to replace alcohol with a safer alternative that would be reversible, so you could take an antidote after a party and drive home sober. That is within the bounds of modern science. The reason it is not happening now is because very few scientists have got the courage to say what I say and no companies have got the courage to take the risk of manufacturing it because they are terrified that it would be called a drug and therefore banned.

So we are currently limiting ourselves to this cesspit of alcohol poisoning because we will not rise to the challenge of using science to improve our lot. I would hope in fifty years that would change. Maybe in China or India they might just move on and do it and then the rest of the world will follow suit.

MF: Ironically, with so much rhetoric bandied around about "innovation", "progress", technology and so on, we are actually standing on the neck of a lot of real, tangible improvements.

DN: We certainly are. Alcohol, I have just given you that example. I could, scientists could make safer versions of MDMA which could be useful therapeutically but companies will not do it because they are scared that the government will ban the

203

drug.

In the USA even these theoretical drugs are banned under analogue legislation. So we are stopping innovation there, we are stopping innovation in psychedelics. Basically wherever the drug laws touch, innovation just withers.

MF: That has been the case for the past fifty years?

DN: Yes, it has been, largely. The whole mephedrone/naphyrone story is an interesting one because that was a scientific program designed with two targets. One was biological control of aphids on plants, which is why it is called 'plant food', and the other was trying to make drugs that were surrogates for cocaine. Both those targets have now essentially ceased because of the banning of mephedrone and naphyrone.

Every time we start to move into an area where there is possible real benefit, the hysteria about possible harms trumps any sensible decision-making and then everything stops and companies no longer work in those fields.

MF: Can I leave you with a parting thought?

DN: Yes.

MF: Arthur Janov,[16] when he wrote about primal therapy, talked about the idea that there was a kind of 'base load' of pain that people absorb as they are growing up and then it expresses itself as neurosis, pathology, and that one must treat the primal pain rather than treating the symptoms.

So when we look at habitual drug use, addictive and self-destructive behaviour, depressive cycles, these seem to bear out some of what Janov was talking about, this idea that underneath a lot of these surface issues you have this primal pain. Society itself seems to suffer from a primal dissonance. Politicians lie to our faces. At all times we are pulled in so many different directions that we get frustrated, bamboozled. Rushing through society so fast, senses of community and belonging diminish.

Every generation feels something essential is being lost or eroded and that it was better when they were younger. Every incoming generation thinks that they are being stepped on by the older people, so there is this consistent sensation of fighting one another, exactly the way you described it, a society at war with itself.

So I was wondering, from your position as an experienced

doctor treating these symptoms of pain, if you could leave us with a thought about that fundamental crux issue.

DN: In terms of primal pain, a lot of the people who end up having major life problems relating to drugs or depression have been traumatised as children. There is no doubt about that at all. We should be maximising the quality of life of children at all levels. When they are in utero we should be supporting mothers to have healthy kids. We should be protecting kids against abuse at all ages.

That would certainly have a significant impact on long-term problems. Also, I am sympathetic to this idea that there might be something deep-seated in individuals that has made them vulnerable. Some of our recent research suggests that people do get locked into mindsets. An abused child will always be a victim, will usually be self-blaming, because as a child you do not understand that the world is unjust, you think you are incompetent and evil. That mindset of negative thinking underplays a lot of long-term problems, from borderline personality to cutting, suicide attempts and depression.

One of the great hopes that I have is for powerful drugs like hallucinogens, like psilocybin. We know LSD, at least for a period, can switch off that mindset and give people a view of another world; it may mean we can actually get them back from those traumatic pathways and bring them into a better life. That really is something I am working very hard to do.

MF: They say ayahuasca[17] is the equivalent of twenty-five years of psychotherapy.

DN: Certainly plenty of people describe fundamental life-changing experiences on many drugs. People are self-medicating with these drugs and we should at the very least be decriminalising them, which is what we are currently trying to do.

MF: We should be guiding each other.

DN: Absolutely. Science should be guiding us, but most scientists either do not know or do not care or are too scared of public opprobrium. We will see.

Ecocities of the Future
with Richard Register

> *"The city is the largest thing human beings create. Why people in the climate change movement, why environmentalists are not saying yeah, redesign the city, it blows my mind."*

Richard was introduced to me by my friend and colleague Sharon Ede, the co-founder of the Post-Growth Institute and blogger at CruxCatalyst. Richard is the founder of Ecocity Builders and has dedicated the past four decades of his life to exploring the ways in which our urban living arrangements can be made friendlier to the environment and more bearable for humans. He was of particular interest to me during the making of Critical Mass because John B. Calhoun, the scientist at the heart of the film, had himself convened a loose affiliation of urban designers and architects called The Space Cadets to look into many of the same things.

I met Richard at his office in downtown Oakland on a sunny day. We talked for an hour and then he took me and my crew to look at one of his projects, the revival of a nearby creek into a community garden.

Richard has obviously put a lot of thought into his answers and he speaks in paragraphs rather than sentences. At times, I get glimpses of a younger Richard angry about Vietnam and the buttoned-down corporate horror of the Nixon administration. World War II, the Cold War, the arms race and the palpable sense of threat in which he must have grown up clearly formed him in a lot of ways, and in a sense we are talking not only about the present and future but also the past. Lessons that were never learnt or acted upon forty-odd years ago have cycled round and trapped us again, inviting us to do better this time. Within this greater cycle, Richard operates as both a weary observer of recurring inaction and a passionate advocate for a hopeful, more fulfilling future.

Mike Freedman: How does revamping a local design change things like consumption, driving patterns, behaviour?

Richard Register: A typical metropolitan area has a big downtown and everything spreads out from that to thousands and thousands of acres off in the distance. People commute half an hour, forty-five minutes one way going to work, then back again. That is an infrastructure that requires massive amounts of energy, pavement eliminating agricultural land etcetera.

If we were to change a city by ecological city design principles, we'd be moving towards more compact areas, taller buildings, much more "mixed use" so that people do not have to travel enormous distances. You would not be designing cities for automobiles and long distance paving and commutes. You would be designing cities so that you could walk around the corner and get many things done.

If you start doing that, we can well imagine cities that run on one-tenth of the energy of average American cities and that take up one-fifth of the landscape. If you just look at a European city with the same population, it runs on one-third the energy and one-third the land.

So what you have then if you start rearranging a city goes something like this:

The metropolitan area has city centres here and there within it, with a rolling back of sprawl development so you open up the creeks, you expand the community gardens, your parks get bigger, your streets get narrower. The downtown gets taller, your neighbourhood centres get taller, more people are accommodated. In the meantime, agriculture and nature is moving back in around these centres.

Little neighbourhoods become village centres in their own right. What used to be a district centre becomes a whole town in its own right. All of these entities would emerge from this miasma of sprawl - a core city with smaller satellite cities that are linked by transit and bicycles. The villages are actually producing food and living on the land and taking responsibility to bring back biodiversity into the landscape with riverfront restoration, ridge lines and creeks which are high biodiversity areas being cultivated instead of being ignored and paved over. So you make room for everything else.

It also defines what green jobs are. The green jobs idea now is entry level work that tends towards installing solar energy and building insulation, which is good - you want to conserve energy.

But if you start understanding that the whole built environment needs this redesign then you see that hey, the cafe around the corner employs a bunch of green workers. How so? Because they don't have to drive a car to get there. They just walk around the corner or take transit.

Suddenly you have this idea that the real green economy is based physically on what we actually build. A city layout determines what the energy systems are going to be, it determines the transportation systems that will actually work. If you try and put public transportation in the suburbs it is not going to work because everybody is so thinly scattered. The car is the only thing that can work there and the car infrastructure damages the entire environment.

So what you really need is to think through the economy - in all these core areas, the green jobs are the normal jobs. Simple as that. I mean, if you are an iron worker in the middle of the city and you are building housing close to jobs you are a green worker. If you are in a village, if you are in a neighbourhood centre and you have a big community garden that is getting bigger adjacent to or in a public park, you are doing a green job. You are growing food in that neighbourhood centre on its way to becoming a real village that produces food for the city, for the towns around it and for itself.

If you can reshape cities in this manner, you would ground the economy in something healthy. Most environmentalists say that we can make the city less damaging. Tune up what you have now, put smog devices on your car, have cars running on electricity. That is a little bit better maybe if the electricity source is not a bad one.

Tuning up what we have now is not the idea. What we really need to do is come up with a different concept of how to build that city. You can make cities so that they build soils. You have human waste, kitchen waste, yard waste, all these organics that you can put right back into the soil. You can design systems to do that.

You can design cities so that they reinforce biodiversity. Rooftop gardens with native plants that attract native birds. I even have a window box in my fourth floor apartment here in Oakland that attracts hummingbirds, butterflies and wasps with a few native plants. So you can run that big time and you can redesign cities so that they build soils, build biodiversity, take up one-fifth of the land and run on one-tenth of the energy.

The city is the largest thing human beings create. Why people in the climate change movement, why environmentalists are not saying yeah, redesign the city, it blows my mind. Climate change people only talk about 'if we invest here and there and if we throw a little bit more energy into the mix from solar, if we have incentives in place to use less carbon'.

The better your car, the worse the city. The more the rationale for continuing the sprawl: keep driving, keep paving and keep spreading the city out, demanding lots and lots of energy. The energy people say "we'll give you lots of energy but it is going to be solar now" - I like solar, but are you going to put solar in suburbia and encourage people to keep building suburbia?

China, Russia, Brazil and India are growing like crazy and their appetite for cars is encouraged by policy, the Word Bank and by their governments. I have been in China thirteen times in the last ten years and I can tell you that they are building for the automobile. The Russian government have just bought two and half million acres of land for low-density single family homes because they want to cultivate capitalistic values. They want more people to become homeowners and have more appetite for more production and keep that whole engine going that suburbia reinforces: consumption and competition with other consuming countries around the world.

So here you have the population of China, Russia, India, Brazil and that is only four countries that want cars. That is nine times as many people as in the entire United States. If people in the United States are catching onto, you know, let's save a little energy here and there, let's go renewable, well, it is a little bit but you have to think, this message has to get out there. The whole infrastructure has to change radically or we are in deep trouble.

America has been the model in the wrong direction. I was living in Los Angeles when it was the poster child city for cars, mobility, the lifestyle of surfers in the sun, but they had the worst smog in the world. When the wind was right the beaches were great but when the wind was wrong, which was most of the time, the beaches were horrendous in Los Angeles. When I was there, they fixed the car. They did not fix the city. They put a smog device on the car, they solved the local air pollution problem and they gave us climate change. The entire planet's atmosphere is different because all the cities in the world started following the model of the car city. We are changing the trajectory of all evolution on the planet by wrecking the climate system and we are doing that by way of our cars.

Why isn't this the number one item from first grade on up in the educational system that we have got to get our cities right? If

Los Angeles led the charge as the automobile city and the automobile city plays the role I think it does in damaging the whole evolutionary course of life on the planet and the climate system and circulation of the oceans, what the hell is going on here? Why can't scientists identify that as something to deal with? The whole system design of a city is one whole system I talk about constantly.

The built infrastructure of cities, town and villages is not enough. The sheer vast numbers of human beings has to be dealt with. Also, the diet-agricultural nexus which is very chemical, heavy on meats getting much worse in that way all over the planet, all at once. We have to deal with that. That takes immense amounts of land. The city take up immense amounts of land too, but agriculture is probably even larger in that regard. The built environment is pivotal in physically determining the entire economy and whether that economy destroys life on the planet or not. I have been doing this thirty five years and I have not been able to get the message across yet but the evidence is building up that this makes a whole lot of sense. We really do have to deal with these things.

MF: Is this something that requires top-down regulation? How much of it is a local issue? How much of it is demanding framework from our governments or best practice from our corporations as either citizens or consumers rather than as local community members?

RR: Top-down and bottom-up are sort of a false argument. Whole systems thinking says you need both. For example recently I was giving a talk in North Adams, Massachusetts and everybody was saying it has to be bottom-up: "We know what we want and what we want is a more ecologically healthy environment, we want to fix the river that runs through town." There are a couple of rivers that run through North Adams. So I say you do need some policy support sometimes, you need some money to get things done, government clearance to do certain things. In fact it was Fish & Wildlife or one of the higher governmental levels said you could not do that because it is not in the regulation. It went all the way up to Washington because if they wanted to do what they wanted to do locally they would be in violation of the procedures of the Army Corps of Engineers and a whole lot of other people.

So if you cannot actually instil the concept that we need to transform the city at all levels simultaneously you are going to find that everyone is at odds with one another. The insight that we need to radically transform the city from a car infrastructure to a human infrastructure is not there. You diddle around a little bit and the new urbanists say well, if we put a little more development around transit that is a transit-oriented development and that is a good deal. Well, it is a step in the right direction, but you have to go way beyond that. You have to subtract suburbia, build new cities, take old cities and transform them so they function like a new city. Anything short of that and we are headed for catastrophe.

MF: What made you want to do this? Why do you still do it after thirty-five years of waiting for the lightbulb to go on?

RR: I am now sixty-seven years old. I am unemployable at anything else so I keep doing it.

I grew up in Santa Fe, New Mexico across from Los Alamos and I knew people that were making hydrogen bombs. Literally. I had Thanksgiving dinner with these guys who were shaking their heads around the dinner table going "oh you know those generals are really nuts!" I said "What do you mean?" He goes "so twice a week I fly from Los Alamos in a light plane out to Livermore and land there and talk to people at Livermore Labs and instruct generals on the use of atomic bombs." And then he says "Those guys are really weird". I was only twelve or thirteen years old when I started hearing this. I started to think "man, this is a scary situation".

So I grew up in the era where you 'duck and cover' under your desk and pretend that would help you if an atomic bomb went off anywhere nearby. At the end of the runway in Albuquerque, New Mexico when I was in fourth, fifth and sixth grade, the B-36s would come in. Now this is a very peculiar airplane. Looks like a long aluminium cigar case with six pusher engines on the back of the wings and four great big jets hanging down from the front of the airplane, a gigantic airplane.

These things would fly in and I would get excited about these gigantic pieces of science fiction coming over and then when they set off atomic bombs in Nevada, the cloud would come over Alberquerque. So the day before our science teacher would say "look at this Geiger counter: click, click, click" and the next day he'd say "They set off an atomic bomb, now listen to the Geiger counter today children: RRRRRRRRRRRRRRRRRR".

So what I am saying is I grew up with this atomic bomb cloud in my mind, the force that human beings can release if they do

211

not use it sanely. Here we have these enormous forces we have unleashed on the planet. So when I start thinking about the city as this force we have unleashed on the planet which is doing the kind of damage that we hypothesised could happen with a nuclear war and we are actually doing it. It is like a slow-burn nuclear war going on.

I did not quite think of it like that at the time I first started getting interested in ecological cities but I had that background. Then I began to realise. I was a sculptor. I was twenty-one years old and I met an architect by the name of Paolo Soleri who said we need to redesign our cities in a very radical way. I liked three dimensions. I could make figures out of clay, metal and stone and really enjoyed it. I grew up in the mountains of New Mexico. I like being able to look out over landscapes, I like getting up high and looking around. It was just natural for me to start thinking about the sculptural city, the three-dimensional city instead of the flat two-dimensional city.

So all these components fit together and as the years went by I began to realise we really are destroying the planet with our city design. How would you design a city that would not destroy the planet? How would you design a city that would actually build biodiversity and increase soil fertility? It can be done but you have to strive to do it or it will not be done.

If you want to be a great pianist do you just dream about being a great pianist? No! You study piano. So if you want ecologically healthy cities the first thing you should do at the grassroots level all the way to the top level is study ecological cities. Try to figure what is going on here. Can we build a city that functions well on this planet? Set that as a major challenge. Almost nobody sets that as a major challenge but if they did we would solve problems galore.

MF: Is there a tipping point past which if we leave it too long we will not be able to find the equilibrium you are looking for?

RR: So many poisons in the system, the climate is changing so fast. Maybe the water is going to go up three feet because all of Greenland is going to melt and it is going to melt faster than we thought. You cannot count on that. It might actually be that that is going to happen to us but you cannot operate on these unknowns especially when you know you can make an enormous difference. I know we can make an enormous difference but also I know we cannot do it if we do not do things that make a whole lot of sense which we have not been doing.

212

We cannot know where we are in that so we have to do the best we can. It just gets down to that.

There are some places in the world where we may have an extraordinary opportunity to do something really city-changing and world-changing.

I went to Detroit two weeks ago and Detroit has tens of thousands of acres of deserted suburban sprawl. Blocks where there used to be thirty houses, there are now three or four of them or none at all in some cases. The open landscape is coming back to Detroit and they are facing something that has looked like a really major disaster for a long time in terms of the city shrinking and losing over half their population, lots of unemployment, but as they have been adjusting, nature is coming back in and people have started doing some really serious farming there.

When I went to Detroit, I was thinking of it as a place where because they are opening up the landscape they are actually thinking seriously about new farms in the city. They are also thinking that 'well, some centres still exist which are pretty good so we will link them up with transit.'

That is good stuff. Then I realised that Detroit saved the world for democracy once upon a time. They didn't really want to but Franklin Delano Roosevelt showed up and said you are going to stop producing cars and start producing airplanes, tanks, guns and bombs because we have a life-threatening situation here. This guy Adolf Hitler is a really nasty player and we have got to deal with him.

They said well, we can still make cars and planes but he said no, you stop making cars. So they stopped making cars in Detroit for almost two years and they won the war for democracy. Michigan is where enormous amounts of material went out from the United States. It was not the only place obviously but I think it is a very valid story that in Detroit they did something really fantastic in defending democracy in the world.

We are in a war right now. Humans versus the rest of the planet. You do not list individual deaths on the other side like the body counts in the Vietnam War, you list whole species as the body count. We eliminate all these species largely due to the way we build our cities. So Detroit could be the city to save the world for biology the way it was once the city that saved the world for democracy. Churchill came to the United States and said America is like a giant boiler. Light a fire under it and there is no limit to what it can produce. That boiler was Detroit. I

213

would look to places like Detroit, shrinking cities in various places that look like they may have problems, and say their problems might be an opening to changing the world in a really positive direction.

Luxury vs. Necessity: The Dilemma of Production
with Claus Conzelmann

"Population growth is something that is inherently positive for any manufacturing company, especially if you are in the food sector."

Like Robert Rapier, I met Claus Conzelmann at the Global Footprint Network's Footprint Forum in Siena, Italy. Among the attendees, Claus was one of only two representatives from the corporate sector. As the Vice-President of Safety, Health and Environmental Sustainability for Nestle, he arrived with baggage that many people were probably not able or willing to see past. Nestle is both the world's largest food and beverage company and also among the most infamous offenders when it comes to environmental impact and labour rights. A boycott of Nestle products has been running since 1977 because of their marketing of infant formula in Africa. Like all multinational corporations, the line of critics is almost as long as the line of shareholders.

However, I was keen to get from Claus the corporate perspective on our converging environmental and economic crises. I did not mention Nestle's past because my intention was to hear how Nestle intended (or claims to intend) to behave in the future. Also, it was clear that those types of questions would not be answered.

Claus is a nice guy with a difficult job. He shakes hands with me and my film crew with a ready smile and patiently waits to be wired for sound. He is impeccably Swiss, speaking with precision and not moving beyond his role as company representative. He obviously cares very deeply about environmental issues, and in him I see flashes of the predicament we're in – a well-intentioned man contributing what he can within a milieu deeply unresponsive to criticism or change. He could be the lone voter with a conscience just as easily as the employee nagging the board about sustainability.

In our conversation, and during the conference at which we met, I feel my heart go out to him even as I find myself left sceptical at best by many of his responses and talking points.

Mike Freedman: In your role, what relationship have you observed between population growth and consumption over the past twenty-five years?

Claus Conzelmann: Working for the world's largest food and nutrition company, population growth is something that naturally increases your customer and consumer pool. So population growth is something that is inherently positive for any manufacturing company, especially if you are in the food sector.

What we have seen over the last ten years is huge populations in the South East Asian countries have not only added population but also purchasing power, which for a consumer goods company makes it even more interesting because we do not only have more people but we also have more people who can afford to buy our products.

At the same time obviously we are seeing that natural resources are being depleted at a frightening rate and that the current growth model as we know it today is unsustainable. So going forward we will have to bring population growth together with the ways of feeding this population sustainably.

MF: How do you reconcile the positivity of population growth with regards to growth in consumer spending with the necessity of lessening your impact on the planet?

CC: For us population growth is a given. We have virtually no possibility to influence it. Basically as a company what you can ask yourself is if there is a 'given' out there, how do you serve that market in the best possible way?

Now traditionally we have been doing that by trying to develop a product that has the best taste and nutrition but increasingly we are also seeing that in addition to taste and nutrition, our corporate objective has to be to produce food at the lowest environmental footprint possible. That is our individual way of trying to address this issue.

Whether that will be enough, only the future will be able to tell, but definitely what we have seen in our area is that in addition to having the economies of scale - making food more affordable to more parts of the population by producing in large volume - we see at the same time the so-called 'ecology of scale'. An industrially pre-cooked or prepared food can actually have a lower environmental footprint than if you home-grow and home-cook it because home-cooking is one of the least energy

216

efficient ways of producing food with all the associated environmental issues. So we definitely believe that there is an opportunity for large scale operations both in farming and in food production to help lower the footprint of individual consumption.

MF: Can you just elaborate this idea that growing some tomatoes in your own garden and making your own pasta sauce at home is less efficient than industrial agri-production and having a massive canning plant? I have never heard that.

CC: Just consider preparing for yourself a plate of pasta and then compare it to preparing pasta for your friends and family, let's say making ten portions of pasta at the same time, just in your own kitchen. Then measure the energy needed just for yourself in one portion and for ten portions. Obviously you will see the specific energy needed is not ten times more by making ten plates of pasta. Our factories are essentially nothing else but a big industrial kitchen where we feed lots of people at one time.

Another associated element is waste in the supply chain. If we have got artisanal supply chains of milk for example, you have loss rates of up to 25% by ferrying some milk by donkey in some individual containers - parts get spilled, parts go off by the time it reaches the consumer. With our very highly optimised supply chains where we have chilling stations already at the farm and at various collection points, we were able to reduce the loss factor from 25% to below 2%.

The people that originally coined the term 'ecologies of scale' were looking at farming of lamb in Europe, Germany and UK versus importing lamb from New Zealand. Because the production systems in New Zealand are much more conducive, for example you do not need to additionally feed those animals in winter, even the transportation getting lamb to Europe is more than compensated by the more environmentally friendly or less environmentally impactful production methods on the other part of the planet.

MF: So for instance the milk example, factoring in running trucks to transport the milk from where it is being pasteurised to where it is being chilled to where it is being distributed down the supply chain, even adjusted for the loss, all of those emissions, all of that energy usage is lower than say having a cow in your backyard and feeding it and taking milk out of it?

CC: Well, if everyone had a cow in the backyard that probably still would be better because they would really have a shorter supply chain but now more than 50% of the world's population lives in urban centres so I think the idea of everyone having a cow in their backyard is probably not a very realistic one.

Somehow that milk has to be brought to these urban centres and if you do that on a small scale the losses are just such that having it in an organised, professional, industrial way, even so that you may use more energy for transportation overall if you compare by individual consumer unit it actually becomes quite favourable.

Let us take another example which is transportation. A few years ago at the early times of food miles, people were just looking at distances but if you transport something from Australia or New Zealand to Europe in big container ships where you have huge volumes transported, the individual energy use per unit of product is in fact far lower than transporting the same goods for 500km by a truck over land. That means it is not the distance as such but it is the efficiency by which you can actually transport and process. Similarly with packaging our basic philosophy has been to save more in terms of preventing product waste than it actually costs in terms of environmental burden. Now obviously there are still some excesses here and there of over-packaging but we have gone after that now for the last twenty years and we have reduced very significantly the amount of packaging used for our products, trying to optimise the ratio between the packaging and the content and we are continuously working further on that.

MF: There are a lot of people who would see your role as being at cross-purposes with the corporate model because you are there factoring in something that to a certain extent cannot be financially quantified. So if part of your role has been to find a way to financially quantify ecological impact that can be factored into the corporate model, I would be very interested to hear how you went about doing that. If your role is simply to make ecological concerns an issue in proposals and in the boardroom, how do you impact the multinational business way of producing and growing in your role as a steward of the land as it were? How do you reconcile your role, which is essentially charitable, with the business role?

CC: I take issue with that notion of charity. It is clear that we are against any charitable acts or philanthropy. What you or I do with our personal money, if we put it into a charitable trust, perfect. But I do not think that any company should waste shareholder funds for charitable acts. Which means everything a company does needs to be associated with a business purpose.

In Milton Friedman's times the saying was 'the business of business is business'. I essentially believe that is still true, but rather than having that kind of contrast between short-term shareholder interests and societal interests, we must actually look at this whole equation from a longer term perspective. Then we are absolutely convinced that anything a company does can only be in the shareholder interest as long as it at the same time is also in society's interest for the long term.

Now, Nestle this year is 144 years old. We are trying to manage the company in a way that another 144 years from today it will still be a very successful company. That you can only do if you look at these societal and environmental constraints that are there. I don't want to pretend that we have found all the answers but that is at least the mindset from which we are addressing the issue. We are not cutting corners, not sacrificing the long term development of our company for any short term gains or profit maximisation.

In addition to this being the fundamental business principle of how Nestle is run, we have focused on three areas in particular: nutrition, rural development and water.

MF: It is interesting you brought up water. What do you see as the world water crisis? How has Nestle reduced its impact on that?

CC: When a lot of people were still focusing on climate change and global warming as the defining issue of the 21st century, Nestle was amongst the first to point towards this other inconvenient truth which is the world's water crisis or 'global drying' as we would like to put it. In addition to that water cycle where we have got rainfall and water sources being replenished there is also a huge amount of fossil water that has been deposited underground over thousands and millions of years, very similar to oil. Once that water is pumped out, it is gone. It is no longer available.

In many parts of the world, not only in China, India or the Middle East but even in the United States, a large part of agriculture is basically fed by these underground water

219

resources that are overexploited at a rate ten, twenty, thirty times more than the natural rate of replenishment. That is really what feeds the world food system at the moment but once that water is gone, like oil, that will mean big problems for agriculture. Climate change will further aggravate all these issues - some parts of the world will have more water when they do not need it but many parts like the Mediterranean basin will not have enough water to feed their agriculture.

MF: How has Nestle contributed to reducing their impact on the water table?

CC: Obviously before you engage in a public policy debate you first put your own house in order which is what Nestle has already done for many years if not decades. Our initial focus was to make sure that all the water we are using in our factories, about 450 factories around the world, we return clean to the environment.

We have been pioneering waste water treatment. In fact in 1929 Nestle was the first industrial entity, the first company to build a waste water treatment plant. Whenever we expanded into other parts in the world even when there was no legal requirements or weaker legal requirements, we put in place a waste water treatment plant and exported our high Swiss or European standards, thereby very often also creating a kind of peer pressure on other companies - politicians come to our factories bringing competitors of ours and say "if Nestle can build a waste water treatment plant here we are expecting it from you as well".

We also in the last fifteen to twenty years had a strong focus on actually reducing our water requirements. We are now using less than 3.5 litres of water to produce one kilo of final product, down more than fifty percent from over 8 litres nineteen years ago.

We are certainly committed to do even more on that but these three to four litres of water we use per kilo of product in our own factories is a drop in the bucket compared to the use of water in agriculture. More than 70% of the world's freshwater resources are used in agriculture where a lot is wasted. It takes about 3000 litres of water on average to produce one kilo of raw materials for us. Simply focusing on our own installations would not solve the issues. We have agricultural advisors in many parts of the world that we employed to help farmers improve their raw material quality, which obviously makes life easier for us in our factories, again nothing to do with charity or philanthropy, it is a clear business purpose to help get us raw materials. We are leveraging this network of agricultural advisors to teach farmers to use water more sustainably, for example by drip irrigation. In Italy we have got a collaboration with some tomato growers that have in this pilot study been able to significantly reduce the amount of water that is necessary.

Then the last part is almost certainly public policy. As the world's leading food, health, nutrition and wellness company we also have an interest that the public policy debate goes in the right direction and we have contributed for example at the World Economic Forum in Davos to this topic. We have also helped to create the United Nations Global Compact and Water Mandate and many other initiatives to highlight the importance of water scarcity but also to highlight the opportunities to address them because solutions clearly are there. We just have to all be determined and work together to realise them over the next ten to twenty years.

MF: Discussing the intensity of farming and the depletion of the water table and also the amount of water it takes to produce raw materials, you said earlier that population growth is a bonus because the more consumers there are the more consumption, the more consumption the more product you sell. It is a very simple equation.

But how do you reconcile the importance of more consumers for a business with the fact that the same consumers that allow Nestle or any other company to sell more product to more people demand the basic conditions that need intense agricultural production and are depleting the water table? How do you reconcile the need that a business has to reach customers and to have more customers year on year for more profit year on year with the fact that resource depletion and overconsumption are linked to the very population that you are serving?

CC: I think what you are describing here is the defining dilemma of the 21st century. On the one hand, on an individual company basis there has to be growth. Any company that stops growing starts dying. On the other hand by expanding ever further we are kind of chopping off the branch on which we are sitting. How to reconcile that on a global level, well I think that really is a defining societal challenge going forward.

Now what can an individual company contribute to that? It is not so much the question of having more consumers, it is how efficiently those consumer needs are being addressed and satisfied. There is an enormous amount of waste still in the food system. Going back to the example of water: in India there are about 20 million motorised water wells now where people get the energy for free so there is absolutely no incentive of using water more efficiently.

So there needs to be first and foremost regulatory frameworks developed by governments to actually make sure that natural resources are not being wasted. Obviously you cannot make farmers in India from one day to the next pay the full price without any sort of accompanying social measures otherwise you will get riots all over the world. So this more appropriate costing of natural resources has to be accompanied by appropriate flanking social measures.

One example which we believe is quite interesting is South Africa. There, based on the insight that water is a basic human right, your first twenty or twenty-five litres per person per day which you need for drinking purposes and sanitation should be free for those who cannot afford to pay. But at the same time water should be a commercial good that is traded because it is not a human right to fill up your swimming pools.

So we have got in many cases public water distribution systems that are subsidised by the broad population where in fact those water systems do not reach the poor and the richest part of the population are getting subsidised. So there we really have to work on some pricing models. South Africa to my knowledge is the first country that provides everyone with the first twenty to twenty-five litres for free whereas those people who can afford to pay for water cross-subsidise the water to the poor.

These are the kind of models where individual companies can certainly lead but where we need legal and regulatory frameworks from government and international organisations in order to make sure these scarce resources are not wasted.

In an example from the Mediterranean basin, farmers in the south of Spain, which is a very water scarce area, only pay about 7% of the true cost of the water for their agriculture. These are the wrong price signals and we will need to correct these if we want to have a chance to feed current or increased world population sustainably.

MF: You made a very interesting distinction between

necessity and luxury. I happen to agree that there is a difference between someone having enough drinking water and washing water for a day versus a guy washing his car, watering his lawn and filling up his swimming pool.

However, drawing the distinction between necessity and luxury, if population growth continues apace, when we do get to the point where there are nine or ten billion people by 2050, do you think that we may find ourselves in a position where Nestle may be told that they cannot produce chocolate bars anymore because people do not need chocolate the way that they need tomatoes, bread and fresh fruit. Maybe there will be a difference between necessity and luxury not just in raw materials but also in products. For instance you could argue that if we get to a point where we have an extra two billion people, the easiest way to provide them with fresh water is not to charge small farmers in developing countries as much as it is to close large industrial plants using large quantities of fresh water to make products that only a percentage of the world's population can even afford, let alone want?

So, how would you define the battle, the balance between necessity and luxury in the context of your business in the future?

CC: Again, you are pointing there to a very challenging question where we believe that it is the price signals that really will have to trigger the right behaviours. Then it will be again up to companies that will use those price signals to develop the products that go in the right direction.

Yes, Nestle is certainly engaged in the super-premium segment with brands like Nespresso where we cater to the well-off part of the population but very deliberately a number of years ago, we also initiated a second strategic pillar which we call the 'Popularly Positioned Products' where we are very specifically trying to cater for the base of the pyramid. C.K. Prahalad, who unfortunately recently passed away, was really one of the big thinkers about this base of the pyramid. We had him on our Creating Shared Value advisory board until very recently and due to discussions with him a lot of these strategies were informed.

So I do not think it is up to individual companies to really decide what direction to go as long as there is a market economy that factors in the appropriate scarcity signals of resources in the price and in the end also in the portfolio. We have been seeing that also in the area of nutrition where over the past fifteen to twenty years there was a very similar discussion as to whether food that was deemed unhealthy should be specially taxed. How we responded to that challenge was to develop products with an inherently superior nutritional value in whatever category there is and in whatever category there is a market for.

We are building on that with what we call 60/40+, meaning every new product has to be preferred from a taste perspective of at least 60% of the consumers but at the same time has to have a nutritional advantage. We also see that every product needs to have an environmental advantage or have a lower environmental impact compared to products in a comparable product category. We believe that is really the way competition between different companies will drive towards a better environmental performance going forward.

MF: The way you discuss it, it seems the profit and growth motives are not at cross-purposes with ecological concerns but necessary to help drive innovation, so sell it to me. How can capitalism in the broadest sense of the word be the cure for overconsumption and overpopulation when it seems to be a driver of overconsumption and creating the life circumstances of overpopulation with lower mortality and higher standards of living? How can capitalism be the cure if that is the underlying logic of what you have been telling me?

CC: Well I am not sure if it is the cure but certainly a market economy, if it is within an appropriate framework where resources are allocated in the best possible way and not distorted like in agri-fuels for example with wrong subsidies, is the most efficient way. So it is not up to individual companies to decide what these frameworks are. Let us allow the market to allocate the resources most efficiently.

Now, whether that will be enough going forward in this century, well, that is not up to us to decide. It may well not be enough. We may well need to have a more sustainable consumption pattern as well as a more sustainable production pattern. Where we can influence that is clearly on the production side to make sure that whatever is being sought after by the consumer is being done with the lowest possible environmental footprint.

We would even go so far as to say we have a certain role to play to communicate with our consumers and give them the information and the transparency to make well-informed choices. Carbon footprints are now popping up on some products in some parts of the world. We believe that carbon footprint is probably too narrow an environmental measurement because something can be good for climate change but it may have negative impacts on water. I believe we need to develop more appropriate tools of communicating the environmental footprints of our products but we are clearly at the leading edge of contributing to these kind of discussions.

For example at the European level there is the European Roundtable on Sustainable Consumption and Production[1] which we are co-leading with a member of the European Commission. We are trying to find on one hand the metrics to actually determine what product has a lower environmental footprint to another one but at the same time to find out an appropriate way of communicating and engaging with consumers in a way that is not just simple brainwashing or where claims are made that cannot be substantiated. By having that engagement with consumers we believe certainly also that we can to a certain extent drive the consumer to make more sustainable choices.

Another element is the product portfolio. We have given up certain parts of our portfolio from a nutritional point of view because it did not fit any longer in the offering of the leading nutrition, health and wellness company. I think there are also some companies that are better prepared than others to face those challenges based on the type of products they are selling. You mentioned chocolate before. I doubt that chocolate is necessarily a product that has a significantly high footprint. I think the much more defining problem is meat consumption. Meat, especially if you are talking about beef, has about a ten times higher footprint because in the first place you need to grow the feed in order to feed the cattle and thereby you have huge losses in the system. So I would not be so comfortable working for a company that is exclusively in the beef business, whereas a company like Nestle is developing a lot of vegetarian alternatives based on soy, corn and maize that give you the same taste of meat with a better nutritional profile and at the same time a much better environmental profile. These are the kinds of things a company can do to contribute to a more sustainable consumption panel over time.

MF: Sum up for me what relationship there is between population and consumption and how you see available resources and population having an impact on the world going forward from here.

CC: I think that the jury is honestly still out on whether it is possible to feed nine billion people with a consumption style based on the Western model today, even with all the big efficiencies that are to be gained. Fifty percent of the world's food is still wasted. If we cut down further on that waste I think larger populations can be fed more appropriately than today based on the current resources but what exactly a sustainable balance will be only the future will be able to tell.

That is the defining question of the 21st century, to figure out what the optimal population size for the world actually is, how to get there and how to do that in the most sustainable way possible.

Better, Not Bigger
with Peter Victor

*"Economic growth has been a very unusual
episode in human history. Only ten generations
of humans have known it out of a hundred
thousand-plus generations of people."*

Peter Victor is Professor of Environmental Studies at York
University in Toronto and a member of the Advisory Council of
the Royal Canadian Institute for the Advancement of Science of
which he was President from 2000 to 2004. He is also the
author of "Managing Without Growth". It is on the back of a
presentation he gave about the central premise of that book that
I contact him for an interview.

He agrees to meet me in the living room of his friend's
apartment at which he is staying in London on his way back to
Canada. He sits in an armchair and answers my questions with
a continuous half-smile, radiating a compassion and emotional
connection to his subject which never fades in the hour and a
bit that we spend together. We speak in hushed tones as the rest
of the household is still in bed.

As Peter concludes his final response, a well-timed doorbell
signals the end of our conversation and the start of the rest of his
day.

227

Mike Freedman: Could you sum up our current macroeconomic model?

Peter Victor: The standard way of thinking about an economy is that it somehow exists in isolation. It is the economy. How often do we hear that term? 'The Economy', as if it is something that is somehow separate from everything else. That is often the way economics is taught to students of economics, that it is a free-standing system involving at its most fundamental level firms who make things and sell them to households or individuals so that you get firms providing goods and services and people providing the money to buy them.

But where do the households get the money? Well, they are the ultimate owners of the land, the labour and the capital that the firms need in order to produce the goods and services. So the firms in this conception of the economy have to pay us, the households, for the use of the land, labour and capital. So you get this circular flow of income. That is the standard conception of the economy.

When you see an economy working in that way there is no reason why it cannot just do more of it. Why does it not just get bigger and bigger and bigger? That is the problem when you see an economy as a free-standing separate entity.

The first thing we know is that the economy is not really separate from society. Where do we get these tastes, preferences and ideas about what we want to achieve as people? It does not come just from the economy, it comes from all of society. When you are raised by a family you learn from your parents, you go to school. To say that it is all the economy is of course ridiculous. There are other important institutions, but as an ecological economist I do not just stop there.

I say that all of humanity is embedded in the biosphere so our society and within that our economy cannot operate unless it is continually bringing in materials and energy from the biosphere and creating waste. So the necessary way to understand the economy today is as something that is included within the biosphere because it has got to the stage where the economy is so large that it is making a measurable impact on the environment within which it is embedded.

So in a sense we are destroying our own home. That is the nature of our economic problem today that is sadly not fully appreciated by all those who should.

MF: Can you briefly summarise your idea of managing

228

without growth?

PV: My interest in managing without growth stems from a real concern that the kind of economy that we have, particularly in the Western world, can no longer be sustained by the capacity of nature to support it. So I have looked at the information and evidence to do with resources, the impact of the waste that we put out on the environment, the extent to which we occupy land and exclude other species. It can look pretty grim.
I think we can do a lot better and one of the clues to doing better is not to pursue economic growth in the way that we have for the last number of decades.

MF: What does modern economics really mean in terms of this demand for growth and consumption? The idea of growth is actually quite recent, isn't it?
PV: Let us first of all say what we mean by the economy. The economy is the part of society where we focus on the production of goods and services. Things that we buy in the shops or services we hire, all of these things go into economic growth.
Another aspect of economic growth is that we go to work. So we produce more and we consume more. We measure the economy by something called the gross domestic product (GDP) and what has happened over the last four to six decades is that governments have said "We have got to make this GDP grow more every year."
They think that without continual growth we will not be able to have full employment, pay our taxes or pay for all of the things that we want either as consumers or as taxpayers.
The question is whether this kind of growth can continue and if it cannot, what are the alternatives?

MF: If you have an ever-increasing number of people you need an ever-increasing number of goods and services to provide for them.

PV: Let me go back to the earliest stage of economics. Adam Smith[1] is sometimes referred to as the father of economics. His most famous book was 'The Wealth of Nations'. He was interested in how nations become wealthier and how Britain was emerging ahead of other nations and becoming richer. Then he was concerned about whether this could continue forever.

He and some other economists more known for their pessimism, such as Malthus[2] and even Ricardo,[3] were rather concerned that the growth process was very temporary. That was in the late eighteenth century and we have had two hundred-plus years of economic growth since then. So those early concerns that economic growth could not continue for a long time were overstated.

Having said that, although we have enjoyed growth for all of these years, the idea that government policy should be specifically devoted to the promotion of economic growth is much more recent. It only came into being maybe in the late 1950s and early 1960s when economists were convinced, with some reason, that unless you had growth you would have massive unemployment.

So the governments of a number of Western countries (US, Canada, UK, Australia) committed themselves to the pursuit of growth, first to deal with unemployment and then secondly in its own right. It became the primary objective of government economic policy.

Now we are in a situation where our economies have grown massively over that period which means we use far more resources, far more energy. We create more waste, we are having a bigger impact on the environment to such an extent that many of us are wondering if this can this continue. If it cannot, what are the alternatives?

MF: Growth is so intertwined with the way we have run our society and also people's perception of how our society remains functional; how do you sell the idea of managing without growth to people who are not ecologists or economists?

PV: Most of us, if you are my age or younger, have known nothing but economic growth and living in a society that says economic growth is so important. So we all sort of take it as normal.

The first thing to realise is it is not that normal. Economic growth has been a very unusual episode in human history. Only ten generations of humans have known it out of a hundred thousand-plus generations of people. So the idea that the kind of life you have will be very different from the life that your children will enjoy is a very novel idea. For most of human history people did not seem to think that. They did not experience rapid change.

230

So to persuade people to consider an alternative to growth, they need to understand that growth is not that normal. It is unusual.

The second thing is that there is some evidence now that once we have reached a certain level of material standard of living, getting richer does not make anybody any happier.[4] One of the main reasons for this is that once you have taken care of your basic needs and a bit more than that, what matters most to people is how they are doing compared to other people. So if everybody gets twice as rich, you are not doing any better in relation to everybody else.

So this concern that relative standing influences our well-being is teaching us that if that is the case then having everybody get richer is not going to make anybody feel better off. Beyond a level of income, roughly speaking twelve or fifteen thousand dollars per person per year, getting richer does not make you feel any better because your neighbour may have got richer as well.

Then you point to what we are doing to our environment which is definitely making us poorer in some fundamental ways. We are living in noisier, more polluted circumstances. We are concerned with destabilising the climate. It is a long list and it really is quite dispiriting but when you put all that together then you have to open your mind up to the possibility that we have to manage without growth. If you are not prepared to do that then you are going to find yourself having to manage without growth anyway but it is going to come as a very unpleasant shock.

Others have observed that humans evolved in circumstances that required us to be good at solving certain kinds of problems. Problems that were pretty immediate in terms of time and space, in other words local problems.

Now we are not in that situation anymore. We have problems which are global and we have problems which are long term. So we have to wonder if we are capable of dealing with those kinds of problems.

The answer to that has been for us to build institutions to work collectively in various ways whether that is through the private sector or through government so that our institutions are in a sense smarter than we are which means they can look further. They have corporate memory. They can think about the long term, they can think globally, they can bring in more information than we can as individuals.

Now here is the trouble: if you look around at how our

institutions are behaving at the moment, they are not behaving like that. They are becoming more and more focused on the short term. How often do we hear about politicians only thinking to the next election? How business is only thinking about the next two quarters worth of profits? This is not the kind of institutional structure we need to get us through the problems that we have now created for ourselves.

This is what concerns me when I think about what humans are capable of and how we have evolved. We are failing, I think, to solve these kinds of problems in our traditional way which is to work collectively and institutionally to solve them.

MF: Could you elucidate the connection between this institutionally myopic behaviour and the need for growth? Obviously businesses only look towards the next quarter, next two quarters because they have shareholders demanding dividends, accountants demanding an effective bottom line. So, link the behaviour to your sphere of interest.

PV: Let me explain why our system seems to need growth. In order to have anything like full employment we need a lot of expenditure in our economy. We have seen in this recent recession that we have been implored by governments to get out and spend. What they have tried to do is take various measures to increase their own expenditure or to free up liquidity so banks will lend more money etcetera.

Why is that? In simple terms, if we do not spend money then people are not employed, factories are not employed, machines are not employed.

Now where does growth come in? Some of that expenditure is for new equipment, to expand infrastructure. So when you look at this over time, we spend money in one year to employ our resources but in so doing we increase the availability of resources in the sense of productive capacity in the following year, so we have to spend even more money in the second year to employ the expanded economy.

If we are adding population or improving the skills of the workforce, we increase further the capacity of the economy to produce. So we get into this sort of dependency cycle: we spend money to keep ourselves reasonably fully employed and in doing so we expand our capacity so we have to spend even more money the next year.

So can we restructure the economy in some way so that we do not have this dependency on growth anymore? What I found in my work is you can come up with arrangements or scenarios hypothetically which show that you can have a stable economy which does not rely on growth each year, where people are still fully employed, where you are still dealing with the eradication of poverty and you are reducing the impact on the environment. There are a lot of good things in the absence of growth.

I do not happen to think this runs against some basic, inherent propensity of humans to seek growth. We have spent most of our lives as humans and in human societies without growth. So I think it is possible to have a stable society that is not based on growth and is viable over the long term.

MF: You said that you believed, at least hypothetically, it is possible to govern and manage a society without growth. How?

PV: One of the first things that I think is important here is we still want to become better at what we do. We want to become more productive, not in terms of more production because for that we need more resources, but we should reduce the amount of time that we spend working as we become better at work. That is a real important key to keeping the rate of unemployment down. It means we can share the amount of work that has to be done out among as many people as we want if we all work a bit less.

Saying that does not mean it is very easy to make it happen. There are a number of institutional barriers, for example those which make it cheaper for a company to pay somebody overtime than to hire a second person because there are certain fixed costs, things that you have to pay every time you take on a new employee. So you prefer to keep the staff you have got working more rather than to share the work hours. Sometimes there are elements in the tax system which do that. So there are obstacles to the capacity to share the work out.

When you ask people if they would take the opportunity to work less, even for less pay, quite a large number of people say yes but of course they do not feel that they have got the choice. The job comes with forty hours a week or no job. If they could work for thirty-three or thirty-five hours a week for less pay, it is very interesting and encouraging that a fair number of people would do that.

Where I live, in Ontario, schoolteachers are able to take eighty percent pay and a year off every fifth year and many of them chose to do that once they had the opportunity. So one of the key components to managing without growth is to make our work arrangements more flexible so people can work less and the work can be spread out.

MF: But once you factor in the demands of the cost of living, even without growth, even if we assume we were going to pioneer the scheme and for the next ten years prices would not go up and money would not lose its value, how do you get people to take a pay cut when they are already just barely covering what they need?

PV: Well I happen to agree with your premise that people are in general just barely covering what they need. Not in a fundamental sense but what you are really pointing to is another problem we have to tackle. How is it in our society that we have developed this notion of what we need? I would make a distinction, as many do, between what we need and what we want.

We are all victims of a tremendous amount of pressure on us to buy. The measure of success in so many ways is translated into what you buy, what you are consuming. A lot of people resent that but it does not seem to be a sufficient critical mass to change the system. We are exposed to literally thousands of ads every day. Wherever you look, whether you go to a men's washroom, walk down the street, drive your car, on the TV, the internet, it is just inundated with ads.

The problem with these ads very often is not just that we don't necessarily need what is being put before us but we are being persuaded that they are of a certain way of life, that a high consumption way life is the way to go. We are shown visual images of people who are very happy and are consuming. If you look around, often some of the happiest people are those who are not visibly consuming, that are taking a step back from that kind of hectic life.

So it is not an easy question to answer: how do you change people's minds about this sort of thing? I think there are two elements. One is to have these kinds of conversations that resonate with some people: "yeah, that is not how I want to live."

That is one of the things we saw in the recession - people realising they were too committed to debt, they had lost control of their lives and they were saying they were not going to let that happen again.

Then there is policy. I think we have to take much stronger

steps than we have done in the past to limit advertising. Advertising needs to be more informative, less persuasive and it has to tell the truth. If you were to simply impose a test on each ad: is it truthful? They show us people driving cars on the open road often in places where you could never drive. Have you seen these vehicles on mountaintops? Or on the beach? This is not the normal experience of driving and yet that is the image that is presented to us in order to persuade us to buy a vehicle. It is not honest, it is not truthful. Until we become more truthful I do not think we are going to make the kind of changes that are necessary.

MF: There are so many dimensions to this issue. You are absolutely right, there is the psychological dimension, consistently reinforcing the idea that your role as a citizen is defined by your level of consumption.

PV: We do not use that term 'citizen' anymore. If you think about how we describe people, we are described as 'consumers', we are described as 'taxpayers'. Sometimes we are described as 'workers' but even that has sort of gone out of fashion. We are seldom described as citizens and I think that is a real shortcoming. We need to think of ourselves as citizens, as members of a society, and to think about what a good society might look like because I do not think what we are living in now necessarily fits that bill.

To get back to the basic theme of this discussion, the kind of society we have got is not sustainable. The resources are not there. We can expect very substantial increases in oil prices as peak oil hits us. We have got to do something to draw back from destabilising the climate. We are acidifying the oceans. Lots of other species are in danger and are dying out. It is just a long, long list of concerns.

So we may think these opportunities for change that I am mentioning are not too attractive, but we are going to have to change. So the challenge for us all is are we going to be somehow in control of that change? Are we going to think through what kind of society we want and try to generate it or are we going to sit back and let these waves roll over us? I think that would be far more painful.

MF: That thing about us never being called citizens, it is a very good point. It is something that I find whenever I am reading an article. There is this issue in the media that even on the most tenuous, theoretical level, any phenomenon, difficulty or inconvenience is always portrayed fundamentally in economic terms.

"So many thousand people a week take sick days, this costs the economy eight billion pounds in lost productivity." How? Being an economist, could you debunk this way that the media portrays issues to us in terms of lost productivity or financial cost to the economy? Do you think calculating the economic cost of behaviour is false or counter-productive?

PV: Well so many issues are translated into terms that in a sense relate to growth. For example we are all accustomed now to seeing people who are promoting the arts tell us not the value that artistic endeavours bring to our life but how many jobs it will create, how much tax revenue will it generate. I have a message for people who take that view of the arts: if you want to generate money in the economy I do not think the arts is the best way to go. You have to make the case for the arts in terms of what art brings to people. An appreciation of the quality of life, an understanding of themselves and their environment, a critical view of life. Art has often been very critical. So it really disturbs me in that one example and there are many others.

I would say the same with sport, I would say the same with virtually anything. Health. When you translate it into dollar terms what you are doing is you are falling into the growth trap. Unless you can persuade people that something is important because it could be measured in dollars, you feel you are not going to win your argument.

I know quite a lot about the methods that are used to convert changes in people's lives into dollar terms. The numbers that come out of those exercises are not very reliable and I would say in many cases not very meaningful.

MF: Can you link the idea of managing without growth to this idea that work is bad and leisure is good? Meaningless repetitive work is bad, but creatively engaging meaningful work has always defined man's experience on this planet.

PV: When I talk about managing without growth, the real focus needs to be on limiting the extent to which we interact with nature as our supplier of materials and energy, for our depository for waste products and how much space we occupy as species.

I think in those three respects (resources, waste and land use) we have gone beyond the boundaries of the planet in terms of what it can do to support us. So we have to pull back and live within some limits that we, I hope, are smart enough to recognise. That is what we are trying to do with climate change for example. We are trying to get a global agreement on the reduction of the emission of greenhouse gases into the environment and to share that out in some reasonably fair way so that we do not destabilise the climate. That is just one example but it is the one we are most familiar with.

Once we have got these boundaries, whatever creativity we can bring forward through our economy and all of our institutions, great! Let us do that!

It is not that zero economic growth should be our objective to replace three percent growth or whatever a country chooses. It is that we need to manage without growth with respect to our impact on the environment in the broadest way defined. Then the economy can be what it is.

Now, having said that, I believe that we can build an economy that can be very creative and offer people very interesting lives. In fact the challenge of living within those limits will be really well worth taking on. When I speak to high school students or undergraduates this is really the way I put it. I say there are wonderful opportunities here to be creative. This is not a totally depressing message, in fact it could be quite the opposite. Engage them in discussions about what kind of lives they could live, how their community life could be stronger, more time with friends and family and more social time.

Social time is what they are into now with all the social networking, which I will not say is free of the use of resources but it is not a resource intense activity as compared with the next car you are going to buy and drive on the highway. So the possibilities of having better lives is really great. There are cultures, religious beliefs that for a long time have said you lead the good life when you recognise certain limits. It is in our culture where we have developed this peculiar idea that the good life is to be defined as always ignoring the limits, always living beyond them. There are no limits. That I think is a formula for tragedy.

MF: The issue with social networking is that there is a lot of resource consumption that goes into getting to that 'neutral' participation. You do not just interface. You consume electricity, you are at a computer. You have a mobile phone. People who do that kind of thing, they still want the car.

237

PV: We will see. This is a transition period. At least they are saying to the people in my generation that being in touch with other people is really important to them but does not necessarily require face-to-face visits all the time. So they have large networks which do not require the same amount of travel. There really is no comparison. You have large numbers of people that you interact with through a social network that you could never interact with physically.

All I am saying is that when you discuss these kinds of changes with young people and you talk about relationships as being important, they understand it. I think they understand it better than my generation, which was more focused on acquiring goods and material things.

I am always looking around for positive signs of change because it is really easy to find the negative stuff in this kind of dialogue. There is a lot of that and the information comes at you all the time through a whole variety of media and it can be very depressing. But the whole message is not depressing. As I say there is a really interesting set of opportunities here for a new generation to build different kinds of lives.

The other thing I often say to younger people is "If you do not like it now, when would you like to have been born? When was it better?"

Pick a decade in the twentieth century, a decade full of tragedy as well as success. Would that have been better? They reflect on this and say yeah, I'll give it a go. Work with what we've got. We have all lived in challenging times but one of the problems of looking at managing without growth is it can be seen as a very negative outlook and I do not think that is the right way to see it. I think it needs to be seen as an opportunity to respond to these challenges and crises. If we do not, we will be looking at a far, far bleaker future and I will regret that.

MF: Is there a tipping point? Where do you stand on this idea that there may or may not be a line that we cross and after we go there, that is it.

PV: I do not think there is one single line that we can cross and probably you do not mean that in your question. There are a range of issues which look to us like they are thresholds that we should not go beyond and we may have gone beyond them in some respects. I think climate change is a good example. I think the loss of biodiversity is another one. The third one, identified in an important article in Nature late last year, is the

238

nitrogen cycle: how much nitrogen we are introducing into the nitrogen cycle because we learnt how to fix it from the air.

But I do not think anybody really has the knowledge to say "oh dear, we have gone so far we will never get back." It is the kind of thing you only ever really understand in hindsight, when you look back and say "look what that civilisation did to itself." So I do not really know the answer to that.

I also want to make one other comment. One of the features of being a living being is that we are not in equilibrium. We work really hard every moment to stay far from equilibrium. That is why we need food to keep our bodies together, to maintain a temperature that is different from the air around us. We are in disequilibrium and that applies also to our economic system. We need to keep feeding that economic system with energy to keep it out of equilibrium.

Economists deal so much with the idea of equilibrium. Demand and supply brings price and quantity into balance and you have an equilibrium but it is a very peculiar use of the term because if we focus too much on equilibrium in that sense we lose track of the fact, thermodynamically, that we are out of equilibrium, we are far from equilibrium and that is what makes life possible. It is a disequilibrium phenomenon.

What makes it possible for us to have these massive economies that produce all these goods and services is access to cheap energy. One of the fundamental concerns of many commentators, I would include myself in this, is that cheap energy does not look like it is going to be with us much longer, even in a narrow economic sense. It is getting more difficult to get our hands on the petroleum that our economies require and has fuelled the economic growth of the last hundred years. We started with coal and we have gone to oil and gas. We still use a lot of coal. Access to cheap fossil fuels has been fundamental for keeping our economies in this far-from-equilibrium state which is characterised by continual growth.

This is a major threat and if we do not make a transition away from a dependency on fossil fuels to renewables we will be in serious trouble. We are going to have to make that transition one way or another but we need to make it in a thoughtful, planned, careful way if we are going to avoid the real downside risks of what happens when growth comes to an end.

MF: There is a lot of inter-relativity between Newton's ideas of physics and the way that human behaviour in relationships and activities function.

PV: Just look around a modern city...take a walk down a city street. Start thinking about how much energy it is taking to keep this thing going? Every vehicle you see moving is being driven by energy. The buildings are being heated or cooled. The food that people eat - modern agriculture depends on cheap energy. What is going to happen as these energy prices really start rising when cheap fossil fuels are no longer available? Those cities are going to look very different.

A lot of the economic work on energy uses the following logic: in the future we are going to have so many people, they are going to want to live like this, so how much energy do we need? Where are we going to get it from?

My approach is to say that the kind of cities that we have, the kind of lives we lead are in a significant way determined by the amount of energy that we have available to us. So suburbia, particularly in North America, came about because of cheap oil and and the automobile. You take the cheap oil away and do not expect to see suburbia looking anything like it does now.

So it is a reversal of causality that is in play here.

MF: How can people make the difference?

PV: When I am talking about managing without growth, I am focusing my interests on the rich countries. I think growth in poorer countries really does bring demonstrable improvements in standards of living provided that growth is shared reasonably.

So in answer to your questions about what people living in wealthy countries can do, there is a dilemma here. There is a real concern that what you do as an individual just does not make any difference so why bother. That is a very sad attitude to have and I contrast it with the attitude that I was exposed to when I grew up in England after the second world war. There was a phrase that was used, still is used occasionally, that runs counter to that. People after the war talked about 'doing their bit'. "I did my bit." Why didn't the same logic work then? Why did they have to do their bit? Their bit did not make any difference, right? Yet they took pride in the fact that they had made their contribution.

Somehow we have got to capture that same spirit and apply it to these problems that we are now facing today. People have got to feel that they have done their bit. Where we see examples of this in Toronto is with waste recycling. When they introduced the blue box, you put it outside your house once a week to show to your neighbours that you were doing your bit.

And you know what? Most people joined in. So the opportunity for people to make an individual contribution is really important. If we can do that in a way that is somehow a shared activity, so that people can see we are all contributing, all doing our bit, then I think that will help us make the kind of changes that we are talking about.

Now the trouble is, that is only ever going to be part of the answer. We also have to work deliberately, collectively through government to set the framework for our individual actions. The blue box again is quite a good example because although it is based upon individual, voluntary behaviour it is a system that is set up by government on behalf of us all. I never thought, even me, someone with a long history in environmental matters, that I would wash out cans before I put them in the garbage but I do. I do not even think twice about it now.

So you can get a change in individual behaviour and it is so much better though if it is done as part of some sort of collective action because then it really does add up to something significant.

Other ways we can change individual behaviour are through tax incentives, reducing subsidies to support behaviour that we know is bad for the environment. Giving a better example to our children. One of the funny things about life today is how often we think that the children give examples to their parents. That is another change in society. It used to be assumed that the older you were the more you understood and the wiser you are. Now that I am getting old I do not see anyone thinking that of me! It is only the kids who really know what is going on. They know the technology. This is why change in the schools is so important, in the messages that children learn and bring home. All these things can help.

I am really quite encouraged by a whole range of voluntary actions that we can see. The transition town movements that started in Britain just a few years ago which has now spread around the world, where people are getting together in their locality and saying "what can we do to deal with the twin threat of peak oil and climate change in our own city?" How do we control the scale of our activities so that we do not keep eating away at efficiency gains by just using more energy?

Then you have got people who are deliberately moving away from a high consumption lifestyle - they are doing it for selfish reasons but they are doing it. You have got the local currency experiments that are taking place in different areas. There is a

241

lot going on and I only have a glimpse of it. This is very encouraging.

Where we are lacking I believe is that level of leadership by governments and corporations who are still working to the old rules, the old visions. Not all of them - there are leaders - but they are few and far between. That is where I think we really need to make the breakthrough.

Part of the transition has got to be done in a way that yes, we are more informed about how we live, what it takes to live, but not that we all have to become our own personal engineers to solve these problems. That would be just too demanding.

There are energy companies now who are trying to provide more alternatives, putting themselves forward as energy service companies as opposed to gas, oil or hydrocarbon companies. So there is some element of change there but this question of how you bring about social change is the big one. How much political action is required? In my own case, I have always contributed a fair amount of my time and expertise to environmental groups because I have seen them as the change agents in our society so I am happy to do that.

So we can say "What are the particular strengths I can bring? What is it that I know that I can contribute?" That is the big thing. Ask yourself that question, not "oh, whatever I do is not going to make any difference" because then we can all sit back and just watch the bad times roll over us.

I do want to emphasise my view that the idea that economic growth is unavoidable, inescapable and inherent in us and that we could not possibly live in a society in which economic growth was not the norm is a mistake.

You can have full employment, deal with poverty, manage the government's finances and deal with environmental issues in an economy that is not growing.

Opening up the possibility of living in an economy that is not continually reliant on growth will then begin to get us to think about a whole range of things that could be different: the food that we eat, the work that we do, the energy that we use, the transportation systems we use, the way we spend our time. All these become interesting subjects for a discussion I really hope we are beginning to see.

The Frenchman and The Canary
with Professor Seyyed Hossein Nasr

*"The first condition for learning anything is to
want to learn. Therefore the first condition for
gaining knowledge is to realise our own
ignorance."*

I came across Professor Nasr whilst researching
environmental movements within the world's major religions.
He is Professor of Islamic Studies at George Washington
University. His books, such as "Man and Nature: The Spiritual
Crisis in Modern Man", have consistently dealt with the conflict
between man's philosophical ideas about himself and his place
in the world and mankind's increasingly deleterious impact on
the planet.

The superficial concept of religious environmental thinking is
that God gave Adam dominion over the earth and all that
dwelled thereon and bade him be fruitful and multiply. This is a
dangerously reductive view of the stewardship role into which
mankind is placed by God in the Scriptures and as such it
marginalises religious thought unproductively. If those who
believe that this planet was created by their God for their use
were equally concerned with its preservation due to the sacred
trust placed in them, would this not constitute a very powerful
alliance on the environmental front?

With this in mind, I approached Professor Nasr in the hope
that he would be willing to shed some light on the ways in
which belief and philosophy have shaped our worldview. I also
hoped to draw him out on this idea of a sacred trust between
God and mankind.

He is a stern speaker, often making me feel that I may have
offended him somehow by being less well-read than he would
like. He speaks in a rich, deep voice that reverberates with years
of study and experience. When we move to global issues or the
question of the future, a weariness creeps into his voice that I
have heard in many of my conversations. It is sobering for a
man of his faith and erudition to be left with such a dim view of
mankind's future.

243

Mike Freedman: Sufism is something that I am quite interested in, obviously from much more of a beginner's perspective than your own. From my understanding, in Sufi training the first step is what I believe is called 'learning how to learn'? I wanted to ask you whether, before we begin our conversation, there was anything you wanted to say to open the field.

Seyyed Hossein Nasr: Yes of course. The fact that you have found and are speaking to me already means that you want to hear what I want to say. In general you can never, as the Zen saying goes, 'put more tea in a cup that is already full'. The first condition for learning anything is to want to learn. Therefore the first condition for gaining knowledge is to realise our own ignorance.

A person who does not realise he is ignorant will never come out of his state of ignorance. There has to be a will on the part of the soul, as well as the intelligence to go with it, to want to learn, to want to know.

When it comes to the question of the environment and the environmental crisis, I was perhaps the very first person, in the 1960s when I gave the series of lectures at the University of Chicago which led to the book *Man and Nature: The Spiritual Crisis in Modern Man*, to have spoken before Lynn White[1] of the deeper religious, spiritual and historical factors which brought the environmental crisis about, but modern society does not want by and large to listen to this. It is suffering from what we call in Arabic and Persian 'composed ignorance', that is being ignorant and not knowing that one is ignorant.

Therefore so much of the debate and discussions talk from the surface of things and do not deal with the deeper causes that have brought these things about. Much of my intellectual life in the last fifty years has been spent with the whole question of the natural environment but always from the point of view of the deeper religious, philosophical, spiritual attitudes, ideas or lack thereof which have led to this crisis.

Therefore I differ to a large extent from many other people who later on came to this field, realising there was an environmental crisis but not wanting to accept the real causes which brought it about, which went to repudiate and reject the very paradigm within which the environmental crisis came about.

MF: You used the phrase ' the real causes'. As I understand from some of the speaking you have done, in Western philosophy we can trace the first steps we took towards the position we are in now to what I believe is called the Cartesian Split, where we began to define the mind as distinct from the body, to separate and compartmentalise things.

SHN: The Cartesian Bifurcation of dualism.[2]

MF: Could you outline for me how that began the journey that has brought us to the point we are at now?

SHN: Certainly. In my Gifford Lectures of 1981, *Knowledge and The Sacred*, which is one of my most important books, I have dealt extensively with this issue, with how step-by-step this took place.

Before Descartes, Western philosophy and theology, like Islamic, medieval Jewish or for that matter Hindu or Buddhist, was based on several levels of reality, what is called The Great Chain of Being later on by intellectual historians and philosophers in the West, by Arthur Lovejoy really. They had that very term in Persian and Arabic long before Lovejoy wrote it. That means that realms of existence are like a chain of being or rungs in a ladder and there are many of them.

The human being was always considered to be composed of several levels of reality and so was the world of nature. These were usually summarised as spirit, soul and body - spiritus, anima, corpus in Latin. This tripartite division was very different from what happened later on. First of all, it did not create a complete separation between the spiritual element of things and the material. It did not create that dichotomy. These three interacted with each other. Secondly these three elements were found both within man and within nature.

What happened with Descartes and with Galileo, these two go together as far as science is concerned, were two elements. First of all is Cartesian Bifurcation, which really impoverished reality for Western man in a way that affected everything. Man was considered to be mind first of all; spirit and soul were no longer categories which were central. Although Descartes himself was a devout Catholic, his philosophy was against the traditional Catholic view.

So the word 'pensée' was used by Descartes. 'Pensée' in French means both 'thought' and 'meditation' but having to do with mental activity; the word 'mind' from the Latin 'mense' became very prevalent. It was not used as a category in medieval or in fact Greek philosophy. We translate it as such but it is not even an important category. There are many faculties to what we call the mind; the mind in the Cartesian sense is a modern invention.

The other pole of reality was considered to be pure materiality. *Res extensa.* Pure quantity. Material here was identified as quantity. So we were left with a very strange world in which nature was pure quantity. Everything which was qualitative was not in nature but was in the mind and nature became a pure 'it', a pure 'thing', totally devoid of any relation with not only our mind and our emotions but the qualities which we see in nature. For example, we see the beauty of a rose. This is totally meaningless in modern science. All modern science is still based on Cartesian Bifurcation. 'The beauty of a rose' does not mean a darn thing. In physics - I have a degree from MIT in physics, I don't just speak through my hat - it does not mean anything. Mention this statement in a physics class and it does not mean anything. It is like you have spoken in Tibetan.

Now, this idea that it does not mean anything goes back to this Cartesian Bifurcation. What Descartes did was take all of reality which was not quantitative out of nature and put it in the other half of the duality which was the mind. *Res cogitans* he called it - the realm of cognition acknowledged.

By this, he first of all created an absolute chasm between man and nature. There are many other things that he caused but since we are talking about the environment I am just sticking to this dimension of it. Secondly, he prepared this materialistic view which is foundational to modern science, a materialistic view of the world of nature in which there are no other substances but what people call the measurable, the quantitative and the material. The soul or the spirit are no longer in the world of nature and if somebody believes in them it's considered to be a poetic statement or imagination. All the matters of self have now been etherealised, become energy. They are not part of the reality of modern Western man and woman. All of Western humanity has been sold on this paradigm. This is the second very important consequence of the Cartesian Bifurcation.

The idea that the goal of science is to dominate over nature, to 'gain power' as Francis Bacon[3] and empirical philosophers said, complemented this Cartesian, more theoretical approach to the understanding of nature, of science and our way of knowing nature. It brought with it the practical aspect of

246

dominating over nature. The goal of science was to gain power over nature. We cannot do any experiments on nature without dominating it.

An experiment is different from observation. If you observe a bird flying from a tree, that is different from taking that leaf from the tree, cutting it up and putting it under a microscope in a lab and studying its molecular structure. You are dominating it. So domination over nature became combined with greed and love of power and led to modern technology and all that followed from that.

So this is very briefly the historical link between the rise of Cartesian Bifurcation, of dualism, and the materialistic or quantitative conception of nature in Galileo's Discourses and Dialogues, his two major scientific works foundational to modern physics and science, although this was rejected by quantum mechanics.

Modern man sees in nature nothing but a source for resources, for food or other things. Of course man always saw in nature this source for food, but that was not the only thing that he or she saw in nature. Today, it is seen only in a material way, to be 'used' in a utilitarian sense for so-called human needs, much of which are artificial because the more needs you create, the more money you make. So the whole aspect of passion and psychology, of domination, greed and so forth, also plays an important role when it comes to the environment, but the philosophical foundation goes back to the Cartesian Bifurcation.

MF: You were discussing the nature of science being one of domination. Traditionally associated with the book of Genesis is this concept of man as the pinnacle of creation being given dominion.

SHN: Trying to blame Judaism and Christianity for the environmental crisis is really a bit of a faux pas because yes, in the Bible man is told that he can dominate the Earth as God's special creature, but he can dominate the Earth precisely because he is God's special creature, not a secular being.

The other half of the formula is really forgotten, that being God's special creature also places responsibility upon man. This is especially emphasised in Islam where there is one sentence that says that 'God made possible the dominion of man over creation' which is true. Look at what we are doing to the Amazon forest or to the ice caps. This is proof that the Quran

247

was right, but it says at the same time that man has a responsibility for creation which somebody dropped out of this argument later on.

Those who will point to this are to some extent right in that once you secularised Christianity and Judaism, you did not take out the idea that man had domination over nature, you took out the idea that man is a spiritual being that also has responsibilities towards nature. So secularised Christianity became the modern worldview of the man-centred anthropomorphic paradigm in which everything on Earth is for the sake of man. No other creation really has a right except in relation to us, and it is in reaction to that that things like animal rights began. It is not accidental that the environmental movement in the West was begun by people who turned against Christianity and Judaism, by and large. That is not what they heard in the churches and synagogues.

When I wrote "Man and Nature", which came out in England in the Sixties, it was strongly attacked by the two Anglican bishops in England who had written about nature. First of all they said "who is this man from the Middle East daring to talk about these matters and criticising us?" A part of it was the colonial mentality which is still very strong even today, but part of it also was the idea that was very prevalent at that time, that it was the glory of Christianity that modern science and technology developed in Christian lands and not in Confucian, Hindu or Islamic lands. That is the 'great proof' of Christianity. Look at the books that were written in the thirties, forties and fifties about this.

Then when the environmental crisis began, at first Christian and Jewish thinkers were not all ready for it, but after a while they realised there was no other way. So both Jewish and Christian environmental movements began.

MF: You made a distinction between the spiritual or mystical counterpart of a religion which may have as the remainder of it a more fundamental power structure layout, like we see the relationship between Sufism and Islam or between Kabbalah and Judaism. Most of the major religions seem to have a mystical/spiritual school that emphasises cycles of life, death and rebirth sometimes not overt in the rest of the religion's teaching, yet the secularisation of culture seems to be a reaction to the material side of the established religions and not the spiritual side.

SHN: It is a bit more subtle than that but there is a grain of truth in what you say. Every religion, as you said, has social and legal teachings for everyday life, like Talmudic law, Islamic law - Christianity does not have laws based on the New Testament but it is drawn from Jewish law and Common Law and so on.

A person is supposed to live by that in order to keep the social order going but when a religion is alive, it always has all sorts of spiritual and mystical inner dimensions, as Christianity in the Middles Ages, as Islam still does. Al Qaeda, these are people issuing ideologically from Saudi Arabia, the one place in the Islamic world where Wahhabism tried to destroy that inner dimension of Islam that is Sufism. It is quite interesting.

If you look at the map of the world, the first religion in which the inner dimension began to be lost was Christianity. It began in the Renaissance. There were Christian mystics in the Renaissance, of course there were, they had not disappeared completely, and there was Christian medicine, but it was the swan song.

Gradually Christianity began dealing more and more with laws and external aspects of things, morality but not with spirituality. If I ask you as an intelligent man, where are the Meister Eckharts and Saint Teresa of Avilas of the nineteenth century? Where are they? Not only in Catholicism but even in Protestantism, the people who lived in the Renaissance who were esoteric, Rosicrucians and so forth and so on, they all disappeared out of sight.

Once that was done, the religion became itself externalised. The externalised aspect of religion provides neither the doctrine nor the method to understanding the spiritual aspect of nature. So this went hand in hand with an externalised science which saw in a tree nothing but a height and a chlorophyll cycle, oxygen coming in and out and the carbon dioxide being absorbed. The spiritual significance of the tree, its symbolism standing for a higher reality, those were all neglected and in fact made meaningless in time following the loss of the inner dimension within religion.

It is very interesting how the most important giants of classical science in the seventeenth century, especially Newton and Kepler, were desperately seeking for mysticism. They were both mystics. Newton wrote more commentaries on the Bible in a mystical vein than he wrote on physics but in order to hide that they did not allow it to be studied. Only now are people studying it. As a young man I tried to get his book on alchemy but they would not show it to me. Newton wrote a book on

249

alchemy. It is very interesting that these two things disappeared together.

MF: The majority of human population growth in the future is going to take place in countries with non-European traditions, particularly Islam. It is already happening that as those traditions filter through to the West, people seem to find a resonance they feel is lacking in their own culture.

Looking forward at this trend of development and growth in those parts of the world that tend to have different criteria for describing the world, the human and reality than we do, what does a future science or a future worldview look like to you if we amalgamate more of these alternative ideas and broader concepts of reality into the Western tradition?

SHN: This is a very important question.

First of all, this is already occurring. It already began in the early decades of the twentieth century when a number of leading Western intellectuals of the highest order discovered non-Western traditions and within them metaphysics, cosmology, spirituality, which had been lost in the West.

Some, through them, rediscovered what was lost in the West. Some in fact went and attached themselves to those non-Western traditions. Non-Western traditions also gradually began to spread in the West itself.

Now we have a very interesting dynamic that is going on in the world. On the one hand, what developed first in the West in the form of modern science and technology and also what goes with it in the social order is spreading rapidly to the rest of the world. Look what is happening in India which is becoming very rapidly industrialised and mechanised. China, whose government is supposed to be Communist, one of the forms of the governments that came from the West.

There are many other examples - in fact, China and India are going faster in this process than the Islamic world. The Islamic world is still holding on to its traditions somewhat more and that is why it is not militarily as powerful as China. That is why the Americans do not bombard China but they keep killing Muslims every night by bombing them, because they are more or less helpless.

The Islamic world in the future is going to become much more powerful and it will be, like India and China - the other two great civilisations of Asia, a major international force, but for the moment it is somewhat segmented, although Turkey,

250

Iran and a few other countries are becoming stronger, but still some ways to go.

You have this trend of Westernisation. Even the Islamic Republic of Iran is doing a great deal of Western technology. They take pride in making airplanes now and sending missiles into the air; they are not taking pride in having a new Rumi in Iran writing mystical poetry. That is a reality. I am a Persian myself, I am Iranian and this is first-hand information.

So whatever type of government you have, you have this flow of materialism and dominance over nature and all of the things that brought about the environmental crisis going from Europe and America to other continents of the world. South America has become more industrialised and mechanised. The consequences for the rainforest in Peru, Brazil and Bolivia you can see for yourself.

You have another wave going the other way, into the original home of all of these forces that continue to destroy the natural environment and destroy us, that is the West, Europe and later on America. Ideas of other civilisations keep flowing in and many people are attracted to them.

There is another dynamic that is going on which will be of some importance in the future. Except for Western Europe, religion is on the rise in every part of the world. It is a very interesting fact. People are asking 'why is this so?' - I said because in France the coffee tastes so good and the steak is so good, that is God for them so they do not bother, the rest of us have to seek alternative meaning elsewhere. I say it jokingly, but this is a great paradox. France, which was called the 'bride of the church' for fifteen hundred years, centre of Catholicism, some of the most beautiful cathedrals in the world, look at the state of religion there: forty percent of people are atheist. Western Europe is an exception.

Religion is on the rise. In India, in China itself, the number of young people going to Confucian, Taoist and Buddhist temples is remarkable. In Beijing and other places, the mosques are full. They have got a tremendous rise of interest in religion and in the Islamic world of course religion is very powerful. Even in the United States religion is on the rise, although it is very externalised.

This movement right now is mostly oriented toward social and economic justice. The more mystical, inward aspect is not being emphasised in many of these new religious movements. There are some, I am not saying none.

As the environmental crisis becomes more difficult to ignore, these movements will have to pay more attention to the mystical inner dimension of their own religion. So it is a very complicated situation.

The Archbishop of Canterbury, Dr. Rowan Williams, a very good theologian who is retiring now, is very much interested in the environment. Ecumenical Patriarch Bartholomew I, the Supreme Head of the Greek Orthodox Church, is called 'The Green Metropolitan' because he is an environmentalist in a certain sense. So you are seeing major changes within the Christian context.

Opposite that, the fundamentalists in North and South Carolina are the first to vote that every caribou be killed in Alaska in order to get the oil flowing. They are completely for the desecration of nature for wealth and are totally oblivious to the environment. Of course in the last four or five years there is a little change in them, so I should not say completely. You see that reflected in American politics where the Republican Party has no interest in environmental issues because its support comes from the twenty percent of the population who are extreme rightists and most of them are fundamentalist Christians from the southern states.

Even a person like Romney, who is a Harvard graduate and should know better, since he has become a candidate he does not speak at all about the environment as any sane person would. So it is reflected in politics.

Now, you have all these trends going together and if you ask me what is going to happen, of course only God knows. I am a Muslim and I believe that the future is known only to God, but as far as we human beings with our limited intelligence and information that we have now are concerned, I think that the best hope for humanity is a major catastrophe. Otherwise it is a slow death, if you understand what I mean.

MF: I do, unfortunately.

SHN: You need something to really shake people out of their slumber so that they are not sacrificing the very air they breathe in the name of economics.

Either we have to change our mindset or nature is going to do it for us. I am one of those who believes that nature will have the last word. There is absolutely no way in which humanity operating within the paradigm of modernism can overcome the problems which that paradigm has caused.

Those who try to keep within that paradigm but say 'We

should save energy', that is cosmetic. It is like somebody who has cancer putting powder on her face so her skin does not look yellow. That is what it is.

I think the fundamental problem is the paradigm within which modernism operates which goes back to that Cartesian Bifurcation and all the other factors that were added later on. Unless we change that, I see no hope except a major catastrophe. Of course if the major catastrophe does not come, and by major I mean something that will kill millions of people and not the whole of the human species, then we might kill the whole of the human species but slowly, like the canary in the coal mine. When the carbon monoxide comes, nobody is aware and the canary drops dead. It does not cry, it does not do anything. It just gradually kills her.

You can forget about man's spiritual needs, about God, you can say we are all superstitious, but we cannot neglect what has happened to the physical earth. It is the only home we have. You cannot neglect what is happening to all the forests of the world, what is left of them.

That is what we are doing. We are already experiencing our own slow death. You might say I am an extremist, but so be it. So be it.

Conclusion

While I was working on this book, the end of the Mayan Baktun cycle happened, touted by the media and tinfoil-hatted ideologues of the world as an apocalyptic moment. December 21st, 2012 came and went eventlessly to I suppose the chagrin of some and the lack of surprise of most.

Buried inside that cultural trope and other apocalyptic memes besides is the linear paradigm of Western science and logic which sees time and attending events as unfolding in one direction towards an end point. Other cultures and frameworks for understanding this mystery we call existence have a different view, that of cycles. Existence is cast in their ideologies as a wheel, an ever-turning and developing movement from now to then, from then to now. Through that lens, the Mayan Baktun was just another cycle that was coming to an end and renewing. In fact, the Mayans had a very developed understanding of astronomy which allowed them to predict fairly accurately not just the length of the year but also the amount of time it takes our solar system to orbit within the Milky Way. It turns out that what some thought of as the end of the world was simply our crossing the galactic meridian and beginning another rotation.

More broadly, what some people believe is the end of the world can also be seen as a new beginning. In the Tarot deck, the card known as Death represents transition and change, not death in the simplistic sense. New work in quantum physics,

254

most notably biocentrism, theorises that death itself is an illusion, a simple release of energy from the limited several state of corporeality into an existence outside of time. Far from being esoteric ideas, these theories and symbols represent a real truth - we think that what we fear is death, but most of the time what we fear is really change.

And so we find ourselves as a species and as a civilisation at the precipice of change, of transition. Whether in the physical sense relating to our changing climate, depleting natural resources, evaporating water supplies, species extinction and fraying threads of diplomacy or in the less literal sense of a shift in perspective and outlook. Our long history has led us from social primate to communal hunter, social farmer to egotistical urbanite. It seems only reasonable that as the world physically alters around us, due largely to our own actions, our inner world will also change.

What will we be as individuals and as societies when the future knocks on our doors? It seems fair to say that those institutions and individuals currently invested in the status quo will continue to direct their time, energy and resources towards its preservation and by extension their own. Those of us who have lived lives of unparalleled plenty in the so-called 'developed' nations will undoubtedly see our much-coveted standard of living decline, either through physical constraint or economic necessity. Those of us who live in so-called 'developing' countries are struggling, with good reason, to secure the basics of survival and the comforts of industrialism as well. Is there enough to go round? Is that even the right question?

In the Tao Te Ching, a book I respect very much, Lao Tzu wrote:

> "He who does not have enough
> will never have enough."

In his 1973 book *Small is Beautiful*, E.F. Schumacher elaborated on Lao Tzu:

> "I suggest that the foundations of peace cannot
> be laid by universal prosperity, in the modern
> sense, because such prosperity, if attainable at
> all, is attainable only by cultivating such drives
> of human nature as greed and envy, which

destroy intelligence, happiness, serenity, and thereby the peacefulness of man.

It could well be that rich people treasure peace more highly than poor people, but only if they feel utterly secure - and this is a contradiction in terms. Their wealth depends on making inordinately large demands on limited world resources and thus puts them on an unavoidable collision course - not primarily with the poor (who are weak and defenceless) but with other rich people. In short, we can say today that man is far too clever to be able to survive without wisdom."

The English language and the Western mentality within which it is embedded does not lend itself to the open discussion of the internal landscape. It is all well and good to debate the visible impact on our planet, the damming of rivers, the draining of wetlands, the felling of forests and the encroachment of desert, but inside us there is also a constant change happening.

Governments of the world have gone to great lengths to regulate certain psychoactive substances but at the same time left relatively unregulated the continuous psychoactive influence of media, politics and education.

In the shadows of trees and buildings, on waterways and in rural villages, we are seeing a continuing groundswell of resistance. Within each and every one of us an even harder and more important battle is being fought. That battle is for our mind, for our heart, for the power to define the terms by which we interact with the world around us.

The name of this book is "The Revolution Will Be Improvised." As I said in my preface, the intention was to show that the future will be what we make it. That answers the question of why I chose the word 'improvised'. Now I will explain why I chose the word 'revolution'.

We will not rise up. We will not bring back the guillotine. Decades of luxury and social acclimation have seen to that. Under the illusion of democracy, we will not even argue about the debts heaped on us by our political leaders and their puppet masters, the financial elite. We will watch as they deconstruct our social system brick by brick to repurpose the materials for their palaces and country retreats. As the surveillance state is

256

more forcefully employed, we will report one another to the authorities and we will walk with our heads bowed beneath the cameras and body scanners. We have walked down this road for long enough now that it is almost inevitable that the worst of what lies ahead is unavoidable.

But a revolution is a sudden change in situation. And that sudden change will come without warning. More importantly, I sincerely believe that sudden change, that revolution, will take place within. You will have many more opportunities to change yourself than you will to change the world. If you meet those opportunities with an open heart and mind instead of fear, you will experience the revolution.

Mike Freedman
London, UK

Acknowledgements

This book would have been impossible without the love and support of my wife, as well as the friendship and collaboration of Ari Abraham, Sharon Ede, and Ben Gregory.

My gratitude also goes to the interviewees, who were so generous with their time and so patient with my questions, as well as to David Cromwell and David Edwards at Media Lens who were so kind in contributing the introduction, to Dr. Nafeez Ahmed who was willing to look over the book and give me his opinion, to Yen Ooi who gave me very helpful advice on how best to release the book, to my brother Emerson who gave me much-needed advice on technical matters, to Bartek Tofel who first introduced me to Desmond Morris's work, and to Michael O'Kelly who many years ago told me about 'The Soul of the Ape' by Eugene Marais.

Endnotes

Introduction

1. Norman Solomon, 'The Military-Industrial-Media Complex: Why war is covered from the warriors' perspective'
    Fairness and Accuracy In Reporting, Extra, August 1, 2005 ;
    http://fair.org/extra-online-articles/the-military-industrial-media-complex/

2. David Cromwell, *Why Are* We *The Good Guys: Freeing Your Mind From The Delusions Of Propaganda*, Zero Books, Winchester, 2012.

3. Edward S. Herman and Noam Chomsky, *Manufacturing Consent: The Political Economy of the Mass Media*, Vintage, London, 1988/1994.

4. Noam Chomsky and Andre Vltchek, *On Western Terrorism: From Hiroshima to Drone Warfare*, Pluto Press, London, 2013, p. 31.

5. Ibid., p. 32.

6. BBC Worldwide, Wikipedia
    http://en.wikipedia.org/wiki/BBC_Worldwide;
    accessed November 11, 2013.

7. See Chapter 2 of David Edwards and David Cromwell, *Newspeak in the 21ˢᵗ Century*, Pluto Books, London, 2009.

8. Jonathan Cook, 'Democratic politics became a puppet show'
    November 12, 2013
    http://www.jonathan-cook.net/blog/2013-11-12/democratic-politics-became-a-puppet-show/

9. Newsnight, BBC2, August 11, 2008, 10:30pm.

10. Emily Maitlis, 'I used to fear being found out, I'm over that now'
    Guardian Professional, Monday 21 October 2013 08.00 BST
    http://www.theguardian.com/women-in-leadership/2013/oct/21/emily-maitlis-newsnight-fear-being-found-out

11. 'The Big Idea', BBC2, February 14, 1996
    http://www.youtube.com/watch?v=GjENnyQupow
    transcript available at http://www.aithne.net/index.php?e=news&id=4&lang=0.

12. Jeff Schmidt, *Disciplined Minds: A Critical Look at Salaried Professionals and the Soul-Battering System that Shapes Their Lives*
    Rowman & Littlefield Publishers, Inc., Lanham, 2000.

13. Noam Chomsky, 'The Clinton Vision', *Z Magazine*, December 1993;
    http://www.chomsky.info/articles/199312--.htm

14. Lisa Hymas, 'E. O. Wilson wants to know why you're not protesting in the streets', Grist magazine, April 30, 2012
http://grist.org/article/e-o-wilson-wants-to-know-why-youre-not-protesting-in-the-streets/

15. 'Good Energy, Bad Energy', Friends of the Earth International website
http://www.foei.org/en/good-energy-bad-energy;
accessed November 11, 2013
David Cromwell, *Private Planet: Corporate Plunder And The Public Fightback*, Jon Carpenter Publishing, Charlbury, 2001.

16. Quoted in Ian Mayes, 'Flying in the face of the facts. The readers' editor on ... promotion, pollution and the Guardian's environment policies', The Guardian, January 24, 2004
http://www.theguardian.com/media/2004/jan/24/pressand publishing.comment

17. 'Silence Is Green', Media Lens media alert, February 3, 2005
http://www.medialens.org/index.php/alerts/alert-archive/2005/376-silence-is-green-the-green-movement-and-the-corporate-mass-media.html

18. Ibid.

The Release Phase - Richard Heinberg

1. http://www.washingtonpost.com/business/us-debt-growing-faster-than-gdp-egan-says/2012/04/09/gIQAyr3q6S_video.html
Source: Bloomberg/The Washington Post

2. http://www.globalpost.com/dispatch/news/regions/americas/120817/midwest-drought-what-dying-corn-iowa-means-the-us-presidential
Source: Global Post, August 17 2012, Faine Greenwood

3. Carrying Capacity: the maximum number of organisms that an ecosystem can sustain (or "carry") given the limits of available food, habitat, water and other necessities.

4. The Return of Tarzan, 1912, Edgar Rice Burroughs

5. Resilience Theory: the capacity of a system to continually change and adapt yet remain within critical thresholds.
Source: Stockholm Resilience Centre

6. "Memories & Visions of Paradise: Exploring the Universal Myth of a Lost Golden Age"; Richard Heinberg; Quest Books 1995

7. Oil Depletion Protocol: drafted by petroleum geologist and founder of the Association for the Study of Peak Oil (ASPO) Colin Campbell as a proposed international agreement on how to cope with an annually decreasing oil supply in order to avoid the worst consequences of

resource shortages and scarcity profiteering.
http://richardheinberg.com/odp/theprotocol

Dr. Colin J. Campbell speaks to David Room of Global Public Media
about the oil depletion protocol and how it would affect the United
States, and the rest of the world, in the face of peak oil.
http://old.globalpublicmedia.com/node/592
Source: Global Public Media

8. "Energy and Equity (Ideas in Progress)"; Ivan Illich;
    Marion Boyars Publishers Ltd, 1974

9. http://www.thetimes.co.uk/tto/news/uk/crime/article3670009.ece
    Source: The Times, Fiona Hamilton, January 28 2013

10. http://www.guardian.co.uk/uk/2011/aug/09/theresa-may-water-
    cannon-riots
    Source: The Guardian, Stephen Bates, August 9 2011

11. Positive Money is a British organisation campaigning to reform the
    money system in the UK, and to raise awareness about monetary
    issues worldwide. http://www.positivemoney.org/

Thinking Outside the Death Camp - Derrick Jensen

1. "Against the Grain: How Agriculture Has Hijacked Civilization";
    Richard Manning, North Point Press 2005

2. Lewis Mumford's two-volume work "The Myth of the Machine",
    published (Vol. 1) in 1967 and (Vol. 2) 1970, is possibly the most well-
    known of his many books. In the Prologue, he sets out his goal: "to
    question both the assumptions and the predictions upon which our
    commitment to the present forms of scientific and technical progress,
    treated as ends in themselves, have been based." His use of the word
    "machine" referred to social structures and the technological and
    cultural values and choices made by them.

3. John Allen Livingston was a well-known Canadian naturalist and
    author. His obituary has a good outline of his life and work:
    https://www.humanesociety.com/index.php/component/mtree/book-of-
    remembrance/In-Memory-of-John-Allen-Livingston;
    Source: Humane Society of Canada, 30 November 1999

4. Herman Daly, considered by many to be the father of ecological
    economics, outlined "uneconomic growth" as follows:

"the economy is a subsystem of the finite biosphere that supports it.
When the economy's expansion encroaches too much on its
surrounding ecosystem, we will begin to sacrifice natural capital (such
as fish, minerals and fossil fuels) that is worth more than the
manufactured capital (such as roads, factories and appliances) added

by the growth. We will then have what I call uneconomic growth, producing "bads" faster than goods – making us poorer, not richer. Once we pass the optimal scale, growth becomes stupid in the short run and impossible to maintain in the long run."
Source: Adbusters #85, interview with Tom Green

5. This definition is cited in various forms but essentially the origin of our modern word 'addict' is the Latin 'addictus' whose meaning included, among other things, to be bound by judicial decree. The word also relates to slavery; a slave was often referred to as an 'addictus', and it could be that this meaning is what relates to addiction in its modern usage: to be a slave to something. Related to this is the long-standing association of chains and debt, in the sense that debt was a metaphorical chain that one agreed to take on; in Roman law, 'manus injectio' (the capture and confinement of a debtor by the creditor) could be, it has been argued, a physical manifestation of this concept.

6. Frederick Winslow Taylor was the father of so-called 'scientific management', which is the practice of concentrating control of the functions of a business in the hands of managers who specify exactly how work is to be carried out by their subordinates, the workers. This quote is from his book, *Principles of Scientific Management*, and appears early in the work as a mission statement as well as a prophecy.

Taylor's ideas were used as the basis for the dystopian future outlined in Yevgeny Zamyatin's fantastic novel *We*. Taylor also is the subject of a brilliant biography by Robert Kanigel called *The One Best Way*.

7. M. King Hubbert was a geophysicist who first put forward the hypothesis (some might say observed the fact) that oil production would peak due to oil's non-renewable nature. He made certain stern predictions about the future which awaited a heavily fossil fuel dependent society in the event that alternatives were not developed in time.

8. "Punishing Saddam", 60 Minutes, May 12 1996, CBS
Source: CBS - http://www.youtube.com/watch?v=x4PgpbQfxgo

An Empty Space Where My Offspring Would Have Been – Les Knight

1. You can check out their official website at http://vhemt.org/.

2. Garret Hardin was an American ecologist and quite a controversial figure. His advocacy for abortion prior to the Roe vs. Wade case which established abortion rights in the United States enraged some, while his interest in eugenics, sterilisation and strict limits on immigration offended others. He was not a particularly sympathetic character - his concept of 'lifeboat ethics', using a lifeboat as a metaphor for individual nations surrounded by hopeful immigrants, advocated stopping new people from entering on the grounds that it eroded the 'safety factor' needed for long-term survival and threatened the prospects of the inhabitants. His view on the 'tragedy of the commons'

was that "Freedom in a commons brings ruin to all".

3.   Desmond Morris is a world-renowned British biologist, anthropologist, primatologist, television presenter and author. His books The Naked Ape and The Human Zoo, written in the 1960s, were instrumental in recasting the human as one among many of nature's species. In his own words, "We must never forget that we are risen apes, not fallen angels."

4.   The interview is in Nina Paley's documentary *Thank You For Not Breeding*. http://ninapaley.com/parasitetreatment.html

5.   Oregon Wild: Bringing Wolves Back Home to Oregon
     http://www.oregonwild.org/fish_wildlife/bringing_wolves_back
     Source: Oregon Wild

6.   An interesting read on this topic is Joseph Tainter's *The Collapse Of Complex Societies*, which contains case studies of societal collapses throughout history and suggests recurring challenges that lead to collapse, primarily the "energy-complexity spiral", which is the way in which an organism or society continually evolves more complexity, which in turn requires more energy to sustain that complexity, until a point of diminishing returns is reached.

7.   Les is referring to the Toba Catastrophe Theory, which posits that a huge volcanic eruption in Sumatra 75,000 years ago resulted in a brutal volcanic winter that almost completely wiped out human beings. In debate since the early 1990s, the theory remains contested, most recently by Dr Christine Lane at Oxford University who conducted a study of sediments in Lake Malawi and considered the results proof that no such volcanic winter took place in that time frame.
     http://www.bbc.co.uk/news/science-environment-22355515

Who Wants To Live Forever? - Aubrey De Grey

1.   Official Website - http://www.sens.org/

2.   Two illustrations of this, at the extremes of the life expectancy chart, are Norway and Afghanistan. Between 1960 and 2015, life expectancy in Norway went from 73 to 81 years, an increase of just over 10%. In that same period, life expectancy in Afghanistan went from 31 to 60 years, nearly doubling.

3.   The "total fertility rate", or TFR, of the world has declined over the past thirty years, and statistics show a correlation between female education, availability of reproductive healthcare (especially contraceptives) and the choice by women to have fewer children. One interpretation, simplistic but defensible, is that when women are given a choice about whether or not they want fewer children, they choose to have fewer children.

Cyberia: The Security-Industrial Complex - Ross Anderson

1. "Robber baron" is a term associated with unfair, unlawful or unethical rent-seeking and other profit-extraction methods by private businesspeople. The word came into common usage in the United States in the 19th century.

2. Facebook's (ab)use of user data is a matter of extensive record, e.g. 'Facebook faces EU curbs on selling users' interests to advertisers'; http://www.telegraph.co.uk/technology/facebook/8917836/Facebook-faces-EU-curbs-on-selling-users-interests-to-advertisers.html; Jason Lewis, Investigations Editor, 26 Nov 2011, The Telegraph

3. http://news.bbc.co.uk/2/hi/uk_news/8159141.stm
    Source: BBC News, 20 July 2009

4. https://trapwire.com/
    Source: Official Website

5. The "Crypto Wars" is the name unofficially given to the US government's struggle to prevent public access to cryptography, i.e. data protection, strong enough to withstand intelligence agency decryption.

6. Also known informally as the Snooper's Charter, the Communications Data Bill is a wide-ranging piece of legislation aimed at increasing the British government's ability to access the public's communications. Originally introduced in 2013, it was blocked by the Liberal Democrats during the 2010 - 2015 Parliament. Theresa May's dedication to the bill is longstanding, and she re-introduced it in a revised form in November 2015. It was passed by the British Parliament and received royal assent on Tuesday November 29, 2016.

7. This handy timeline by the American Civil Liberties Union gives a good overview of US government surveillance since September 11, 2001: http://www.aclu.org/timelines/post-911-surveillance

8. Bruce Schneier is a well-known technologist and author, most recently of the book Data and Goliath. He maintains a blog at www.schneier.com.

No Free Lunch - Robert Rapier

1. The Crude Truth About Oil Reserves
    http://online.wsj.com/article/SB10001424052748704107
    20457447070700973579402.html
    Source: Wall Street Journal, Leonardo Maugeri, 4 November 2009

2. "We were wrong on peak oil. There's enough to fry us all.";
    http://www.guardian.co.uk/commentisfree/2012/jul/02/peak-oil-we-we-wrong; Source: The Guardian, George Monbiot, 2 July 2012

3.   The Breaking Point
     http://www.nytimes.com/2005/08/21/magazine/21OIL.html?
     pagewanted=all&_r=0
     Source: The New York Times, Peter Maas 21 August 2005

4.   Has Obama stifled oil production?
     http://articles.chicagotribune.com/2012-02-27/news/chi-obama-and-
     oil-production-20120227_1_oil-production-barrels-president-obama
     Source: Chicago Tribune, Steve Chapman, 27 February 2012

5.   "Climate Change in the Indian Mind"
     Yale Project on Climate Change Communication
     http://environment.yale.edu/climate/publications/climate-change-
     indian-mind/
     Source: Yale University Website

6.   "The Magic Washing Machine", Hans Rosling, filmed December 2010
     http://www.ted.com/talks/hans_rosling_and_the_magic_
     washing_machine.html

7.   Ethanol Production Slows From Drought Pushes Gas Prices Higher
     http://www.huffingtonpost.com/2012/08/13/ethanol-production-
     slows-drought-pushes-gas-prices-higher_n_1772104.html
     Source: Reuters, Steven C. Johnson, 13 August 2012

8.   Chu: DOE working to wean U.S. off oil
     http://www.politico.com/news/stories/0212/73408.html
     #ixzz1nlwKN38K
     Source: Politico, Alex Guillen, 2 March 2012

9.   350.org Director Bill McKibben Does The Colbert Report
     http://www.sofreshandsogreen.com/2011/11/16/video-350-org-
     director-bill-mckibben-does-the-colbert-report/

10. Ed Markey is a long-serving politician in the Democratic Party, first as
     a Congressman (1976 - 2013) and then as a Senator (2013 - present).
     His work in office has been focused on energy policy.

11. Josh Fox is an American filmmaker whose breakthrough documentary
     is "Gasland" - http://gaslandthemovie.com/. It looked at the
     environmental and social impact of hydraulic fracturing, or "fracking",
     an oil industry practice whereby large amounts of water and a cocktail
     of chemicals are forcefully injected into bedrock to fracture it and
     release the gas it contains.

The Three Dimensions of Power – Michael Marmot

1. http://www.who.int/social_determinants/en/

2. http://www.hpa.org.uk/web/HPAweb&Page&HPAwebAutoListDate/Page/1278943917079
    Source: Public Health England Official Website

3. http://life.mappinglondon.co.uk/#
    Source: Official Lives On The Line Website

4. http://www.bbc.co.uk/news/uk-scotland-glasgow-west-15368400
    Source: BBC News Website

5. http://acs-social-state.findthedata.org/compare/22-44/Massachusetts-vs-Texas
    Source: Find The Data Website

6. The Health and Social Care Act was a controversial bill that received Royal Assent on 27 March 2012, thereby becoming law in the UK. Among its many provisions, it removed the Health Secretary's responsibility for the health of British citizens, something that had been law since 1948 when the National Health Service, the UK's internationally admired public healthcare provider, was created. Other provisions included drastic changes to the structure of the NHS and how it is funded. Many critics saw this as evidence of a drive towards privatisation of the NHS, while the government declared those accusations as "ludicrous scaremongering".

7. http://www.britsocat.com/Body.aspx?control=HomePage
    Source: Official Website

Redefining the Situation - John Darley

1. Catherine "Kitty" Genovese was stabbed to death in New York City on March 13, 1964. At the time, their were numerous reports of neighbours who stood by and did nothing, or who did not respond to her calls for help, or who did not even call the police.

2. Broadly speaking, the Bystander Effect is what happens when a number of people witness something in which, under normal circumstances, social norms would expect that they intervene, yet they do nothing. John Darley's research into this topic was groundbreaking and, while considered by many critics to be inconclusive or downright mistaken both in its premise (the Kitty Genovese case, the circumstances of which have been disputed) and its conclusion, his arguments are persuasive and based on painstaking research and experimentation.

3. "The Unresponsive Bystander", by Bibb Latane and John Darley, is still a core psychological text. The central conclusion of the book is summed up perfectly in the authors' own words: "A victim may be

more likely to get help...the fewer people who are available to take action."

4. Washington Post - ABC News Poll
    http://www.washingtonpost.com/wp-dyn/content/article/2009/11/24/AR2009112402989.html
    Source: The Washington Post, 25 November 2009, Juliet Eilperin

5. Normalcy bias is a cognitive bias whereby people base their assumptions about the future on their present situation, i.e. everything is normal now so it will continue to be normal going forward.

Why Do The British Not Eat Horses? - Iain Overton

1. Not long after we met, Iain Overton was involved in a scandal in which a major political figure associated with the Conservative Party was outed by him on social media as being the subject of an investigation into allegations of paedophilia, an allegation which later was disproven and led to Iain's resignation.

2. Robert McKee is a famous story-telling guru who writes books and gives seminars on screenplay structure and narrative.

3. Alan Yentob is a stalwart of the BBC, a TV executive and presenter who has spent his entire career there.

4. High frequency trading having greater impact on commodities
    http://www.theglobeandmail.com/globe-investor/high-frequency-trading-having-greater-impact-on-commodities-study/article534321/
    Source: The Globe and Mail, Javier Blas, 26 March 2012

5. "We'll make a killing out of food crisis," Glencore trading boss Chris Mahoney boasts
    http://www.independent.co.uk/news/world/politics/well-make-a-killing-out-of-food-crisis-glencore-trading-boss-chris-mahoney-boasts-8073806.html
    Source: The Independent, James Cusick, 23 August 2012

6. Russia, Crippled by Drought, Bans Grain Exports
    http://www.nytimes.com/2010/08/06/world/europe/06russia.html?_r=0
    Source: The New York Times, Andrew E. Kramer, 5 August 2010

7. Use your loaf: why food prices were crucial in the Arab Spring
    http://www.guardian.co.uk/lifeandstyle/2011/jul/17/bread-food-arab-spring
    Source: The Guardian, Rami Zurayk, 17 July 2011

8. Privatisation of water supply in Delhi opposed
    http://www.thehindu.com/news/cities/Delhi/privatisation-of-water-supply-in-delhi-opposed/article3960536.ece
    Source: The Hindu, 3 October 2012

9. Prostitution and trafficking - the anatomy of a moral panic
http://www.guardian.co.uk/uk/2009/oct/20/trafficking-numbers-women-exaggerated
Source: The Guardian, Nick Davies, 20 October 2009

Inquiry fails to find single trafficker who forced anybody into prostitution
http://www.guardian.co.uk/uk/2009/oct/20/government-trafficking-enquiry-fails
Source: The Guardian, Nick Davies, 20 October 2009

10. Naming the Dead
http://www.thebureauinvestigates.com/2013/02/04/naming-the-dead-bureau-announces-new-drones-project/
Source: The Bureau of Investigative Journalism, 4 February 2013

11. The Long Tail
http://www.wired.com/wired/archive/12.10/tail.html
Source: Wired, Chris Anderson, October 2004

12. Paul Lewis's Twitter handle is @PaulLewis;
https://twitter.com/PaulLewis

13. Newspaper's key to boosting circulation is planning to be better
http://www.guardian.co.uk/media/organgrinder/2011/may/09/newspaper-gaining-readers-through-planning
Source: The Guardian, Emily Wilson, 9 May 2011

14. Richard McGregor at the Financial Times wrote an article entitled "Zhou's cryptic caution lost in translation" in which he quotes an interpreter who was present at the time. The quote "It's too soon to tell" or in other versions "It's too early to judge", often falsely attributed to Mao Tse-tung, is actually from Zhou Enlai, then Prime Minister of China. The famously misunderstood comment was actually in reference to the Paris student uprising of 1968 rather than the French Revolution of 1789.
Source: Financial Times, Richard McGregor, 10 June 2011

To avoid the pay wall, try
http://mediamythalert.wordpress.com/2011/06/14/too-early-to-say-zhou-was-speaking-about-1968-not-1789/
Source: Media Myth Alert, W. Joseph Campbell, 14 June 2011

15. How the Bureau investigated Bell Pottinger
http://www.thebureauinvestigates.com/2011/12/05/how-the-bureau-investigated-bell-pottinger/
Source: The Bureau of Investigative Journalism, Melanie Newman, 5 December 2011

16. The idea of the 'filter bubble' is put forward by Eli Pariser in his book "The Filter Bubble: What The Internet Is Hiding From You". There is a link from his website to his excellent TED talk on the subject.
Source: http://www.thefilterbubble.com/

17. "The Secret Policeman was screened amid a storm of publicity in October 2003."
http://news.bbc.co.uk/1/hi/programmes/panorama/7650207.stm
Source: BBC News, 3 October 2008

18. "Last week six people were jailed for their role in abusing patients at [Winterbourne View] near Bristol after an investigation by BBC's Panorama."
http://www.bbc.co.uk/news/uk-20140421
Source: BBC News, 30 October 2012

19. Iraq: The War Logs
http://www.guardian.co.uk/world/iraq-war-logs
Source: The Guardian / Wikileaks

20. Tax havens: Super-rich 'hiding' at least $21 trillion
http://www.bbc.co.uk/news/business-18944097
Source: BBC News, 22 July 2012

21. All sides must be clear on bank transparency
http://www.telegraph.co.uk/finance/comment/james-quinn/9653321/All-sides-must-be-clear-on-bank-transparency.html
Source: The Telegraph, James Quinn, 3 November 2012

22. Reality check: how much did the banking crisis cost taxpayers?
http://www.guardian.co.uk/politics/reality-check-with-polly-curtis/2011/sep/12/reality-check-banking-bailout
Source: The Guardian, Polly Curtis, 12 September 2011

23. Revealed: 50% of Tory funds come from City
http://www.guardian.co.uk/politics/2011/feb/08/tory-funds-half-city-banks-financial-sector
Source: The Guardian, Nicholas Watt & Jill Treanor, 8 February 2011

24. Tories in 'cash for access' scandal
http://www.dailymail.co.uk/news/article-2120010/Peter-Cruddas-Tory-treasurer-resigns-selling-secret-meetings-David-Cameron-250k.html
Source: Daily Mail, Graham Smith & Chris Parsons, 25 March 2012

25. "The Leader's Group is the premier supporter Group of the Conservative Party. Members are invited to join David Cameron and other senior figures from the Conservative Party at dinners, post-PMQ lunches, drinks receptions, election result events and important campaign launches."
http://www.conservatives.com/Donate/Donor_Clubs.aspx
Source: Conservative Party Official Website

26. http://www.dailymail.co.uk/health/index.html
Source: The Daily Mail Official Website

27. Libel laws explained
http://www.guardian.co.uk/technology/2006/aug/31/

The Word Bookshop Ltd.
314 New Cross Road London SE14 6AF
020 8355 9378

Regd. No. 10101794

Revolution Will Be Improvi	£10.00
total.	£10.00
al.	**£10.00**

ment
h: £20.00
nge: £10.00

------ VAT SUMMARY ------

@ 20%. £0.00

e   30-Nov-2017 20:10:22
eipt 12,346

news.politicsandthemedia
Source: The Guardian, James Sturcke, 31 August 2006

28. Times libel ruling restores Reynolds public interest defence
http://www.guardian.co.uk/media/2012/mar/21/times-libel-reynolds-defence
Source: The Guardian, Owen Bowcott, 21 March 2012

29. Putin: The richest man on earth?
http://www.thebureauinvestigates.com/2012/04/19/putin-the-richest-man-on-earth/
Source: The Bureau of Investigative Journalism, Maeve McClenaghan, 19 April 2012

30. Was the Big Bang good for the City of London and Britain?
http://www.telegraph.co.uk/finance/financialcrisis/8850654/Was-the-Big-Bang-good-for-the-City-of-London-and-Britain.html
Source: The Telegraph, David Kynaston, 26 October 2011

31. Greek political elite blames crisis on everyone else but not on itself
http://www.grreporter.info/en/mark_mazower_greek_political_elite_blames_crisis_everyone_else_not_itself/7993
Source: GR Reporter, Anastasia Balezdrova, 24 October 2012

A Game of Shadows - Sven Hughes

1. Sefton Delmer worked for the British government during World War Two as a propagandist, broadcasting against Hitler by radio from England.

2. Trying To Pull Together: Africans are asking whether China is making their lunch or eating it
http://www.economist.com/node/18586448
Source: The Economist, April 20 2011

3. No, it wasn't. It was Lord Palmerston: "Nations share no permanent friends or allies. They only have permanent interests."

4. David Stirling was the founder of the Special Air Service, or SAS, an elite group within Britain's military. He was also a main character in Adam Curtis's excellent documentary "The Mayfair Set".

5. Coltan is a rare earth mineral and a key ingredient in many modern electronics, especially mobile phones.
http://www.friendsofthecongo.org/resource-center/coltan.html;
Source: Friends of The Congo website

6. IMF calls for dollar alternative:
http://money.cnn.com/2011/02/10/markets/dollar/index.htm
Source: CNN Money, Ben Rooney, February 10 2011

7. I was only half right. It is from Shakespeare's King Henry VI, Part III, Act III, Scene 2. However, it is Richard III who says it:

"Why, I can smile and murder whiles I smile,
And cry 'content' to that which grieves my heart,
And wet my cheeks with artificial tears,
And frame my face for all occasions"

A Society At War With Itself – Dr. David Nutt

1. Drug harms in the UK: a multicriteria decision analysis, Prof David J Nutt FMedSci a, Leslie A King PhD b, Lawrence D Phillips PhD c, on behalf of the Independent Scientific Committee on Drugs
Source: The Lancet
http://www.thelancet.com/journals/lancet/article/PIIS0140-6736(10)61462-6/abstract)

2. 'Cocaine users are destroying the rainforest'
http://www.guardian.co.uk/world/2008/nov/19/cocaine-rainforests-columbia-santos-calderon
Source: The Guardian, Sandra Laville, 19 November 2008

3. The geopolitics of drug trafficking in Afghanistan
http://www.opendemocracy.net/daniel-nguyen/geopolitics-of-drug-trafficking-in-afghanistan
Source: OpenDemocracy.net, Daniel Nguyen, 24 November 2012

4. http://drugscience.org.uk/
Source: Official Website

5. http://www.herc.ox.ac.uk/icohde/datasets/239
Source: University of Oxford Interactive Compendium of Health Datasets for Economists

6. http://reformdrugpolicy.com/beckley-main-content/conventions/
Source: The Beckley Foundation

7. The 1912 Hague International Opium Convention
Source: UNODC - http://www.unodc.org/unodc/en/frontpage/the-1912-hague-international-opium-convention.html

8. Ladies' Temperance Leagues were a phenomenon of the pre-Prohibition era United States. They were groups of women who campaigned for laws against drinking and drunkenness from the angle that it was bad for their husbands, sons, fathers etc. One famous slogan was "Lips that touch liquor shall not touch ours".

9. 53% of those surveyed supported either decriminalisation or one form or another of legalisation.
Source: Ipsos Mori poll
http://www.tdpf.org.uk/Ipsos_MORI_TPDF_poll.pdf

10. http://www.labour.org.uk/labour_crackdown_on_cannabis
Source: Labour Party Website

11. I was a little carried away there. The truth is much more moderate. "From international comparison, it is concluded that trends in cannabis use in the Netherlands are rather similar to those in other European countries, and Dutch figures on cannabis use are not out of line with those from countries that did not decriminalise cannabis. Consequently, it appears unlikely that decriminalisation of cannabis will cause an increase in cannabis use.";
http://www.parl.gc.ca/Content/SEN/Committee/371/ille/presentation/korf-e.htm;
Source: Parliament of Canada website

12. "Iran has 1.2 million "drug-dependent users,"... 2.26 percent of the population aged 15-64 is addicted to opiates."
http://www.foreignpolicy.com/articles/2011/11/18/iran_opium_chasing_the_dragon
Source: Foreign Policy, Roland Elliott Brown, 18 November 2011

13. "...on average, traffic fatalities in [Colorado and Montana] fell nearly 9 percent after medical pot became legal."
http://abcnews.go.com/blogs/health/2011/12/02/driving-stoned-safer-than-driving-drunk/
Source: ABC News, Clayton Sandell, 2 December 2011

14. "The Soul of the Ape", Eugene Marais, published posthumously in 1969

15. http://news.bbc.co.uk/2/hi/uk_news/england/lancashire/3767537.stm
Source: BBC News

16. Arthur Janov is a renowned psychologist who created primal therapy, a therapeutic system whereby patients re-experience primal pain and are thereby purged of its ill effects.

17. Ayahuasca is a psychoactive brew made from the *Banisteriopsis caapi* vine found in the Amazon. It contains DMT, which is present in the human body naturally but which our brains do not react to due to an inhibitor we produce. The vine is brewed with an additional plant, often *Psychotria viridis*, that blocks this inhibitor, thus allowing the DMT in the vine to be absorbed by the body and to produce a reaction. When smoked in crystal form, DMT has instant psychoactive effects. Dr. Rick Strassman conducted extensive research into DMT and made an excellent documentary called "DMT: The Spirit Molecule".

Luxury vs. Necessity: The Dilemma of Production - Claus Conzelmann

1. European Food Sustainable Consumption and Production Round Table: An initiative by the European Commission and food suppliers aimed at 'sustainable consumption and production in Europe.'
Source: Official website - http://www.food-scp.eu/

Better, Not Bigger - Peter Victor

1. Adam Smith is often cited as the father of modern economics. His work is still central to a great deal of economic thought. While he has been adopted by certain schools of thought as a leading thinker sympathetic to their cause, most notably the Adam Smith Institute, which regularly calls for deregulation and privatisation, it is worth bearing in mind that Smith himself was unequivocal in his interpretation of the motives of profit-seeking business when left unchecked: "People of the same trade seldom meet together, even for merriment and diversion, but the conversation ends in a conspiracy against the public, or in some contrivance to raise prices." (The Wealth of Nations, Book I, Chapter X)

2. Thomas Malthus was a British scholar who is credited with the first modern formulation of the argument that unrestrained human population growth creates pressure on society and on the environment. His observation that human population grows exponentially while food supply is only increased arithmetically, known as the 'Mathusian' view, has so far not been borne out historically, although diminishing returns from technological farming and recent UN studies have indicated that the mid-term future, approximately sixty years from now, is a possible point when his observation may be proved correct. Essentially, the simplistic reduction of Malthus's view is that humans will eventually outstrip their food supply if their population grows unchecked. He was also not in favour of welfare, since he saw it as an encouragement for the poor to breed. While not a sympathetic character, his central view remains fairly logical: humans require natural resources to survive and, like other animals, may one day run out of those resources if there are too many people or if there is too much consumption.

3. David Ricardo is another pillar of modern economics along with Adam Smith. He is also credited with articulating the argument for free trade, in the form of a concept that has come to be known as 'comparative advantage', which is the idea that if goods are produced in the nations where their production is the most efficient, and other nations trade with those producer nations using goods that they themselves produce most efficiently, then the result is a stable and beneficial system of global trade where each nation specialises in that which it can produce most efficiently, even if each nation could also produce itself the thing that they are obtaining from another nation.

4. "The research shows that six out of 10 Europeans are now better off than they were 15 years ago. In Britain, Spain and Germany the difference is especially clear. Households in these countries are around 90% wealthier in real terms than they were 30 years ago, but they are not as satisfied. Around 10 years ago nearly 70% of Europeans were happy with their standard of living. But now only 45% of those questioned said they were happy with their quality of life.";
http://news.bbc.co.uk/2/hi/uk_news/2005529.stm;
Source: 23 May 2002, BBC News

273

The Frenchman and The Canary – Seyyed Hossein Nasr

1. Lynn White was a well-respected professor of medieval history. He
    posited a connection between medieval Christian thought and the
    development of ecologically destructive technology and social
    behaviour. In 1966 he gave a lecture called "The Historical Roots of
    Our Ecologic Crisis". He deserves to be quoted at length:

    "...the impact of our race upon the environment has so increased
    in force that it has changed in essence. When the first cannons were
    fired, in the early 14th century, they affected ecology by sending
    workers scrambling to the forests and mountains for more potash,
    sulphur, iron ore, and charcoal, with some resulting erosion and
    deforestation. Hydrogen bombs are of a different order: a war fought
    with them might alter the genetics of all life on this planet. By 1285
    London had a smog problem arising from the burning of soft coal, but
    our present combustion of fossil fuels threatens to change the
    chemistry of the globe's atmosphere as a whole, with consequences
    which we are only beginning to guess. With the population explosion,
    the carcinoma of planless urbanism, the now geological deposits of
    sewage and garbage, surely no creature other than man has ever
    managed to foul its nest in such short order."

2. The 'Cartesian Bifurcation' or 'Cartesian Split' refers to the theory of
    the French philosopher Rene Descartes that the mind and body are
    not actually related to one another and are in fact totally separate
    things. Outlining his belief that the mind represents the true self, has
    nothing to do with the body and can therefore be separated from the
    body without a meaningful loss of consciousness, Descartes wrote:

    "I rightly conclude that my essence consists only in my being a
    thinking thing or a substance whose whole essence or nature is merely
    thinking. And although I may, or rather, as I will shortly say, although
    I certainly do possess a body with which I am very closely conjoined;
    nevertheless, because, on the one hand, I have a clear and distinct idea
    of myself, in as far as I am only a thinking and unextended thing, and
    as, on the other hand, I possess a distinct idea of body, in as far as it is
    only an extended and unthinking thing, it is certain that I, that is, my
    mind, by which I am what I am, is entirely and truly distinct from my
    body, and may exist without it." (*Meditations 6, paragraph 9*)

    This is directly opposed to thousands of years of esoteric wisdom
    which holds that it is in fact thought which is deceptive and false, and
    that a direct connection to one's living body is the surest way of
    maintaining a meaningful relationship to oneself, the world and
    ultimately life itself. One can trace a line from the Cartesian Split
    directly to the transhumanist movement best exemplified by Ray
    Kurzweil's belief that a 'singularity' in computing power will allow
    humans to upload the content of their brains into computers and
    thereby live forever.

3. Not the painter. The other one.

CPSIA information can be obtained
at www.ICGtesting.com
Printed in the USA
FSOW02n1535201017
40009FS